9/2002

To Stan,
    an inspirational
pastor,
    With admiration,
        Connie

GOD &
CAESAR

GOD &
CAESAR

Troeltsch's
Social Teaching
as Legitimation

Constance L. Benson

with a foreword by Cornel West

Transaction Publishers
New Brunswick (U.S.A.) and London (U.K.)

This book is printed on acid-free paper that meets the American National Standard for Permanence of Paper for Printed Library Materials.

Library of Congress Catalog Number: 98-46219
ISBN: 1-56000-384-7
Printed in the United States of America

Library of Congress Cataloging-in-Publication Data

Benson, Constance L.
    God and Caesar : Troeltsch's Social teaching as legitimation / Constance L. Benson ; with a foreword by Cornel West.
        p. cm.
    A revision of the author's doctoral thesis.
    Includes bibliographical references and index.
    ISBN 1-56000-384-7 (alk. paper)
    1. Toreltsch, Ernst, 1865–1923. 2. Church and social problems—History. 3. Church history. I. Title.
HN31.T7523B46   1998
261.8'3—dc21   98-46219
                                                        CIP

Contents

To Brian D'Agostino
My husband, colleague, friend and love.

Acknowledgements

I wish to thank the following persons who carefully read, offered detailed suggestions for improvement and publicly endorsed my research: John H. Kautsky, professor emeritus of political science at Washington University in St. Louis; Walter Struve, professor of history, the Graduate Center of the City University of New York; Shelley Baranowski, associate professor of history, the University of Akron, Ohio.

I am also especially grateful to Cornel West, professor of Afro-American studies and the philosophy of religion at Harvard University for reading my manuscript and providing his public support. James McBride, assistant professor of religion and social ethics at Fordham University has also earned my gratitude for his continued moral and professional support.

I must also thank the following for their attentiveness to and courageous support of my work: Jerrold Atlas, professor of history, Long Island University, Brooklyn, New York; church historian Manfred K. Bahmann, Ph.D.; Renate Bridenthal, professor of history, Brooklyn College of the City University of New York; Mary C. I. Buckley, professor of theology emeritus, St. John's University; Susan Buck-Morss, professor of political philosophy and social theory, Cornell University; Joseph J. Fahey, professor of religious studies, Manhattan College, Riverdale; Thomas Ferguson, professor of political science, University of Massachusetts; Elisabeth C. Gladir, German instructor; Amy Newman, research associate and visiting faculty member at Harvard Divinity School at the time of her support; Bertell Ollman, professor of political theory at New York University; Dr. Leonore Siegele-Wenschkewitz, lecturer at Johann Wolfgang Goethe University, Frankfurt; Paul Surlis, associate professor of moral theology at St. John's University; Joseph L. Walsh, professor of philosophy and religion, Stockton State College, New Jersey.

I am grateful to the following for publicly supporting my right to engage in controversial research: Leonard Minsky, executive director,

National Coalition for Universities in the Public Interest; David Noble, co-founder, National Coalition for Universities in the Public Interest and professor of history, York University, Toronto;

A special mention goes to psychotherapist Milton Klein, Ph.D., for testifying to the psychological damage caused by the suppression of research.

I am indebted to the following who formally supported my legal appeal: Peter Becker, Esq., Becker, Buettner & Partner, Marburg, Germany, an expert on administrative and academic law; Jack H. Schuster, professor of education and public policy at the Claremont Graduate School; Michael Arthur Simon, professor of philosophy at the State University of New York at Stony Brook; adjunct professor of Law, Benjamin N. Cardozo School of Law, Yeshiva University; and the Honorable Edward C. Sullivan, member of the Assembly of the State of New York and chair of the Assembly's Committee on Higher Education.

I am particularly indebted to John Ranz, executive director of Holocaust Survivors U.S.A. and The Generation After, president of the Buchenwald Concentration Camp Survivors, U.S.A., adjunct professor of European history, Brooklyn College. He not only formally supported my appeal—he also helped me to grasp the significance of my findings for the present and future.

I am grateful to Professor Robert Thurman, chair of the Columbia University Religion Department, Professor Manning Marable, Columbia University, and Professor Dennis Dalton, Barnard College, for their negotiating efforts on my behalf. Thanks also to Morton Frank, Ph.D. for a careful reading of my manuscript.

A major debt of gratitude is owed to my former advisor, Professor Frank Moore Cross, Harvard biblical scholar, who taught me the use of contextual methods for the critical interpretation of canonical texts. I thank also the Center on Violence and Human Survival at the City University of New York, particularly Charles Strozier and Robert Jay Lifton, for their ongoing intellectual, professional and moral support.

I appreciate the History of Christianity Section of the American Academy of Religion (AAR) for providing me the opportunity to present an earlier version of this research in 1990 at the national annual meetings; also the AAR Mid-Atlantic Region, for giving me forums in 1993 for two other anticipatory papers on Troeltsch and Lagarde, and Troeltsch's racial theories.

Despite our differences, I must express my gratitude to the Troeltsch Society for paying my full travel expenses, plus room and board so that

I could present a paper at their triennial Congress in Augsburg, Germany in September 1988. Their generosity made it possible for me also to attend the annual conference of the *Bund der Religiösen Sozialisten* and a major international conference on Karl Kautsky on the 50th anniversary of his death, held around the same time.

I appreciate the German Christian socialists for opening their conference, archives and homes to me; especially, Dr. Ulrich Dannemann, Rev. Christiana Dannemann and Karlheinz Lipp of the *Leonhard Ragaz Institut* in Darmstadt; Rev. Jürgen and Ursula Finnern, Udo Fleige, Rev. Dr. Reinhard Gaede, Rev. Erhard Griese, Dr. Martina Ludwig and Helmut Pfaff of the *Bund der Religiösen Sozialisten*.

This book would not have materialized without the generous financial and moral support of Rev. Judith and Dr. Marshall Deutsch; Daniel Richardson, Riverside Printing Service; Drs. Olivier and Claire Mathey; Michael Bereza; Rev. Robert Hemstreet and Wendy Moscow; Nicholas and Marion D'Agostino; and my parents, Rev. Donald and Alice Benson.

Gratitude also goes to publicist Dr. John Halberstadt of Cambridge for his personal support and professional assistance with *Benson v. Columbia*.

For legal counsel in my quest for an impartial and rule-governed evaluation of this research in the context of my Ph.D. program at Columbia University, I wish to thank my attorneys, David M. Slater; Donald M. Bernstein of Tressler, Soderstrom, Maloney & Priess; and Eric A. Seiff and Abigail Pessen of Seiff & Kretz. For additional legal assistance I am also grateful to David Abraham, professor of law; Frank Askin, Esq.; Charles E. Bruzga, Esq.; Bob Keach; Leonard Marks, Esq.; Beth Minsky, Esq.; Ronald Podolsky, Esq.; Judith Vladeck, Esq.; and Peter Weiss, Esq. I am especially thankful for the dedication, professionalism and generosity that these legal experts brought to an exceedingly difficult case.

A special acknowledgement goes to Irving Louis Horowitz and Laurence Mintz of Transaction Publishers for their valuable editorial guidance.

Finally, Dr. Brian D'Agostino, to whom I dedicate this book, has been my political science consultant, legal aide and unfailing partner. I will always remain in his debt.

Foreword

Ernst Troeltsch is one of the most respected and renowned figures in modern Christian thought. I shall never forget the sheer intellectual excitement and delight of reading the grand dissertation of H. Richard Niebuhr on Troeltsch's philosophy of religion in the library of Union Theological Seminary. Niebuhr's powerful interpretation of Troeltsch as a subtle historicist has shaped our view of Troeltsch for over seventy years. Sarah Coakley's superb work on Troeltsch is a fine example of this viewpoint and influence.

Yet Constance Benson's book shatters certain crucial aspects of Troeltsch's image as a liberal religious thinker. In fact, her work forces us to revise Niebuhr's Troeltsch—despite his subtle historicism. Benson's controversial thesis is that Troeltsch's magnum opus, *The Social Teaching of the Christian Churches* (1912), is shot through with xenophobic elements that are guided by a deep political conservatism. Similar to the celebrated cases of intellectual giants like Martin Heidegger and Paul de Man who succumbed to the worst racist ideologies of their time, Benson highlights Troeltsch's link to Paul de Lagarde, an exemplary and influential anti-Semite in pre-Nazi Germany. She also argues that Troeltsch's classic text was primarily a polemic against the Marxist thinker Karl Kautsky's view of the political teachings of the early Christian churches in his pioneering work, *Forerunners of Modern Socialism* (1895). In this way, Troeltsch's "liberal" Christian project was deeply conservative in content and xenophobic in character. And the recent revival of Troeltsch studies in contemporary Germany—especially those inspired and informed by Emanuel Hirsch, an unrepentant Nazi theologian—build on this retrograde endeavor.

Benson's courageous book is the most challenging critique of Troeltsch's politics we have—an unsettling critique that forces us to revise the beloved Troeltsch so many of us had come to admire and cherish. This significant attempt to discuss certain silences and blindnesses of most Troeltsch scholars not only deserves a fair hearing; it also reveals how difficult it often is to shake off the encrustations and

remove the protective mechanisms that hover over certain iconic figures in the pantheon of Western thought. Let the robust and uninhibited
quest for truth about Ernst Troeltsch's political thought now really begin!

Cornel West
Professor of Afro-American Studies
and the Philosophy of Religion
Harvard University

1

Introduction: The Theologian
and the Revolutionary

In 1985, I would have never imagined finding myself at the center of a major academic and religious controversy. To be sure, I had a long-standing habit of asking tough questions, which always put me on a collision course with religious and political orthodoxies of all kinds. But now I was in an environment with an international reputation for rewarding critical thought and innovative inquiry. I was attending Columbia University in the City of New York, enrolled in a Ph.D. program in religion offered jointly with the Christian Ethics Department of Union Theological Seminary, on the other side of Broadway.

Little did I know that even such institutions have their icons. And in choosing my dissertation topic, I had inadvertently stumbled upon one of them—Ernst Troeltsch's 1912 classic, *The Social Teaching of the Christian Churches*.[1] Seven years later I defended a Ph.D. dissertation that was essentially the same as the book you are now reading. Given the controversy that then erupted,[2] I feel it is important to reconstruct at the outset my original intentions in undertaking this research, and why I came to revise my views regarding Troeltsch.

In 1985, I was personally dissatisfied with the eclecticism of the liberal Protestant community in which I found myself, and was searching for a more coherent religious identity. I therefore asked my academic advisor, Roger Lincoln Shinn, if there were a foundational liberal Protestant theologian whom I could read to provide a frame of reference for my intellectual and existential search. He answered, without hesitation: Ernst Troeltsch (1865–1923), especially his thousand page *magnum opus, The Social Teaching*.

The image of Troeltsch that I inherited from Shinn, and that he inherited from Reinhold and H. Richard Niebuhr, is still the prevailing conventional wisdom, both within and outside the liberal Protestant subculture. Troeltsch, according to this view, was an enlightened critic of what is today called Christian fundamentalism. His *Social Teaching* is generally believed to be a pioneering application of modern sociology to the history of Christianity,[3] and is today one of the pillars of the advanced curricula in mainstream Protestant seminaries throughout the world.

With an open mind, and indeed with a favorable predisposition inherited from Shinn and the Niebuhrs, I decided to undertake a serious reading of Troeltsch's massive *Social Teaching*. This decision coincided with my need to develop a dissertation topic. However, the Ph.D. program I had chosen in the first place reflected my personal religious and existential concerns, and I now chose this specialized research topic for the same reasons. I emphasize these "purely religious" motives at the basis of my research, because many observers have erroneously concluded—given my iconoclastic findings regarding Troeltsch—that I must have approached *The Social Teaching* with an iconoclastic intent. Nothing could be further from the truth.

My task now, of course, was to formulate an even more specialized research topic that could make some contribution to existing scholarship on my chosen subject. As I became familiar with the vast secondary literature on Troeltsch, it became apparent to me that interpretation in this field had been almost entirely limited to traditional text-based methods. My contribution would be to reconstruct the original historical context of *The Social Teaching* and Troeltsch's intentions in writing it as a basis for a fresh interpretation. While I hoped this methodology would advance Troeltsch studies, I had no intention of challenging the Niebuhrian paradigm of Troeltsch as an enlightened liberal.

At this point in my inquiry, I knew that Troeltsch had been influenced by the contemporary Marxist intellectual, Karl Kautsky. Filtering this information through my Niebuhrian lens, I imagined that Troeltsch had appropriated what was positive in socialism, perhaps anticipating modern liberation theology. What I discovered from the historical record, however, made it clear that he was actually arguing *against* such a view, advocating equality "in Christ" as a purely spiritual and individual alternative to a Christianity based on an apostolic "communism of goods." In fact, as I eventually learned, Troeltsch went so far as to align himself with Paul de Lagarde, a right-wing Protestant mystic and a notorious architect of what later became Nazi ideology.

These findings were startling enough in their immediate implications: that Troeltsch was arguing primarily against the left, not against the religious right. Their broader implications were even more startling, given Troeltsch's preeminent position in modern Protestantism. It would appear that the Protestant establishment—who promoted Troeltsch's fortunes and for whom he spoke—has been more conservative than is generally realized. Conversely, it would appear that many Protestants in Imperial Germany were more receptive to revolutionary interpretations of Christianity than is commonly thought, otherwise Troeltsch would not have devoted his *magnum opus* to refuting such interpretations.

In summary, modern Protestantism—which is widely perceived to be above the fray of politics—has been in fact highly politicized. Although I came to this realization in part through original historical research, I am not, of course, the first to discover this. Fritz Fischer, a pioneer in the historiography of modern Germany, documented this view in rich detail in the 1960s and more recent scholarship on the period remains indebted to his work.[4]

Troeltsch may have "won" his debate with Kautsky and the Christian socialists in the sense that Troeltsch's interpretation of Christianity, not theirs, came to dominate the curricula of mainstream Protestant seminaries. However, this state of affairs conceals the political and ideological struggle for the soul of Christianity that raged in Imperial Germany and that rages throughout the world today.

The same polarization between rich and poor that created German socialism, and more recently, Black and Latin American liberation theologies, continues to afflict today's world. Now, as then, believers as diverse as Ralph Reed and Peter Berger interpret Christianity as a path of salvation for individual souls only. Others, such as Cornel West, Jean Bertrand Aristide, and certain Latin American bishops, view Jesus as a liberator of women and the poor, an outspoken critic of oppression and exploitation, and a martyr in the struggle for a new community based on love and the sharing of wealth.

To be sure, many believers try to harmonize these alternative theologies. It would appear, however, that the individualistic and social interpretations of Christianity are what Weber called "ideal types." Since they arise as characteristic responses to an objective social predicament, the conflict between these theologies is likely to continue as long as society remains polarized between rich and poor. This theological debate took one form in Troeltsch's Germany, a somewhat different form in recent U.S. and Latin American history, and will undoubtedly produce further variations as capitalism, Christianity, and the relationship between the two continue to evolve.

This conceptual approach reflects my attempt to understand religion and its relationship to political and economic power in a genuinely dialectical manner. Only from this vantage point will it be possible to do justice to both Troeltsch and Kautsky and to grasp what is really going on in their debate. Kautsky correctly saw that the communism of goods was a distinguishing feature of early Christianity, but then explained that feature reductively in terms of political economy. Troeltsch was no less reductive, but in the opposite way, viewing Christianity as a purely spiritual teaching having nothing to do with the communism of goods.

From a dialectical perspective, the real question is precisely how the specifically religious concerns of Jesus and his movement related to their communism of goods. Although this question cannot be answered in detail here, I will summarize my own view inasmuch as it inevitably informs my reconstruction of the Troeltsch-Kautsky debate.

My understanding of Christian teaching is that the essence of God is love (John 15:9; I John 4:8,16; cf. Deut. 4:37,7:7), that the ultimate fulfillment of all human beings is to participate in this divine love (Matt. 5:43–48; John 15:12; I Cor. 13; I John 4:11–12), and that Jesus's own mission was to establish a path through which all persons could so participate, thereby establishing the Kingdom of God "on earth as it is in heaven" (Matt. 6:10). For Christianity, therefore, the first principle is spiritual, but the authenticity of any human being's spirituality is measured by his or her embodiment of God's love in relationships with other human beings (I John 4:20–21). This teaching leads naturally and inevitably to a communism of goods, since a wealthy Christian could not possibly love a less fortunate member of the community in the radical way Jesus intended without also sharing his or her economic surplus (Matt. 19:21, 25:31–46; Acts 2:44–46; James 2:15–17). A community characterized by such sharing would have no need for private property and would naturally turn to a social administration of economic matters.[5]

What lends weight to this interpretation in the present context is that Troeltsch, to be internally consistent, could not dispute the importance of the communism of goods in Christian tradition without also subordinating "love" to "religious individualism" within the specifically *religious* teaching of Christianity. The question then becomes why Troeltsch held this theological view, which I can only begin to answer here and which requires further biographical and historical research.

Let us begin with the central thesis of this book: that Troeltsch, in disputing Kautsky's theory that the essence of early Christianity was its communism of goods, was delegitimizing the socialist movement of his own day. Assuming Troeltsch held this ideological and political agenda, the question would still remain whether it was his primary concern, or whether it was itself a mere by-product of his religious and scholarly concerns, which were the real driving forces behind his life and work. My conclusion is that Troeltsch's primary concern was political, and my reasoning is as follows.

Had Troeltsch's primary agenda been political and anti-socialist, he would have had to refute any theory that the communism of goods is central or necessary to Christianity. This in turn would have required him to reject Kautsky's theory of Christianity and any theory centered on a theology of love, which leads inevitably to the communism of goods, as I have argued above. Troeltsch's embracal of religious individualism is therefore consistent with the theory that his primary motivation was political.

Had Troeltsch been concerned in the first instance with religious individualism and/or its centrality for Christianity, however, he would have had no reason to reject socialism, since there is no conflict between religious individualism *as such* and either the communism of goods or the contemporary program of German socialism. Religious individualism—the belief that the essence of authentic religion is the private mystical experience of the individual—is compatible both with socialist and conservative political agendas.

In fact, Kautsky himself defended religious individualism, which he found exemplified in Schiller, as an authentic religious alternative to the corrupt, organized Christianity of his day. As for the early Church, Kautsky's focus on its organized social expression—the communism of goods—was fully compatible with Troeltsch's theory that its inner experiential essence was religious individualism. Indeed, Troeltsch's own typology *required* him to classify every form of Christianity *both* in a sociological dimension (church vs. sect) *and* in an inner experiential dimension (mystical vs. non-mystical), as explained in chapter twelve.

In summary, Troeltsch's claims to be defending the true spiritual character of Christianity from Kautsky's Marxist reductionism obfuscates the real nature of their dispute, which was overwhelmingly political. The two men could have agreed on religious individualism and its applicability to Christianity. Their bone of contention was the communism of goods *as such* and its modern counterpart, the program of the German Social Democratic Party.

The relevance of the Troeltsch-Kautsky debate, seen as a clash of conservative and revolutionary ideal types in the ongoing history of Christianity, is not the only justification for the present study. Troeltsch in his own right is at the center of an important intellectual revival in Germany today. This revival began in the 1960s with the founding of the Ernst Troeltsch Society and has continued along with the revival of other conservative German thinkers during that country's ongoing economic and political ascendancy. In 1988, I received a travel grant from the Society and presented a preliminary version of this research to its triennial Congress in Augsburg.

Before my arrival at the conference, the Society had not been aware of my critical perspective on Troeltsch, and I had not been aware of the extent of the Society's political and cultural conservatism. Like many American interpreters of Troeltsch, including religious and political liberals such as James Luther Adams, I knew little about the politics surrounding Troeltsch studies in Germany. Although the Society did not seem pleased with my findings, they had no major scholarly criticism to offer except my failure to discuss Troeltsch's then untranslated essay, *Political Ethics and Christianity*, an omission that has been corrected in chapter ten, below.

What I learned in Germany about the politics of Troeltsch studies went beyond the Troeltsch Society's racial and gender homogeneity, its wealth, politically conservative connections and its control over theological appointments in southern Germany.

I also learned that a core of co-founders and leaders of the Society were admirers of the late Emanuel Hirsch, an eminent Nazi theologian. Hirsch was a member of the *Sturmabteilung* ("Storm Section") or SA, Hitler's paramilitary organization. According to *Mein Kampf*, the purpose of the SA was to control the streets by force, and to combat the Jews and Marxists who Hitler claimed dominated the Weimar Republic.[6] Hirsch was forced to formally retire from his post at the University of Göttingen after World War II. Unlike many Nazis whose careers were on the line in the postwar period, Hirsch refused to be rehabilitated and remained openly loyal to his Nazi beliefs for the rest of his life. While he could not be formally reinstated as a professor of theology, he was allowed to maintain an informal group of students in his home near the university.[7]

Indeed, it was only after the war that Hirsch published the bulk of his writings. He was to remain a prominent figure in German Protestantism into the 1960s, and was so revered that he was honored at a major celebration on his seventy-fifth birthday in 1963. A German Lutheran pastor, who was a theological student at Göttingen at the time, described to me how he saw Hirsch, old and blind, appear at an upper window and acknowledge the expectant celebrants below.

On this occasion, the Nazi theologian was presented with a *Festschrift* entitled *Truth and Belief*, to which a number of prominent theologians contributed.[8] Among the contributors were Hans-Joachim Birkner, a co-founder of the Ernst Troeltsch Society, and the late Wolfgang Trillhaas, who had been an eminent member of the Society. In fact, for Trillhaas, Hirsch was "the last prince" of Protestant theologians.[9] Another prominent Society member, Hermann Fischer, is also cited in the *Festschrift* for his assistance with its publication.[10]

The link between Hirsch and leaders of the Troeltsch Society documented here is consistent with what is known about Troeltsch's own politics. As discussed in chapters five and eight, Troeltsch in 1913 dedicated the second volume of his collected works to Paul de Lagarde (1827–1891) and highly praised the *Deutsche Schriften* (*German Writings*) in which Lagarde proposed a mystical Germanic religion of the pure German *Volk* ("folk"). Lagarde—who called for the extermination of the Jews two generations before Hitler—was the most notorious anti-Semite and racist of late nineteenth-century Germany and a major architect of what later became Nazi mystical ideology.[11] While some German theologians including Albrecht Ritschl rejected such mysticism, Troeltsch—who was deeply influenced by Lagarde's ideas at the University of Göttingen—warmly embraced it.

Given his prominent position in German Protestantism, Troeltsch played an important role in legitimizing Lagarde's proto-Nazi ideology in the Christian mainstream.[12] Troeltsch thereby helped create an understanding of Christianity that contributed to the subsequent collaboration of most mainstream Christians in Germany with the Third Reich. Indeed, many leaders of the mainstream churches—such as Kittel, Althaus, and Hirsch—were to actively support and participate in Hitler's regime.[13]

These pivotal connections call into question the conventional wisdom that the mysticism and religion of the Third Reich was only pagan, and that the Protestant churches of the period staunchly resisted the Nazi regime.[14] The present study has implications for a reconstruction of such developments, including the tradition linking Lagarde, Troeltsch, Hirsch, and leaders of the Troeltsch Society.

When confronted with the link between Troeltsch and Lagarde, American Troeltsch Society member Garrett Paul reportedly argued that Troeltsch eventually rejected his own pre-World War I conservatism.[15] Does this mean that he repudiated the project he had undertaken in *The Social Teaching*? If so, it would appear long overdue for Protestant seminaries to retire such a questionable text from their curricula.

As I point out in chapter 8, however, it is misleading to say that Troeltsch moved politically and ideologically to the left after World War I. To be sure, with Imperial Germany defeated and a socialist government in power, the entire political spectrum in Germany moved to the left. In this new political universe, however, Troeltsch's German Democratic Party stood to the right of center, just as his National Liberal Party had in the prewar political spectrum (see chapter 8).

Nor did Troeltsch ever repudiate his prewar writings. On the contrary he explicitly affirmed them in his 1922 "My Books."[16] His official biographer argues that *The Social Teaching* was Troeltsch's favorite work and central to his entire corpus.[17] In "The Place of Christianity Among the World Religions," which appeared just months before Hitler's 1923 Beer Hall Putsch, Troeltsch reiterated his earlier racialist theories of the world religions and called Christianity "the religion of all Europe."[18]

One might well ask how American religious and political liberals such as Reinhold Niebuhr and James Luther Adams could have overlooked this "shadow" side of Troeltsch. Conventional methods of text interpretation are undoubtedly part of the problem. Like other classics, *The Social Teaching* has been generally read as if it stands outside and above the ideological debates of the author's time and place. As church historian Roland Bainton put it: "in many quarters [Troeltsch] is treated as a veritable gospel, and his conclusions are accepted with an uncritical devotion wholly alien to his own spirit."[19] The present book breaks new ground by applying critical methods of historical and contextual interpretation to this icon of mainstream Protestantism.

Veneration such as Bainton describes is not unique to the case of Ernst Troeltsch. Indeed, it is so common that the history of ideas is generally understood as a succession of "great books," which are read without reference to the ideological universes in which their authors were actively involved. The reconstruction of these ideological contexts as a basis for interpreting the "great books" is therefore revolutionizing the secondary literatures.

This methodological revolution occurred early on in nineteenth-century Biblical studies. More recently, Cambridge University Professor Quentin Skinner has pioneered the application of this method in political theory.[20] Skinner historically reconstructs the way ideas legitimize and delegitimize various political agendas in the historical situations of their authors. The study of modern religious thought, however, is still dominated by older methods in which ideas or texts are interpreted primarily on their own terms or in relation to other ideas and texts.[21]

The debate between Troeltsch and Kautsky particularly lends itself to Skinner's history of ideologies approach. Like Kautsky's work, *The Social Teaching* opens by addressing not the teachings of early Christianity as one might expect in a work of history, but rather the contemporary debate over the "Social Problem."[22] While Troeltsch's historical account ends in the eighteenth century, he continually interrupts his chronology to refer to issues, groups, and personalities linked with debates of his own day.

Methodological inertia helps explain why even German interpreters of Troeltsch, who understand more of his original political context than, say, liberal Americans, fail to adequately apply such knowledge in interpreting *The Social Teaching*. For example, members of the Troeltsch Society indicated to me in 1988 that they had been aware of Troeltsch's debate with Kautsky.[23] From the perspective of a contextual method, this debate and the historical circumstances out of which it arose are central to illuminating the obscurities of Troeltsch's "great book."

Yet in spite of the numerous references to Kautsky in *The Social Teaching*, none of the Troeltsch Society members had undertaken to systematically interpret it in light of this debate, nor did they cite any other study comparable in this regard to the present one. For persons confined to older methods of text interpretation, this powerful interpretive key remains unused and the single most important door to Troeltsch's intentions in writing *The Social Teaching* remains unopened.

As I will show in detail in the remaining chapters, *The Social Teaching* was largely a polemical reply to contemporary socialist interpretations of Christianity, especially Karl Kautsky's 1895 study, *Forerunners of Modern Socialism*.[24] This view revolutionizes the conventional wisdom that Troeltsch was primarily replying to the religious right. To be sure, Troeltsch did criticize Martin von Nathusius, the conservative Christian author of *Cooperation of the Church in the Solution of the Social Question* (1904). But H. Richard Niebuhr and other interpreters incorrectly identify Nathusius as Troeltsch's primary antagonist, while ignoring the much more important role of Kautsky.

In fact, Nathusius was a parochial figure in Troeltsch's ideological universe. By contrast, Kautsky was one of the leading thinkers in Europe and a successor to Marx and Engels as theorist of the international socialist movement. There are many more references to Kautsky in *The Social Teaching* than to Nathusius, and Kautsky's interpretation of Christianity is overwhelmingly the main object of Troeltsch's polemic.[25] Indeed, as he makes clear in a footnote, Troeltsch's opening salvo in chapter 1 of *The Social Teaching* is directed at Kautsky:

> To put it quite plainly: Christianity was not the product of a class struggle of any kind; it was not shaped, when it did arise, in order to fit into any such situation; indeed, at no point was it directly concerned with the social upheavals of the ancient world.[26]

Yet in the secondary literature on *The Social Teaching*, Kautsky is hardly mentioned. In fact, the polemical thrust of Troeltsch's opening statement goes virtually unnoticed. For example, H. Richard Niebuhr, Wilhelm Pauck, Roland H. Bainton, James Luther Adams, Claude Welch, Wilhelm F. Kasch, and Robert J. Rubanowice do not mention Kautsky.[27]

This neglect of the original historical context of *The Social Teaching* by leading interpreters of Troeltsch justifies the large proportion of this book devoted to reconstructing it. The purpose of this reconstruction is entirely ancillary to the interpretation of Troeltsch's *Social Teaching* and two related texts by Troeltsch and Kautsky. While my interpretations of Troeltsch's texts constitute original research in the history of ideas, this research necessarily rests on a foundation of existing historical knowledge, which is presented in chapters 2 through 9.

In these chapters, I make no claims to original scholarship nor do I make any effort to review current scholarly debates on specialized issues in the history of Wilhelmine Germany. My purpose is to summarize established and uncontroversial historical knowledge based on the most authoritative secondary sources available, as well as select primary sources. This reconstruction of Wilhelmine Germany can serve as a general introduction to the period for readers unfamiliar with it. Since I have also told the story with a view to illuminating the Troeltsch-Kautsky debate, these introductory chapters can also serve for Troeltsch scholars as a review of specific historical information bearing on that debate, but which previously has not been applied to understanding it.

Chapters 2 through 9 cover the broad social and political context. I begin in chapter 2 with an examination of the "Social Problem," the explicit focus of concern in the introduction and conclusion of *The Social Teaching*. This necessarily leads into a description in chapters 3 through 5 of the German state, the universities, and the Protestant churches—the three major arenas in which Troeltsch was active while writing his massive work.

The Social Problem also leads naturally to a look in chapter 6 at the role of Social Democracy as the catalyst of political change, and its influence on Protestantism in chapter 7. Against this backdrop a quest for the historical Troeltsch is undertaken in chapter 8, and the issue of his intellectual stature is reassessed. Chapter 9 rings down the curtain on the overall historical context by focusing on what had been gathering force on the horizon all along: World War I.

The more immediate intellectual context to *The Social Teaching* is then examined; in chapter 10, Troeltsch's programmatic essay on political ethics (1904), and in chapter 11, Kautsky's social history of Christianity.

Only on the basis of this reconstruction of the social and intellectual contexts can chapter 12, which provides a fresh interpretation of *The Social Teaching*, be adequately understood. The summary in chapter 13 presents the "big picture" that has emerged; since it is also dependent on all the preceding chapters, this picture has not been extensively discussed at the outset. In my conclusion, I relate the thesis of this book to recent religious trends—including the debate between Peter Berger and advocates of Black and Latin American liberation theologies—and reflect on its significance in the context of the present global crisis.

In my quotations in English from *The Social Teaching*, I have used the authoritative translation by Olive Wyon wherever possible. In the few instances where I found this inadequate, I have explicitly noted that the translation is my own.

Notes

1. Ernst Troeltsch, *The Social Teaching of the Christian Churches*, trans. Olive Wyon (New York: The Macmillan Co., 1931; reprint ed., Chicago: The University of Chicago Press, 1981).
2. Ron Grossman, "Doctorate Denied: Constance Benson's Standing as a Scholar is More than an Academic Question," *Chicago Tribune* (December 8, 1993), Section 5:1–2; Peter Kadzis, "Cornel West for the Defense," *The Boston Phoenix* (November 26, 1993), Section 1:1; Jeffrey Goldberg, "Blindness or Insight? Is the Ernst Troeltsch Affair a Christian Coverup, or Merely a Matter of Grad Student Incompetence?" *Lingua Franca* (February, 1994), 44–49; Tom Weidlich, "A Thesis Fracas Comes Down to Procedure," *The National Law Journal*, 17: 36 (May 8, 1995), A12.
3. See Hans-Georg Drescher, *Ernst Troeltsch: His Life and Work* (Minneapolis, MN: Fortress Press, 1993), 222–223.

4. Fritz Fischer, "Der deutsche Protestantismus und die Politik im 19. Jahrhundert," Chap. in *Probleme der Reichsgründungzeit 1848–79*, edited by Helmut Böhme (Cologne und Berlin, 1968), 49–71. French, British, and American social historians have built on Fischer's work. In Germany, however, Richard J. Evans notes that: "The strength of the theological faculties in German universities, their explicit confessional allegiances and the tight grip which they have exercised over ecclesiastical history have prevented the emergence of a confessionally neutral, sociologically informed history of religion." Evans, *Rethinking German History: Nineteenth-Century Germany and the Origins of the Third Reich*. (New York: HarperCollins Academic, 1987), 129.

5. For this understanding of Christianity, I am largely indebted to Chiara Lubich, leader and principal founder of the international, ecumenical, and interreligious Focolare movement. Originating among Italian Catholic women during World War II, the Focolare movement now has local communities in over 180 nations and has over 200,000 persons in its core group. Chiara Lubich's writings on Christianity bring together rigorous scholarship on the origin and history of Christianity with a practical spirituality that aims to embody Christian principles in daily life, including the apostolic communism or communion of goods. She is the recipient of numerous honors, including the 1977 Templeton Prize for Progress in Religion and the 1996 UNESCO Education for Peace Prize. For a biography of the Focolare Movement and its founder, see Jim Gallagher, *A Woman's Work: Chiara Lubich* (Hyde Park, NY: New City Press, 1997).

6. The SA functioned like a street gang, engaging in gratuitous acts of violence to claim and control its territory. The SA was to the SS what the U.S. Army is to the Green Berets, according to Prof. Ulrich Herbert of the University of Freiburg, Germany, an expert on the Nazi SS, in conversation with this writer. It was also formed much earlier, before Hitler actually came to power. Adolf Hitler, "Basic Ideas Regarding the Meaning and Organization of the SA," *Mein Kampf*, Vol. II, translated by Ralph Manheim (Boston: Houghton Mifflin, 1925, 1971), 518–553; Ulrich Herbert, "Werner Best and the Intellectual Leadership of the Nazi SS," Paper presented at the City University of New York Graduate School, October 28, 1997; idem, *Best* (Bonn: Dietz, 1996).

7. Robert P. Ericksen, *Theologians Under Hitler: Gerhard Kittel/Paul Althaus/Emanuel Hirsch* (New Haven, CT: Yale University Press, 1985), 176.

8. *Wahrheit und Glaube: Festschrift für Emanuel Hirsch zu seinem 75. Geburtstag*, edited by Hayo Gerdes (Munich: "Die Spur", Itzehoe Herbert Dorbandt KG, 1963).

9. Wolfgang Trillhaas, "Repräsentant und Aussenseiter einer Generation: Nach dem Tode von Emanuel Hirsch," *Evangelische Kommentare, Monatsshrift zum Zeitgeschehen in Kirche und Gesellschaft*, 5 (1972), 602.

10. Trutz Rendtorff, former president and co-founder of the Ernst Troeltsch Society, in his eulogy of Wolfgang Trillhaas, emphasizes the pivotal roles that Hans Joachim Birkner and Wolfgang Trillhaas both played in the Troeltsch Society. Rendtorff, "In memoriam Wolfgang Trillhaas (1903–1995)," *Mitteilungen der Ernst-Troeltsch-Gesellschaft* IX (Augsburg, 1995/96), 1–2.

11. The Troeltsch literature is virtually silent on the link between Troeltsch and Lagarde, with the exception of the works of Troeltsch Society members Sarah Coakley and Hans-Georg Drescher. In his recent Troeltsch biography, Drescher makes no reference to Lagarde's notoriety. On the contrary, he describes Lagarde as "a deeply pious person." See my discussion of Lagarde in chapters 5 and 8. Drescher, *Ernst Troeltsch: His Life and Work*, 350 note 84; 21, 45, 349 note 82, 350 note 85. See also Drescher, "Ernst Troeltsch und Paul de Lagarde,"

Mitteilungen der Ernst-Troeltsch-Gesellschaft III, (Augsburg, 1984), 95–115; Sarah Coakley, *Christ without Absolutes: a Study of the Christology of Ernst Troeltsch* (Oxford: Clarendon Press, 1988), 48.

12. See Constance L. Benson, "Mainstreaming the Radical Right: Ernst Troeltsch's Appropriation of Paul de Lagarde," paper presented to the American Academy of Religion, Mid-Atlantic Region, March 4–5, 1993, Temple University, Philadelphia, PA.

13. Robert P. Ericksen, *Theologians Under Hitler: Gerhard Kittel/Paul Althaus/ Emanuel Hirsch*, 176.

14. In June 22, 1946, Pastor Martin Niemöller wrote a letter to Hans Assmussen, head of the Chancellery of the Evangelical Church of Germany, complaining, "'in the territorial churches there prevails everywhere a scarcely concealed politics of restoration and reaction, not the Word of God.'" Hannes Karnick and Wolfgang Richter, *Niemöller: Was Würde Jesus Dazu Sagen? Eine Reise durch ein Protestantisches Leben* (Frankfurt: Roderberg Verlag, 1986), 75.

    Shelley Baranowsky has written about the "myth of resistance" and the purpose it served to legitimate the Federal Republic of Germany within NATO during the Cold War period. Baranowsky, *The Confessing Church, Conservative Elites and the Nazi State* (Lewiston, NY: Edwin Mellen, 1986), 105–128.

15. Goldberg, *Lingua Franca*, 47. See also Garrett E. Paul, "Why Troeltsch? Why today? Theology for the 21st Century," *Christian Century* (June 30–July 7, 1993), 676–81.

16. "Meine Bücher," *Gesammelte Schriften*, vol. 4 (Tübingen: J.C.B. Mohr, 1925).

17. Drescher, *Ernst Troeltsch*, 222.

18. See chapter 8, page 93 of this book for a fuller treatment. Ernst Troeltsch, "The Place of Christianity among the World Religions," *Christian Thought: Its History and Application*, edited by Baron F. von Hügel (London: University of London Press, 1923), 24–5.

19. Roland H. Bainton, "Ernst Troeltsch—Thirty Years Later," *Theology Today* 8:1 (April 1951), 71. Bainton himself overlooks the context of *The Social Teaching* primarily because he has chosen to focus on its historical accuracy, rather than its ideological thrust within its own time and place.

20. Quentin Skinner, "Meaning and Understanding in the History of Ideas," *History and Theory* 8 (1969), 3–53; idem, "'Social Meaning' and the Explanation of Social Action," *Philosophy, Politics and Society*, Series IV, ed. Peter Laslett, W. G. Runciman and Quentin Skinner (Oxford: Blackwell, 1972), 136–57; idem, "Motives, Intentions and the Interpretation of Texts," *New Literary History* 3 (1972), 393–408; idem, "Hermeneutics and the Role of History," *New Literary History* 7 (1975–6), 209–32; idem, preface to *The Foundations of Modern Thought, vol. 1: The Renaissance* (Cambridge: Cambridge University Press, 1978), ix–xv.

21. For an example of the traditional history of ideas approach in the field of Christian ethics, see Waldo Beach and H. Richard Niebuhr, eds. *Christian Ethics: Sources of the Living Tradition*, 2nd ed. (New York: John Wiley and Sons, 1973). A work by H. Stuart Hughes provides the strong case of the traditional "history of ideas" approach: H. Stuart Hughes, *Consciousness and Society* (New York: Alfred A. Knopf, 1961).

22. Donald E. Miller, "Troeltsch's Critique of Karl Marx," *Journal for the Scientific Study of Religion* 1 (October 1961), 117. Note that the "Social Problem is a direct translation from the German: *das Soziale Problem*, Troeltsch, *Gesammelte Schriften*. Vol. 1, *Die Soziallehren der christlichen Kirchen und Gruppen* (Tübingen: J.C.B. Mohr, 1923), 8. Martin von Nathusius refers to the issue in

the title of his book as "the social question" [*die soziale Frage*]. Nathusius, *Die Mitarbeit der Kirche an der Lösung der soziale Frage* (Leipzig: J. C. Hinrichs, 1904).

23. Hans-Georg Drescher does refer in passing to Kautsky in his official biography of Troeltsch. However, he does not recognize Troeltsch's negative dependency upon Kautsky's earlier work on the history of Christianity. Rather, he uncritically adopts Troeltsch's own claim that with the publishing of *The Social Teaching*, a new discipline had been born. Drescher, *Ernst Troeltsch*, 222.

24. Karl Kautsky, *Die Vorläufer des Neuren Sozialismus*, 2 vols. (Stuttgart: J.H.M. Dietz, 1895).

25. Troeltsch, *The Social Teaching*, 166n. In fact Troeltsch explicitly cites Kautsky for refutation at least ten times (once in the body of the text): ibid., 28, 165–6n [3x], 169n, 175n, 176n, 355n, 399n, 399n and 821n. Related references include one on Marxism: ibid., 407n; on monastic communion of goods, ibid., 419n; on Christian socialism, ibid., 903n, 962n. Troeltsch also replied to other socialists such as Albert Kalthoff, 166–8n. For the sake of brevity I have focused upon his main antagonist, the one who made the most serious reconstruction of the communism of the early church.

26. Ernst Troeltsch, *The Social Teaching*, 39.

27. H. Richard Niebuhr, introduction to *The Social Teaching*; idem, *Ernst Troeltsch's Philosophy of History*, Ph.D. Thesis, Yale University Microfilms 1924, 1964; Wilhelm Pauck, "Ernst Troeltsch," in *Harnack and Troeltsch: Two Historical Theologians* (New York: Oxford University Press, 1968; idem, *From Luther to Tillich: The Reformers and Their Heirs*, ed. Marion Pauck (San Francisco, 1984); Roland H. Bainton, "Ernst Troeltsch—Thirty Years Later," 70–96; James Luther Adams, "Why the Troeltsch Revival?" *The Unitarian Universalist Christian* 29 (1974), 4–15; idem, "Ernst Troeltsch as Analyst of Religion," JSSR 1 (1961), 98–109; idem, "Troeltsch, Ernst," *Encyclopedia Britannica*, XXII (London/Chicago: William Benton, 1963), 489; Claude Welch, "A Social History of Christianity," *Protestant Thought in the Nineteenth Century*, vol. 2 (New Haven, CT: Yale University Press, 1985), 291–97; Wilhelm F. Kasch, *Die Sozialphilosophie von Ernst Troeltsch* (Tübingen: J.C.B. Mohr, 1963). Kautsky is also not mentioned by any of the contributors to the volume edited by John Clayton, *Ernst Troeltsch and the Future of Theology* (Cambridge: Cambridge University Press, 1976). Nor is he mentioned in the works of Benjamin A. Reist, Robert J. Rubanowice or Robert Morgan and Michael Pye. The omission by Rubanowice is particularly serious given his emphasis on Troeltsch's political writings. Benjamin A. Reist, *Toward a Theology of Involvement: The Thought of Ernst Troeltsch* (Philadelphia, PA: The Westminster Press, 1966); Robert J. Rubanowice, *Crisis in Consciousness: The Thought of Ernst Troeltsch*, with a foreword by James Luther Adams (Tallahassee: Florida State University, 1982); Robert Morgan and Michael Pye, *Ernst Troeltsch: Writings on Theology and Religion* (Atlanta, GA: John Knox Press, 1977).

The more recent works of Bryce A. Gayhart and Sarah Coakley also treat the subjects of *The Social Teaching* and Troeltsch's interpretation of Jesus in an apolitical way, failing to take account of the political debate that Troeltsch was engaged in with the Christian and secular left. Even though Coakley specifically refers to Troeltsch's section in *The Social Teaching*, "Christian Thought Dependent on Social Factors," she fails to interpret it in light of Troeltsch's debate with Kautsky. As usual, Gayhart mentions only Nathusius as Troeltsch's foil for *The Social Teaching*. Neither Gayhart nor Coakley reconstruct Troeltsch's socio-political context. Bryce A. Gayhart, *The Ethics of Ernst Troeltsch: A Com-*

mitment to Relevancy (Lewiston, NY: The Edwin Mellen Press, 1990), 181–212; *Sarah Coakley, Christ Without Absolutes: A Study of the Christology of Ernst Troeltsch* (Oxford: Clarendon Press, 1988), 193f.

From a Christian left perspective, Gary Dorrien misinterprets Troeltsch's *Social Teaching* as providing legitimation for social reform, because he also fails to read it in context. He mentions neither Kautsky nor the Evangelical Social Congress. Gary Dorrien, *Soul in Society: The Making and Renewal of Social Christianity* (Minneapolis, MN: Fortress Press, 1995), 4–5.

In his official biography of Troeltsch, Hans-Georg Drescher does draw a cursory link between Troeltsch and Kautsky. However, he uncritically echoes Troeltsch's opening dismissive statement towards Kautsky. He does not refer to Kautsky's earlier history of Christianity which provides a counterpoint for Troeltsch as he develops his alternative social history. Drescher, *Ernst Troeltsch*, 222–225.

Harry Liebersohn provides quite a good synopsis of *The Social Teaching*, even though he does not mention Kautsky's role. Liebersohn does place Troeltsch's *magnum opus* against the backdrop of the politics of the Evangelical Social Congress. From that standpoint, he views the work as serving a conservative, legitimizing purpose. Harry Liebersohn. *Religion and Industrial Society: the Protestant Social Congress in Wilhelmine Germany* (Philadelphia, PA: American Philosophical Society, 1986), 55–57.

2

Troeltsch's "Social Problem": Revolutionary Movements in Imperial Germany

Paul Göhre was a theology student who voluntarily spent three months working in a factory in industrial Saxony of the early 1890s in order to write about why the working class was flocking into the Social Democratic party. Göhre's report on what he found was a startling revelation for the affluent, cultured classes of Germany.[1] Göhre skillfully took his readers on a tour of the overcrowded, squalid living conditions which even skilled laborers had to endure:

The most wretched lodgings which I saw were those of another of our workmen. Here, the arrangements were actually unfit for human beings. The man was a machinist of long standing in the factory; no longer so young, well over fifty, an honest, good-natured little fellow with whom I liked to talk. His wife was sickly and half decrepit, subject to hemorrhage. He told me the story of their life and love in endless detail, as the people do, yet not without a certain touch of romance, and with the absolute ingenuousness and friendly confidence that springs up so quickly in such places between comrades young or old. Their children were already grown up and married. They had with them only one grandchild, affectionately cared for, but, on the other hand, they lodged five strangers. This man's dwelling-place was as follows: one "room," one alcove, a chamber with one window and a loft. In the small chamber were two beds, in one [p. 24] of which a horse-cardriver slept, and in the other two masons, Bohemians. The invalid wife slept in the alcove alone; for years she had been unable to have anyone lie beside her, and her husband slept, therefore, on a sofa in the living-room, which was used by all the members of that household for talking, eating, and smoking, from early morning until ten o'clock in the evening, which, for these people, means late into the night and into their time for sleep. The two masons having drunk their coffee prepared in this same room, left the house at half-past four in the morning, and the cardriver came home from his hard work at half-past nine in the evening, and must then have his supper. How was a really refreshing night's rest possible for the husband and wife? Yet the worst remains to be told. In the garret were also two beds, one of them sublet to a young newly-married pair who were out at work all day, and had literally nothing they could call their own; in the other slept the grandchild, a girl twelve years of age. The condition of affairs in this and other similar households, even with the best intention on the part of all the members, may easily be imagined.[2]

Thus, Göhre portrays eight people stuffed into four cramped rooms without privacy. He also provides a close-up of the prevailing twelve-hour work day and six-day work week:

[D]uring factory hours we had only two recesses for eating; twenty minutes for breakfast, from eight o'clock until twenty minutes past eight, and the dinner hour from twelve until one. The nearly eleven hours of labour, from six in the morning until six in the evening, were otherwise uninterrupted. Only the apprentice lads were allowed a half-hour's recess at four o'clock in the afternoon; all others who felt the need of food snatched a hasty mouthful at their work. The afternoon recess, which had formerly been the universal custom, had been given up voluntarily by the men themselves, in order to leave off work at six o'clock.[3]

Such was the human suffering that the rapid industrial expansion of the late nineteenth century brought to the German people. An enormous human sacrifice was demanded to create what would become the leading industrial nation in Europe by the turn of the century. Millions of factory workers crammed into the inner cities of the industrial Ruhr valley and other urban areas. Through the organizing efforts of the Social Democratic party the teachings of Marx spread like wildfire through their ranks, and labor unions were organized. Göhre wrote:

For proof of this I may quote some perfectly spontaneous expressions taken at random from all kinds of working men, and all conveying the same sentiment. "Every one of us, to the last man, voted the social-democratic ticket." "Working men are all social democrats, and vote for social democrats." "Every workman is a social democrat." "I vote for my kind." And especially sententious, "Everything here is social-democratic, even the machines."[4]

Göhre's report only confirmed the worst fears of members of the German elite. From their perspective, this was a nightmare scenario: not only masses of workers but even the very machines themselves rising up to overthrow the established order. As much as he sympathized with the workers' plight, Göhre was also disturbed by the subversive effect this was having on Christian loyalties:

More than once it has been said to me in the factory, in so many words: "What Jesus Christ has been in the past, Bebel and Liebknecht will be in the future."[5]

In other words the "Social Problem," as it was delicately phrased, referred not only to massive human sufffering in the wake of industrialization. By Troeltsch's day it had become the most burning political and religious issue as well.[6]

While the class issue loomed large, there were other social problems which are reflected in *The Social Teaching*. These include the oppression of women, Jews, Catholics, and the colonies.

In Imperial Germany, the ideal woman was a gracious creature, busily tending hearth and home as a haven for her work-wearied husband. Therefore, there was every reason to keep women out of the public domain: to keep them from voting, from joining labor unions, from prosecuting abusive husbands in court, or from entering higher education and the professions.

For example, no secondary schools for girls existed that rivaled the *Gymnasien* in quality until just before the start of World War I. Throughout the nineteenth century the universities barred entrance to women students except those from other countries. Even after German women began to be admitted, they still could not take the civil service examination or earn advanced degrees. Only after World War I would the first German woman gain a Ph.D. degree, namely, Ricarda Huch, an eminent historian and novelist, and she had to earn it in Switzerland.

Most German men shared the sentiments of a Catholic who bemoaned in 1912, the year that *The Social Teaching* appeared, that all too many women wanted to fly from their quiet nests and become participants in public life.[7] By the turn of the century there were over 850 associations with a total of about 1,000,000 members dedicated to the improvement of working conditions, wider opportunities for employment, the pursuit of civil liberties and equality for women.[8]

Yet despite the political agitation on the part of the suffragettes, little progress was achieved before World War I. Gordon Craig wrote:

> [The Imperial German] ruling class was as intent upon keeping the female population in a state of dependence as it was upon combating socialism. All the expedients of the law, every form of financial and moral pressure, were employed to maintain male dominance in state, society, and the home.[9]

The author of this critical assessment, it should be noted, was not a feminist scholar of women's studies, but one of the most mainstream historians of late nineteenth-century Germany.[10]

The Jews also had their segregated place in German society. One of the most important by-products of rapid industrialization in Germany was the revival of anti-Semitism. With the stock market crash of 1873 the myth of a Jewish conspiracy, of the Jewish banker corrupting society, took on new life. Articles in newspapers such as the *Kreuzzeitung* commonly referred to German economic policy as "Jewish policy," and argued that the great banking houses were headed by Jews such as Herr von Bleichröder. Jewish bankers were accused of influencing the selection process of government officials and turning state ministers into Jewish puppets.[11]

Anti-Semitism was particularly strong in Berlin where by 1880 there were as many as 45,000 Jewish residents compared to only 46,000 Jews in all of England and only 51,000 in France during that time. A German writer of the time wrote that Berlin might as well be the capital of a Jewish Reich,

> since one meets the haughty Jew in all areas of the public sector...the flea-market, commercial and stock market Jew, the newspaper and literary Jew, the politician Jew, the theater and music Jew, and culture and charity Jew, and—what is unique to Berlin—the city official Jew. Nearly half of Berlin's city administrators...are Jewish...and, with their control of the newspapers and stock-market, they actually dominate all of city government.[12]

Many educated Berliners expressed a more nuanced form of anti-Semitism, preferring to make a distinction between the "good" Jews, such as Felix Mendelssohn, who had contributed their talents to culture, and the moneylenders and speculators, who through their get-rich-quick schemes, caused the market to crash.

The Jews were also accused of criticizing the internal affairs of the Christian churches, which, of course, were state-sponsored. Earlier, Schopenhauer had chastised the Jews for what he saw as their brashness and aggressiveness. By the end of the nineteenth century, cultured Germans of all political and social persuasions increasingly agreed with him and felt resentful of the perceived economic, cultural, and political dominance of the Jews.[13]

In a particularly notorious article in the *Preussische Jahrbücher* in November 1879, the historian Heinrich von Treitschke wrote, "the Jews are our national misfortune."[14] Theodor Mommsen and other academics publicly opposed his attacks. However, Treitschke's brazen anti-Semitism did not prevent him from subsequently becoming the editor of the prestigious *Historische Zeitschrift* and admitted to the Prussian Academy.

Treitschke's anti-Semitism was shared by many of his colleagues, as the statistics on professorial appointments suggest. Although there were many Jewish university instructors during the prewar years (1,909—about 12 percent of the total), there were far fewer professors and not one Jewish full professor in Berlin during those years.

In fact it was the university professors, the "bearers of culture" (*Kulturträger*), who more than any other group in society developed the stereotype of Jewish materialism—that while Germans were concerned with spiritual values, the Jews had sold out to Mammon.[15] Further, as long as Germany was identified as a Christian nation, Jews were perceived as foreigners. Within the theological disciplines, the Biblical scholars sought to cut off the Jewish roots of Christianity. For example, Ernest Renan in his *Life of Jesus* (1863) typically argued that Christ proclaimed a timeless religion of warmth and humanity as opposed to Old Testament dogmatism and intolerance.[16]

Arguably the most notorious anti-Semite of his generation was Paul de Lagarde, professor of biblical studies and ethics at Goettingen University and a mentor of Troeltsch.[17] His *German Writings*, which Troeltsch praises, are filled with invective against the Jews, whom he viewed as a cancer on the German nation.[18]

In addition to anti-Semitism, discrimination against the Catholic Church was resurgent in Germany in the decade before World War I, when Troeltsch was writing *The Social Teaching*. There was talk of another *Kulturkampf*, resurrecting memories of Bismarck's ruthless policies of the 1870s. Seeking to consolidate Prussian hegemony over the predominantly Roman Catholic south, Bismarck had dissolved Jesuit schools, banned most monastic orders, and imprisoned or deported Catholic clergy in large numbers. The persecution backfired, however, and the Catholic "Center Party" actually doubled its votes, forcing Bismarck to repeal the repressive legislation in 1879.

The National Liberals, Troeltsch's party, enthusiastically supported the *Kulturkampf*. As Craig remarks, "In the name of freedom they underwrote laws that denied it, and placed their party, which pretended to maintain the cause of the individual against arbitrary authority, squarely behind a state that recognized no limits to its power."[19]

In 1905, about the time Troeltsch was beginning his work on *The Social Teaching*, the Catholic Center Party and the Social Democratic party opposed proposed increases in military spending. Catholic politician Matthias Erzberger also published a series of embarrassing reports about the German government's financial involvement in South West Africa and brutality towards the indigenous peoples. In retaliation, Chancellor Bülow moved against the Catholic Center and Socialist parties by uniting the liberal and conservative parties behind a campaign of nationalism, militarism, antisocialism and renewed anti-Catholicism. The people were fed conspiratorial theories that Germany's enemies were hoping for a union of Catholics and socialists that would spell the doom of Imperial Germany.[20] Red-baiting now went hand in hand with Catholic-bashing. Troeltsch's National Liberal Party made anti-Catholicism the primary theme of its 1907 Reichstag campaign, raising the specter of a new *Kulturkampf.*

Used against the Catholics and socialists, colonialism and militarism were important rallying cries for maintaining loyalty to the German regime. While laborers, women, Jews, and Catholics were challenging social arrangements from within, colonial expansion helped power-holders rally the nation under their conservative leadership, a contributing cause of World War I. Troeltsch was writing *The Social Teaching* during a high water mark of European colonialism.[21]

Germany was a relative latecomer in the scramble to acquire colonies. As the German leaders observed Britain, France, and Italy busily dividing Africa and the Pacific islands among themselves, they acted to catch up. German industrialists pointed to overproduction, the rapid growth of the Social Democrats, and the need for new markets abroad as reasons to leap into the race for colonies.

By the 1880s the German leadership set out to acquire South West Africa and parts of the Fiji Islands. Germany hosted a major international conference on the administration of the Belgian Congo and other aspects of European colonialism in Africa. In 1906 colonialism gained popularity with the discovery in South West Africa of rich diamond and copper deposits.

In Germany, as elsewhere, top academics and opinion makers provided the ideological legitimation for colonial policies made by business leaders and government officials.

Professors Adolf Wagner, Gustav Schmoller, Heinrich von Sybel, and Heinrich von Treitschke supported Germany's goal to expand its colonies.[22]

Virtually all the student organizations were swept by nationalism, militarism, anti-Semitism, and anti-Catholicism during the period of Imperial Germany. During Troeltsch's student years in the 1880s, they had regressed into "beer-swilling, duel-fighting, song-bawling fraternities."[23]

Influenced by this trend, Max Weber, Troeltsch's colleague and close friend, joined a dueling fraternity as a student at Heidelberg and soon carried the conventional dueling scar on his face. When he visited his mother in Berlin, she was so shocked at how her son had taken on the look of an Imperial German that she slapped him across the face. His mother's wrath did not deter young Max from serving a year in the army soon thereafter and eventually becoming a reserve officer.

Recalling those years Weber later wrote: "The usual training for haughty aggression in the dueling fraternity and as an officer has undoubtedly had a strong influence on me. It removed the shyness and insecurity of my adolescence."[24] Far from sharing his mother's disgust with this "training for haughty aggression," Weber believed that it had made a man of him. This incident, combined with women on the march, suggests a "gender gap" concerning the values of Imperial Germany in Troeltsch's own day.

In summary, the growth of an industrial proletariat and the rise of Social Democracy was by no means the only "social problem" of the day. Women had organized into a number of politically active associations, the Berlin Jews were making their presence increasingly felt, and Roman Catholics had organized their own political party. Imperial German leaders responded with a politics of social reaction, African colonialism, and militarism. Their main target was Social Democracy, the one political force with the potential of overthrowing the established order.[25]

Social Democracy exercized such political power in part by reaching beyond its primary social base among industrial workers and embracing the causes of other oppressed groups. Social Democrats spoke and wrote on behalf of the women's movement, of the Catholic working class, of Jews, and even of indigenous peoples in the colonies. They spoke out against the traditional ideologies of the family, nationalism, and militarism, seeing them as legitimations not only of capitalism but of patriarchy and imperialism as well. This overarching analysis was an important element of Social Democracy's organizing success.

Before examining in more detail this threat to the power structure of Imperial Germany, it will be helpful to turn now to the structure itself.

Notes

1. Paul Göhre, *Three Months in a Workshop: A Practical Study*, trans. A. B. Carr (New York: Charles Scribner's Sons, 1895; repr., New York: Arno Press, 1972), viii.
2. Ibid., 23–4.
3. Ibid., 29.
4. Ibid., 112.
5. Ibid.
6. Karl Kupisch, "Einleitung," *Quellen zur Geschichte des deutschen Protestantismus (1871–1945)* (Göttingen: Musterschmidt Verlag, 1960), 12. Virtually

all that H. Richard Niebuhr said about the "Social Problem," is that it had to do with "the human problems attendant on the rise of industrial society." He neglected to describe the political controversy accompanying industrialization in Germany. Niebuhr, "Introduction," *The Social Teaching*, 7. Rubanowice, a leading interpreter of Troeltsch's political writings, makes no reference to a Social Problem. He argues that "living standards of the masses had never been so high" in the wake of industrialization. Rubanowice, *Crisis in Consciousness*, with a foreword by James Luther Adams, 2.

7. Gerhard A. Ritter and Jürgen Kocka, eds., *Deutsche Sozialgeschichte: Dokumente und Skizzen*, vol. 2: *1870–1914* (Munich, 1974), 426.

8. "Introduction: Imperial Germany and World War I," *When Biology Became Destiny: Women in Weimar and Nazi Germany*, eds. Renate Bridenthal, et al. (New York: Monthly Review, 1984), 1–5.

9. Gordon A. Craig, *Germany: 1866–1945* (Oxford: Oxford University Press, 1978), 207.

10. Nor were suffragette women the only Imperial Germans to endorse what we today would call gender reform. Craig prefaced the observation cited above with this quote from Troeltsch's contemporary Ernest Rhys: "'The woman's predicament is the test of the moral and human worth of any given state of society.'" Ibid.

11. Ivo N. Lambi, *Free Trade and Protection in Germany, 1868–1879* (Wiesbaden: F. Steiner, 1963), 84f.

12. Konstantin Frantz, *Der Föderalismus als das leitende Prinzip für die soziale, staatliche und internationale Organisation unter besonderer Bezugnahme auf Deutschland*, (Mainz: Kirchheim, 1879), 268.

13. Paul W. Massing, *Rehearsal for Destruction: A Study of Political Anti-Semitism in Imperial Germany* (New York: H. Fertig, 1949), 313f.

14. Treitschke quoted in Craig, *Germany 1866–1945*, 204.

15. Fritz Ringer, *Decline of the German Mandarins* (Cambridge, MA: Harvard University Press, 1969), 46, 135–37.

16. George L. Mosse, *Toward the Final Solution: A History of European Racism* (Madison: University of Wisconsin Press, 1985), 129–30.

17. Fritz Stern, *The Politics of Cultural Despair* (Berkeley: University of California Press, 1961), 63.

18. Paul de Lagarde, *Deutsche Schriften* (Göttingen: Lüder Horstmann, 1903); Ernst Troeltsch, *Gesammelte Schriften* Vol. 2, *Zur religiösen Lage, Religionsphilosophie und Ethik* (Tübingen: J.C.B. Mohr, 1913), 19–21. I discuss Lagarde's influence on Troeltsch more fully in chapters five and eight.

19. Craig, *Germany 1866–1945*, 78.

20. Peter-Christian Witt, *Die Finanzpolitik des deutschen Reiches von 1903 bis 1913* (Lübeck: Matthesen, 1970), 158.

21. Troeltsch was influenced by and himself contributed to an ideology of race that legitimized European colonialism. I discuss this point more fully in chapters eight, ten and twelve.

22. Hans Ulrich Wehler, *Bismarck und der Imperialismus*. (Cologne: Kiepenheuer and Witsch, 1969), 142.

23. Craig, *Germany: 1866–1945*, 206.

24. H. H. Gerth and C. Wright Mills, *From Max Weber: Essays in Sociology* (New York: Oxford University Press, 1958), 7.

25. Richard Evans and other recent historians of Imperial Germany correctly emphasize the central role that these challenges to established authority played in the politics of the regime. The challenges arose from both left and right ends of

the political spectrum. Evans argues, "...the rise of the feminist movement was only part of a far broader political mobilization of German society, including workers, peasants, nationalists, anti-Semites, agrarians and many others, that was going on in the 1890s." He also avers, "It was out of such social upheaval, seen in a general sense, and not out of social stagnation, that Nazism was eventually born." Richard J. Evans, *Rethinking German History: Nineteenth-Century Germany and the Origins of the Third Reich* (New York: HarperCollins, 1987), 6, 2; see also Geoff Eley, *From Unification to Nazism* (Boston: Allen & Unwin, 1986), 243.

3

"Blood and Iron":
The Military-Industrial Complex

On January 18, 1871 when Troeltsch was about six years old, King William I of the Prussian House of Hohenzollern stood in the court of Versailles and became the Emperor of the Second Reich.[1] William's coronation in the halls of the French kings spelled humiliation for his freshly defeated neighbor. It also symbolized the unification of Germany and its rise to preeminence on the European Continent.

What a contrast this achievement was to the failed Revolution of 1848! A wave of democracy had swept Europe then, driving Metternich out of office, the French king from his throne, and William himself to institute limited democratic reforms. But in most places, the democratic forces could not govern effectively, and the old regimes returned. In Frankfurt, a constitutional assembly drafted a democratic plan for German unification and offered William the crown, which he contemptuously rejected to their dismay. Willian then ordered the military to disband the assembly forcibly.

Not only was the drive to popular sovereignty quashed, but democratic ideas were also scrapped in favor of authoritarian ones. Bismarck's oft-quoted statement captured the views that dominated the media of the day: "Not through speeches and majority resolutions are the great questions of the day decided—that was the great mistake of 1848 and 1849—but through blood and iron."

William had appointed Prince Otto von Bismarck his chief minister in 1862, upon the recommendation of his minister of war. Not long after his appointment Bismarck proposed increased military spending and put the issue to a vote in the Prussian parliament. When the measure was defeated, Bismarck simply flouted parliamentary legality and found a way to fill the Prussian war chest through other means. Through a program of military aggression culminating in the Franco-Prussian war of 1870, Bismarck then unified the German states under Prussian domination. By the 1880s, not only had Germany become the most powerful nation in Europe, it had joined Britain and France as a major colonial power.

Notwithstanding the dubious constitutionality of his actions, Bismarck's success convinced the educated German public that authoritarian leadership, a time-honored German tradition harking back to Frederick the Great, was preferable to democracy and the ideals of the French Revolution.

Such was the cultural climate in which Troeltsch was born and raised. It was precisely during his formative years that this authoritarian Prussian heritage with its emphasis on the military was given new life.[2]

Bismarck and Emperor William I united the highly disciplined Prussian military with the latest organizational and technological developments to produce a fighting machine of unprecedented power. To the time-honored, feudal tradition of the officer corps was added the institution of the general staff, which made possible modern military planning, strategizing, and mobilization. Such German innovations were state-of-the-art and soon emulated by the other European powers, including Britain.

Science and industry were also put to work designing new weaponry. The great powers were soon mass producing chemical weapons, mines, submarines, torpedos, more destructive and heavily armored warships, and artillery and ordnance with unprecedented destructive power. This militarization of industry took on a momentum of its own, fueling an arms race that proved highly profitable for Krupp in Germany, Schneider in France, and other captains of industry.

The rise to power of Emperor William II in 1888 and his dismissal of Bismarck as Reich Chancellor in 1890 signalled the rapid breakdown of what had been Bismarck's carefully crafted system of diplomatic alliances. The new emperor and his chief naval advisor, Admiral Alfred von Tirpitz, set out to strengthen further the German navy so as to narrow the gap with the then unequaled British navy. Britain responded in kind, and the naval arms race between the two countries escalated. Meanwhile, German and French land forces threatened one another on the continent, and by 1890 German military planners had formulated a preemptive first-strike strategy.

The escalating arms race consumed vast amounts of funds which were raised through unprecedented tax hikes. For example, in 1903 Emperor William II demanded the passage of yet another military spending bill in the Reichstag to further strengthen the navy. It would mean tax increases on tobacco, beer, and brandy. Reich Chancellor Bülow realized that the only way these tax hikes could be approved would be to make concessions on some social reform legislation. At this point, Bülow arranged a series of consultations between the emperor and the Protestant theologian Adolf von Harnack, an older colleague of Troeltsch, to convince the monarch of the wisdom of this strategy.[3]

The dominance of military-industrial interests and authoritarian rule in Imperial Germany limited the power of democratic institutions. It was clear that the Empire was created by the royal houses of Germany.

> There was, in short, to be no nonsense about popular sovereignty in the new Empire. The German people were not to be allowed to claim the dangerous powers that the American people, for example, could demand on the basis of their Declaration of Independence and the preamble of their constitution. On the contrary, it was to be clear from the outset that the Reich was a gift that had been presented to them and that, if it were not properly appreciated, it might be withdrawn.[4]

To understand how limited democracy actually was, consider the composition of the houses of parliament. The upper house of the imperial parliament, or Bundesrat, was made up of representatives from the state governments. Of the thirty-five total votes, Prussia controlled seventeen, by far the largest and most decisive share (the next being Bavaria with only six votes). Under the Constitution, Prussia had absolute veto power over legislation dealing with the military, taxes and the constitution.[5] Such was the dominance of Prussia in the Empire that nothing indicated where the Prussian king's powers left off and the emperor's began.[6]

The lower house of the German Empire, or the Reichstag, had very limited powers, but was nevertheless a perennial irritation to the rulers and was closely monitored. The Reichstag was disbanded and new elections called whenever it threatened to intervene seriously in matters of state. It was elected by universal male suffrage, but the voting districts were not reapportioned to reflect urbanization, giving conservative rural voters much more electoral power than industrial workers. By 1907, for example, the Social Democrats were outpolling the agrarian-based Conservative party nearly three to one, but received fewer seats in the Reichstag. This undemocratic bias also favored the Catholic Center Party, with its largely rural social base, over the urban-based SPD.[7]

The lower house of the Second Reich officially opened with Emperor William I presiding on March 21, 1871. The assembled delegates were divided into five major political parties or groups. From the political right to left there were the Conservatives, the Free Conservatives, the National Liberals, the Catholic Center party, and the Social Democrats (who at this time were not organized into a single party).[8] The Conservatives were the party of the Prussian landed nobility, with their seat of power east of the Elbe River. The Free Conservatives, who represented the new industrialists as well as agrarian interests, gave unswerving support to Bismarck's policies and received many positions in his government.

The National Liberals were a procapitalist party, favoring laissez-faire economics and increased governmental centralization but under the constraints of a constitutionally limited monarchy. Their educated and upper middle-class members—including many university professors and government officials—were concentrated in Saxony, Hanover, Baden and in the industrial areas adjacent to the Rhine.

The National Liberals were comprised of two factions. The more conservative of the two, which included Troeltsch, supported Bismarck's repressive and militaristic policies. The more liberal faction, which included Lujo Brentano and the would-be revolutionaries of 1848, split off in 1880 to form the Progressive Party. They continued to criticize Bismarck, pushing especially for greater parliamentary democracy and civil liberties.

Founded in 1870 to protect the rights of Roman Catholics in an officially Protestant country, the Center Party was larger than either of the Conservative parties, drawing its strength from Bavaria, Silesia, the Polish provinces of Prussia and the Rhineland. The party was economically progressive, combating the evils of capitalism through workers' cooperatives and Catholic trade unions, and it was critical of colonialism and militarism. But it promoted a culturally conservative program of religious schools, traditional morality, the patriarchal family, and feudal institutions such as monarchy.

Finally, at the left end of the political spectrum stood delegates representing the urban workers and secular trade unions, who were to form the Social Democratic Party in 1875, as discussed chapter 6.

When the lower house of the Empire opened in 1871, the National Liberal party held the dominant position. Encompassing progressives in its own left faction and forming coalition with the Free Conservatives to its right, it was able to control a majority of the votes. By 1912, after a history of remarkable growth, the Social Democrats would gain the dominant position, despite the very unrepresentative apportionment of seats and various other obstacles the government put in its way.

Despite the Industrial Revolution that transformed Germany during this period, the landed nobility remained the wealthiest stratum of society until 1914 and thereby bolstered economically their continued social and political dominance. Throughout Germany the new bourgeoisie never developed their own autonomous social, cultural, or political institutions by which to challenge the supremacy of the old society. Rather they coveted and vied for aristocratic privileges and titles, steering their sons into joining dueling fraternities, and their daughters into marrying the sons of aristocrats.

In turn the emperor annually bestowed titles of nobility on certain industrialists who proved their loyalty to the values and traditions of the old order.[9] The continued dominance of feudal institutions was most strikingly illustrated by the ease with which the young Emperor William II fired Bismarck from the chancellorship in 1890 on grounds of insubordination. Bismarck had been the architect not only of the Second Reich, but also of German modernization, and was the most powerful statesman in Europe.[10]

In summary, Imperial Germany witnessed the resurrection of crown, sword, flag—and altar as we shall see in subsequent chapters. Neither the churches nor the universities, themselves feudal institutions in their origins, were to pose a serious challenge to this arrangement.

Furthermore, the ideals of the French Revolution—equality, liberty, fraternity and the perfectibility of man based on belief in his essential goodness—gave way to the appeal to "practicality," to nationalism and the military-industrial state. While certain liberal values such as democracy, welfare, and universal education did not disappear, they were eclipsed in the aftermath of the failure of the Revolutions of 1848.

The only major political force that persisted in espousing these liberty values was Social Democracy. Herein lay the awesome threat that it posed. It was nothing less than the vehicle of a continuing fundamental challenge to the old authoritarian order.

Notes

1. Germany's "First Reich" was the Holy Roman Empire. I use the terms, "Second Reich," "Second Empire" and "Imperial Germany" interchangeably.
2. Troeltsch was born February 17, 1865 just outside of Augsburg during the process of unification. See chapter 8.
3. Brose cites General Field Marshal Alfred Grafen von Waldersee's records of these consultations held on the dates of January 11, January 19, February 2, and February 8, 1903. Eric Dorn Brose, *Christian Labor and the Politics of Frustra-*

tion in Imperial Germany (Washington, DC: The Catholic University of America Press, 1985), 187.

4. Craig, *Germany: 1866–1945* , 44.
5. Arno Mayer, *The Persistence of the Old Regime* (New York: Pantheon Books, 1981), 158–9.
6. Ibid., 147.
7. Ibid., 168–69; Tenfelde discusses the various ways in which the working class was denied political power by an authoritarian state apparatus. Klaus Tenfelde, "Germany," *The Formation of Labour Movements, 1870–1914*, vol. I, edited by Marcel van der Linden and Jürgen Rojahn (Leiden: E.J. Brill, 1990), 254–55.
8. Viewing the parties along this single continuum, of course, simplifies political reality. While standing to the left of most National Liberals on labor and foreign policy issues, for example, the Catholic Center Party generally stood to their right on many cultural issues. After the formation of the Progressive Party in 1880, I locate the Center Party to the right of the Progressives. Like any other conceptual model, this linear view of the partisan landscape is useful provided that its limitations are kept in mind. In my understanding of the political parties in Imperial Germany, I am indebted to Gordon Craig, *Germany: 1866–1945*, 62f.
9. Mayer, *Persistence of the Old Regime*, 96–97.
10. Craig, *Germany: 1866–1945*, 171–79; Tenfelde uses the term "defensive modernization" to refer to the influence of the French Revolution upon Germany. The German establishment grudgingly modernized to absorb and manage this influence. Tenfelde, "Germany," 248.

4

The Professors: Guardians of the Citadel

In his post-World War I memoirs, the historian Friedrich Meinecke, a close friend of Troeltsch, contrasted the political decay and the robust intellectual life of the Second Reich.[1] But he wrote approvingly of the union of state and culture during the preceding Prussian reform period at the beginning of the nineteenth century:

> In those years culture and intellect [*der deutsche Geist*] freely merged with the state, and springs were tapped that irrigated all of German life, far beyond the immediate goal of liberating the country. Earlier achievements, when the German spirit yearned only to perfect itself, undoubtedly reach farther into eternity. But by descending to the state, the spirit not only preserved its own endangered existence as well as that of the state, it secured a reservoir of moral and psychological wealth, a wellspring of creative power for later generations.[2]

Meinecke's description of how the German spirit "freely merged with the state," refers to the period when the German intelligentsia embraced nationalism. While viewing this development somewhat critically as a "descent" compared to the Golden Age of Bach and Kant, Meinecke nevertheless believed that culture and government both benefitted from the merger. What he neglected to take into account, however, was the way culture would provide legitimation to existing political structures.[3] The overwhelming majority of writers, artists, and academics of Imperial Germany reflected and actively legitimated, rather than challenged, prevailing political and social values. The theologians, whether orthodox or modernist, were no exception.

In the face of growing nationalism, militarism, and urban blight, the majority of Germany's novelists and poets chose to flee into "inwardness" (*Innerlichkeit*). The rise of German Impressionism and cultivation of aestheticism reflected the artists' retreat from the disturbing political and economic events of the day. What is striking about the novels, short stories, and articles of the late 1890s is the absence of political content. The poets of the day—Richard Dehmel, Detlev von Liliencron, Stefan George, Richard von Schaukal, Rainer Maria Rilke, Hugo von Hofmannsthal—did not focus on political themes, but rather on subjective states of mind and stream of consciousness.[4]

> Others must by a long dark way
> Stray to the mystic bards,
> Or ask someone who had heard them sing
> Or touch the magic chords.
> Only the maidens question not
> The bridges that lead to Dream;
> Their luminous smiles are like strands of pearls
> On a silver vase agleam.
>
> The maidens' doors of Life lead out
> Where the song of the poet soars,
> And out beyond to the great world—
> To the world beyond the doors.[5]

There were a few lonely exceptions who engaged in social criticism of Wilhelmine society. For example, the dramatist Frank Wedekind, who paved the way for the twentieth-century theater of the absurd, poetically expressed the prevailing mood of the day:

> Finally the great day has come
> Already the past is dreadfully near,
> Though the future is already blurred;
> While the present is no more.
>
> God and humans and the cosmos have vanished,
> What once has been, glows in the dawn;
> Quietly stands the otherwise so hasty hour,
> And now lying still are also the dead.
>
> Out of the night a horror gathers strength,
> A thunderous voice calls: "I am!"...
> With a thunderclap piercing suddenly
> The broad, desolate expanse therein.
>
> All stare anxiously round about,
> No one looks another in the eye;
> Out of the deep there gently moans
> A ghostly voice: "I am not!"...
>
> A maiden from the far north
> Miraculously has arrived at the solution:
> The poet had been a philosopher
> And the philosopher's insane.[6]

About the time Troeltsch was writing *The Social Teaching*, novelist Heinrich Mann denounced his contemporaries for studiously ignoring or even actively supporting the authoritarian German state.[7]

The professors—especially in the social sciences and humanities—were the vanguard of an elite class of cultural leaders or "mandarins" also comprised of doctors, lawyers, artists, clergy, government officials and secondary school teachers.[8] Meinecke had good reason to praise the German scholarship of the late nineteenth century, for it was an age of humanistic accomplishment. This grew out of devotion to the Greek ideal of *paideia*, a wholistic cultivation of the person, as the goal of education. Therefore, even while the sciences flourished, German universities were often judged by the strength of their humanities faculties.[9] A brief look at the dominant figures should illustrate the renaissance of their fields in Imperial Germany.[10]

In philosophy, Kuno Fischer, Hermann Cohen, and Heinrich Rickert began a Kantian revival in the 1870s centered at Heidelberg.[11] Along with Eduard von Hartmann's "philosophy of the unconscious," this signalled a break from Hegelian dialectics and from system-building in general.[12] Cohen's student, Ernst Cassirer, turned to symbolic forms while Edmund Husserl at Göttingen developed the phenomenological method.[13] Wilhelm Windelband, one of the most noted neo-Kantian philosophers of the late nineteenth century, was a formative influence on Troeltsch. Windelband gave a rectoral address at Strasburg in 1894 that contrasted sharply with the philosophies of Darwin and Comte based on naturalism and materialism.[14]

Philology also thrived and expanded into the new fields of romance studies in Bonn and Near Eastern and Asian studies in Berlin. The brothers Jakob and Wilhelm Grimm had established Germanic studies as a major field at the beginning of the century.[15] With the unification of Germany the field became a vehicle for instilling a spirit of patriotism. It was, in the words of one historian, "not merely a science but a handmaid for the salvation of the nation."[16]

Leopold von Ranke's historical critical method was a great contribution to the field of history. Although a professor at the University of Berlin since 1825 and seventy-five years old when German unification took place, Ranke continued to labor for another sixteen years.

After 1871, several major historical works appeared including Adolf von Harnack's *History of Dogma*,[17] Eduard Meyer's *History of Antiquity*,[18] the final volume of Theodor Mommsen's *History of Rome*,[19] and Ranke's *Universal History*[20] which unfortunately did not reach completion. These were works of great scholarly erudition and written with literary flair.

Ranke's approach to history focused on the role of the state, an approach which became more popular in the wake of German unification. Political historians commanded the terrain, including Heinrich von Sybel of Bonn who wrote the multivolume *Founding of the German Empire by William I* and Heinrich von Treitschke of Berlin whose *German History* was a paean to German nationalism.[21]

Wilhelm Dilthey was to break with the traditional methods of the political historians and begin to place more emphasis on intellectual history (*Geistesgeschichte*). Ernst Troeltsch and Friedrich Meinecke were among those to follow Dilthey, who in his *Introduction to the Cultural Sciences* (1883) charged that the political historians were too narrow and parochial in scope.[22] In 1908 Meinecke brought forth *Cosmopolitanism and the National State*, a pioneering effort in the history of ideas.[23] Four years later, Troeltsch's *Social Teaching* appeared, taking a very similar historiographic approach.

The political historians dominated the field of history, while the intellectual historians such as Troeltsch comprised an important minority approach. By contrast, a third group, the pioneers of social historiography, were given a chilly reception by the Wilhelmine academic community. These social historians included Karl Lamprecht, Otto Hintze, Kurt Breysig, and of course Karl Kautsky.[24] Even Meinecke joined the orthodox critics of the new method. At a gathering of historians in 1908, when Breysig described the social historian's goal of synthesizing the intellectual, political, and economic dimensions of a given period, he was told not to let his imagination get out of hand. Hintze's groundbreaking work in institutional and comparative history went virtually unrecognized in his lifetime.

This important difference between intellectual and social history, which caused so much conflict at the time, has been neglected by some recent commentators. Claude Welch, for example, classifies *The Social Teaching* as a form of social history.[25] Michael Pye also fails to make this distinction when he refers univocally to "the method" of Marx and Troeltsch.[26] To be sure, Troeltsch was also influenced by Weber's sociology. As discussed below, however, Weber himself was more in the tradition of German idealism than of social history. In any case, most interpreters of Troeltsch compare his method to that of other theologians rather than historians of his time.

In summary, Troeltsch wrote at a time when political and intellectual history emerged as largely separate sub-disciplines, a division of labor that continues to influence the practice of historiography today. Pioneering efforts in social history, however, remained outside the academic mainstream in Imperial Germany.

The social sciences began to come into their own during this period. Economics forged ahead through Gustav Schmoller, Adolf Wagner, and Lujo Brentano who saw their discipline as more an inductive and empirical science than an elaboration of theory.[27] They generally took exception to laissez-faire economics, although Brentano favored free trade in opposition to the landed gentry. A member of the Progressive Party, Brentano raised eyebrows among his colleagues with his activism on behalf of coal miners and female mill workers.

Psychology was still in its infancy when Wilhelm Wundt, who taught philosophy, opened the first psychological laboratory in the world at Leipzig in 1879.[28] Kiel instructor Ferdinand Tönnies launched modern German sociology with his 1887 work *Community and Society*.[29] Analysing the process by which a society based on traditional values could become based on reason, Tönnies help set an intellectual agenda for his successors before 1914, most notably Georg Simmel and Max Weber.[30]

Like Dilthey's method of *Geistesgeschichte* in the field of history, Weber's sociology provided a mainstream academic alternative to Marxist social analysis. In his 1904–1905 *The Protestant Ethic and the Spirit of Capitalism*, Weber examined the impact of culture on political economy. His emphasis on the subjectivity (*Sinn*) of historical agents and the reconstruction of such subjectivity (*Verstehen*) by sociology placed Weber in the German idealist tradition.[31]

Clearly, the impressive scholarly accomplishments summarized above cannot be reduced to mere legitimation of the power structure of Imperial Germany. To the extent this scholarship addressed social and political issues, however, it increasingly conformed to and legitimized official opinion, as is most clearly revealed in the work of political historians such as Treitschke. This was the case despite the self-image of the professors as disinterested champions of *Veritas*. Professor Werner, the protagonist of a novel published in 1865, proudly states:

> No royalty is nobler, no dominion more powerful than ours. We shepherd the souls of the people from one century to the next; it is our duty to guard their learning and their thoughts. We are their champions against error and against the ghosts of the dead past, which still wander among us, clothed in the appearance of life. What we consecrate for life, lives, and what we condemn, withers away. The

old virtues of the apostles are expected of us, to ignore what is passing, but to expound truth.[32]

Despite this self-idealization, the German professors habitually lent their names in support of government policies that eventually proved to be reckless and irrational.[33] They were socially critical to the extent that they did see their world caught in a crisis of culture. But it was not the expansion of the Prussian officer corps that bothered them as much as the rise of the entrepreneurial class, the proletarianization and political awakening of displaced peasants, and the advent of the machine age which rapid industrialization ushered in.

They developed a doctrine of the state as the protector and sustainer of the intellectual and spiritual life of the nation. This legitimation of the state was an alternative to theories of divine right or theories of popular sovereignty. As Meinecke emphasized, this doctrine in effect attributes sovereignty to the learned *Kulturträger* or bearers of culture, rather than to the monarch or the people.

What began as a progressive doctrine in the context of absolute monarchy, such as that of Frederick the Great, became increasingly conservative by the end of the nineteenth century. Earlier, the German mandarins wholeheartedly supported the development of constitutional law to which the monarch must be subject. They also developed the concept of a private-public split, which began progressively as a defense of civil liberties in which the monarch had no right to intrude.[34] In addition, their defense of academic freedom for both students and professors won international renown for German universities.

Intrinsic to this doctrine of the state was the concept of individualism (*Individualismus*) and of the individual's relation to the state. Meinecke's description of the formative Romantic period makes this clear:

> Out of this deepening individualism of uniqueness, there henceforth arose everywhere in Germany, in various different forms, a new and more living image of the State, and also a new picture of the world. The whole world now appeared to be filled with individuality, each individuality, whether personal or supra-personal, governed by his own characteristic principle of life, and both nature and history constituting what Friedrich Schlegel called an "abyss of individuality."[35]

Using the word *Individualität*, Romantics such as Wilhelm von Humboldt, Novalis, Friedrich Schlegel and Friedrich Schleiermacher stressed the unique, the subjective, the qualitative and incomparable dimension of the person as opposed to a quantitative, atomized, and abstract emphasis that is usually attributed to the Anglo-French Enlightenment. When the term *Individualismus* came into usage in the 1840s through the writings of Karl Brüggemann, a German liberal, it was used in much the same way to denote that which is irreplaceable, infinite and whole—and also transpersonal or "suprapersonal."[36] It was a quality increasingly imputed to the personified state.

As in Meinecke's statement above, it is most important to note that the German understanding of individualism easily slides from a reference to an individual person to reference to the collective ("whether personal or supra-personal"). Georg Simmel, Max Stirner, and Ernst Troeltsch are also frequently cited thinkers who use the word in this way. In fact, Troeltsch's essay, "The Ideas of Natural Law and Humanity in World Politics" (1922), is particularly illustrative of the close relation between German *Individualismus* and the doctrine of the state:

> The decisive factor in this connection was a feeling, half mystical and half metaphysical, which interpreted the idea of individuality as meaning the particular embodiment from time to time assumed by the Divine Spirit, whether in individual persons or in the super-personal organisations of community-life. The basis of Reality was regarded as consisting, not in material and social atoms on a footing of equality with one another, or in universal laws of nature by which these atoms were combined, but in personalities constantly moving to different specific forms, and in plastic forces constantly at work on a process of individualisation.[37]

Here, Troeltsch contrasts the "half mystical and half metaphysical" German understanding of individualism to an Anglo-French understanding based on universal social laws. His understanding quickly shifts from separate persons to include the "suprapersonal" dimension. Then he proceeds to show how this different understanding results in a different relation of the individual to the state:

> The result of that conception, in turn, was a different theory of Community. Contract and rationally purposive construction were no longer regarded as the factors which created the State and Society out of individuals. The true factors were rather to be found in super-personal spiritual forces, radiating from individuals who laid the foundations of social life; in the National Mind [*Volksgeist*]; in the 'Idea' of the Good and the Beautiful.[38]

Note here the emphasis upon "the individuals who laid the foundations of social life," namely the bearers of culture who most purely embody the "National Mind" (*Volksgeist*). Also, observe Troeltsch's dismissal of community based upon a social contract. In other words, it is the culture-bearer, the philosopher, who is foundational to society and the state, who is the subject of history. It is the "National Mind" as embodied in certain great thinkers, not a social contract among separate individuals, which brings the state into being and provides it with legitimacy. Troeltsch goes on:

> Along with this different idea of Community there goes a different ideal for mankind in general—not the ideal of a final union of fundamentally equal human beings in a rationally organised community of all mankind, but the ideal of a wealth of national minds, all struggling together and all developing thereby their highest spiritual powers.[39]

Popular sovereignty and equality do not play the primary role in forming the state, as in the Anglo-French Enlightenment traditions.[40] Rather, this constitutive role is played by the charismatic leaders and leading lights of the various nations. To emphasize the stark contrast he is making, Troeltsch adds:

> You abandon a world where men are always seeking, on the basis of equality and by a mere process of incessant climbing, to increase [p. 212] the range of reason, well-being, liberty and purposive organisation, until they attain the goal of the unity of mankind. You enter a world in which there is a hierarchy of qualitatively different cultures—a world in which the people that from time to time enjoys the hegemony hands on the torch to the next.[41]

Writing after World War I, Troeltsch consciously abandons the model of a league of equal nations organized democratically, to embrace a hierarchical model of inherently unequal nations, which vie with one another for the dominant position. Yet he employs the language of individualism in service of this starkly authoritarian view.

Troeltsch's emphasis upon the state as the vehicle and sustainer of *Geist* is characteristic of German idealism. In this philosophical tradition, the word *Geist* meant mind, spirit or soul, a transcendental consciousness realized in the world of created matter. As the German name for the humanities (*Geisteswissenschaften*) suggests, the German mandarins were involved with the investigation of *Geist* in its external manifestations.[42]

Applied to the study of history, idealism was associated with an emphasis upon great leaders and the personification of cultures, eras, and nations as each containing its own unique *Geist*. This raised certain methodological problems which the German mandarins debated among themselves. For example, organic models or references to "immanent" processes of unfolding were employed, in the manner of Hegel. The diversity of actual historical facts were understood to be individualized expressions of *Geist*. How could one describe the ongoing trends in history without falling into this trap of utilizing unhistorical categories?[43]

For Troeltsch, previous idealist solutions to the problem of history were unsatisfactory. This problem was the focus of his inquiry in *Die Absolutheit des Christentums und die Religionsgeschichte* (1902) and also *Der Historismus und seine Probleme* (1922).[44] He was never able to arrive at a solution. While writing *The Social Teaching*, he worked within the neo-Kantian paradigm. In his autobiographical "My Books" (1922) he wrote: "I entered into close personal relations with Windelband and Paul Hensel and independently of them I was very strongly moved and furthered by Rickert's sharp logic."[45] Referring to his own work in the philosophy of history, Troeltsch reaffirmed this position:

> I devoted myself to a thorough critical examination of the theories of the philosophy of history advanced in the last hundred years.... I also sought to substantiate my own systematic thought, above all in conversation with Rickert and Windelband, who seemed to me to afford the most useful foundation in the contemporary situation.[46]

At the end of his life, Troeltsch knew that he had failed to solve the problem of history within the neo-Kantian framework. He clearly states, however, that he was never able to develop a better framework:

> The results of these reflections are now in the process of taking shape; but I cannot bring myself to reveal them as yet. I would only suggest that the solution seems to me to lie approximately in the direction of Malebranche, Leibniz, and Hegel.[47]

His late interest in Hegel also makes clear that, although the problem of history disturbed him greatly, Troeltsch would never venture beyond a German idealist framework.[48]

As Karl Kautsky himself acknowledged in *The Materialist Conception of History* (1927), Troeltsch was the most important philosopher of history of his time.[49] Troeltsch, Kautsky continued, believed that history was shaped by great personalities who create something entirely new all by themselves. These creative acts and thoughts come about through "inspiration" and defy any further explanation. "No wonder that it comes down to an obscure mysticism that shoves everything off onto God, who, to be sure, is also unknowable."[50]

As with the concept of "individualism," the concept of "freedom" had a very different meaning in German idealist, than in Anglo-French Enlightenment thought. For Troeltsch and his fellow mandarins, *Freiheit* did not mean the liberty of the individual, but rather involved a mystical understanding of "submission" (*Hingabe*) and "inwardness" (*Inner-lichkeit*), as found in German Lutheranism. In their secular form these concepts evolved into an ideal of voluntary submission to the community. The concept of freedom became the inner freedom of the highly developed personality. The state became the symbol of the German soul or *Geist*, to which even the monarch was to submit.

Whether the antecedents of German political theory are said to be found in romanticism, idealism, or German Protestantism, the same cluster of closely related themes surfaces repeatedly which diverge from Anglo-French liberal traditions.[51]

As described above, German mandarin political theory had been progressive within an earlier context of monarchical absolutism, where it served to place the king under constitutional law. With the development of a constitution and a state bureaucracy, the political power of the university men as official interpreters of the constitution greatly expanded. Under constitutional monarchy, they were to achieve their high-water mark within German society.

As the nineteenth century progressed, however, the political landscape began to include movements toward democracy, popular sovereignty, and universal suffrage. The mandarins became increasingly conservative in relation to these emerging social forces, often aligning themselves with the monarch. Their social position in Wilhelmine society was threatened by capitalism, socialism, and by modernity itself. They longed for the continuation of earlier social structures.[52] Thus, a "crisis of culture" haunted the mandarins professionally as well as spiritually.[53]

The fate of academic freedom in the Second Reich illustrates how the professoriate increasingly functioned to legitimize power.[54] The concept of academic freedom had been developed in Germany to an unparalleled degree and involved three things: first, freedom of the university itself—that a university should be administered by the faculty with the deans, whom they elect. Second, freedom of individual faculty members, who were to follow their own convictions unfettered by political pressures both in teaching and research. Such freedom was necessary, it was argued, if truth-seeking was to be the goal of intellectual inquiry. Third, there was the freedom of students, who were not to be bound by rigid curricula and could freely choose their course of study as long as they could pass the final examinations.

In reality, such freedoms were limited to begin with and were restricted still further after German unification. For one thing, the dependence of the universities on state financing greatly increased as the growth of science and technology gave rise to the need for expensive laboratory facilities. In fact, state financing to universities quadrupled between the years 1871 and 1908. Given this growing financial dependence, the universities became ever more reluctant to challenge the government on how subsidies should be used. Therefore, in practice, academic self-government was greatly curtailed.

Because the universities were state institutions receiving large subsidies, government officials made the final confirmation of academic appointments. Normally this was done in accord with the faculty's choice of candidates, but not always and automatically. This hands-off rule was increasingly violated as the century came to a close, particularly under Friedrich Althoff, the interventionist Prussian minister of education from 1897 to 1907. Freedom of the universities was flagrantly violated several times under his administration.

For example, Althoff created a Catholic Theological Faculty at the University of Strasburg and appointed Catholic medievalist Martin Spahn in an effort to improve relations with the Vatican. Acting without consulting the university's faculty, he created a storm of protest in Strasburg and Munich in the form of a petition from the university. Theodor Mommsen of Berlin pointed out that appointments based on political considerations would jeopardize the future of German scholarship. Although this protest included eminent scholars of the time, it made no impression on Althoff, who had the support of the emperor. The Spahn appointment and the new Roman Catholic faculty were upheld.

Furthermore, Althoff told university faculties that he would not tolerate their public dissent on current political issues. He made good on this threat, and tried to dismiss Hans Delbrück, professor of history in Berlin and editor of the *Preussische Jahrbücher*. Delbrück managed to keep his chair, partly through the support of colleagues, and partly by delivering a public address in support of the government's policy of naval expansion.

Ferdinand Tönnies was less fortunate. He refused to take the oath of personal service to the king of Prussia which was expected of all professors as civil servants, because he felt it would deprive him of freedom of thought. In 1893, Tönnies refused Althoff's demand that he leave the Ethical Culture Society, known to be a bastion of liberalism. Consequently, he failed to win a promotion in Kiel and had to wait until Althoff died fifteen years later to become an associate professor. For his part, Max Weber felt that Althoff tried to prevent his joining the faculty in Freiburg in 1893.

Of course, Karl Kautsky and other Social Democrats were simply off the map when it came to an academic career. In 1896, the teaching credential of Leo Arons, a young physics lecturer at the University of Berlin, was revoked by the Ministry of Education because he was an active socialist. Though the rest of the faculty argued that Arons' socialism had nothing to do with the teaching of physics, Althoff took matters into his own hands. In 1898, the Prussian government passed a law declaring that active support of Social Democracy posed a conflict of interests with teaching at a royal university. Arons was thereby forcibly removed from his lectureship.

In another noteworthy case, a young sociologist named Robert Michels, one of Max Weber's most promising students, was blocked from becoming a lecturer at Marburg because he too was a socialist. Despite Weber's protests on his behalf, he was forced ultimately to look for teaching work in Italy.[55] In a letter to the *Frankfurter Zeitung* in 1908, Weber forcefully challenged the claim that academic freedom was respected in the German universities of his time.

Red-baiting sprang up fairly early in the history of socialism. Quite apart from Althoff's interventions, it became commonplace for business leaders and junkers to talk about academic freedom as providing a shield for the "red professor."[56] Fabricating tales of the intellectual slaughter of innocent students at the hands of socialist instructors, such ideologues anticipated the kind of right-wing hysteria that surfaced periodically in the United States in the 1920s, 1950s, and 1980s.

Paul Anton de Lagarde, a Biblical scholar and ultra-right Pan-German political theorist, argued against democratic education. Instead, a Christian elite should be put through a rigorous training emphasizing both physical skills and Germanness (*Volkstümlichkeit*) as preparation for ruling the nation. The "masses" should be restricted to learning elementary skills. The prospect of widening educational opportunities to new social groups created a risk of German culture being overtaken by barbarism, Lagarde believed. Indeed, pure German learning and culture had already suffered a serious decline. He felt that the German professors were living off the intellectual legacy of the past and destroying their students' capacities for creative thought. He wanted to see a vanguard of heroes, created by a few elite schools, who would save the nation from the soullessness of modernity.[57]

Lagarde's cultural pessimism is later expressed in the deeply conservative philosophies of Oswald Spengler and Arthur Möller van den Bruck; their views on education anticipate the educational practices of

Heinrich Himmler during the Third Reich.[58] As mentioned, Lagarde was a major influence on Troeltsch.[59]

A few professors like Lujo Brentano heroically defended themselves against the red hysteria. When the conservative press attacked Brentano for sympathizing with Hamburg strikers, he cried foul. Some people seemed to think, he declared, that university professors had relinquished the freedoms of citizenship. He himself thought otherwise.[60]

Unfortunately, few professors had the courage and moral integrity of Brentano. Rather, the majority chose the easy road of making peace with the established order. Many of them like Friedrich Naumann were convinced that the best way to entice the masses away from Social Democracy and to unify the country was through promoting patriotic and nationalist feelings. The Pan-German League that was established in the 1890s had a large percentage of professors in its ranks. Also, as mentioned in chapter 2, feudal attitudes and practices as well as anti-Semitism flourished in the universities, among faculty and students alike.

In summary, while German intellectuals had been a vanguard for the Revolution of 1848, a major retrenchment within their ranks occurred after its defeat. Although pioneering work continued with Ranke's historical critical method and similar intellectual achievements, the professoriate increasingly conformed to and legitimized government opinion whenever addressing political issues. Meanwhile, as they embraced nationalism, they broke with the liberal ideals of the French Revolution that had fueled the Revolution of 1848. They became champions of a state based not on the social contract, equality, or popular sovereignty but rather on *Geist* and *Kultur*, of which they themselves were the custodians.

The newer social forces of both capital and labor threatened the comfortable niche the German mandarins had carved out for themselves within a constitutional monarchy.

Their understanding of individualism revolved around the personified nation endowed with *Geist*. Their understanding of freedom emphasized the merit of submission to the nation. Yet their philosophical idealism gave them the impression of standing outside and above the political conflicts of their own time and place. In this ideological retrenchment during the time of the Second Reich, Troeltsch was no exception.

Indeed there was a union of the state and the "German spirit" in more ways than Meinecke may have wished to admit. Gordon Craig concluded, "it is not an exaggeration to call [the professors], as they were called before 1914, the intellectual bodyguard of the Hohenzollerns."[61]

Troeltsch was both an academic and a Protestant theologian. It is therefore appropriate to ask, did this level of social and political conformity also prevail within the Protestant churches?

Notes

1. Friedrich Meinecke, *Erlebtes 1862–1901* (Stuttgart: K. F. Köhler Verlag, 1964), 167–68.
2. Friedrich Meinecke, *The Age of German Liberation 1795–1815*, ed. Peter Paret, trans. Peter Paret and Helmuth Fischer (Berkeley: University of California Press, 1977), 3. Also cited in Ringer, *Decline of the German Mandarins*, 118.
3. Ringer, *Decline of the German Mandarins*, 3.
4. Craig, *Germany: 1866–1945*, 218–19.
5. Rainer Maria Rilke, *Poems*, trans. Jessie Lemont (New York: Columbia University Press, 1943), 28.
6. Frank Wedekind, *Prosa, Dramen, Verse* (München: Albert Langen, 1924), 42–43.
7. Craig, *Germany: 1866–1945*, 222–23.
8. I am indebted to Fritz Ringer for his typology of the German "mandarins," inspired by Max Weber's study of the Chinese literati. Ringer, *Decline of the German Mandarins*.
9. Craig, *Germany, 1866–1945*, 193.
10. For the following survey I am primarily indebted to Gordon Craig's summary of the intellectual accomplishments of the Second Reich. Craig, *Germany: 1866–1945*, 194–98.
11. Kuno Fischer, *A Commentary on Kant's Critique of the Pure Reason*, trans. John Pentland Mahaffy (New York: Garland Publishers, 1976); idem, *Geschichte der neueren Philosophie* (Heidelberg: C. Winter, 1909); Hermann Cohen, *Kants Begründung der Ethik* (Berlin: Dümmler, 1877); Heinrich Rickert, *Die Heidelberger Tradition in der Deutschen Philosophie* (Tübingen: J. C. B. Mohr, 1931); idem, *Kant als Philosoph der Modernen Kultur* (Tübingen: J. C. B. Mohr, 1924).
12. Eduard von Hartmann, *Philosophy of the Unconscious*, trans. William C. Coupland (London: Routledge and Kegan Paul, 1950).
13. Ernst Cassirer, *The Philosophy of Symbolic Forms*, trans. Ralph Manheim (New Haven, CT: Yale University Press, 1953–57); Edmund Husserl, *Ideas Pertaining to a Pure Phenomenology and to a Phenomenological Philosophy*, trans. F. Kersten (Boston: Kluwer, 1982).
14. Wilhelm Windelband, *Präludien, Aufsätze und Reden zur Einleitung in die Philosophie* (Tübingen: J. C. B. Mohr, 1915).
15. Jakob and Wilhelm Grimm, *Grimms' Tales for Young and Old*, trans. Ralph Manheim (Garden City, NY: Doubleday, 1977).
16. Craig, *Germany: 1866–1945*, 194.
17. Adolf von Harnack, *History of Dogma*, trans. Neil Buchanan (New York: Russell and Russell, 1958).
18. Eduard Meyer, *Geschichte des Altertums*, 5th ed. (Basel: B. Schwabe, 1953–58).
19. Theodor Mommsen, *The History of Rome*, trans. W. P. Dickson (London: E. P. Dutton, 1911).

20. Leopold von Ranke, *Universal History*, trans. D. C. Tovey and G. W. Prothero (New York: Harper and Bros., 1885).
21. Heinrich von Sybel, *The Founding of the German Empire by William I*, trans. Marshall L. Perrin (New York: T. Y. Crowell, 1890–98); Heinrich von Treitschke, *History of Germany in the Nineteenth Century*, trans. Eden and Cedar Paul (New York: McBride, Nast, 1915–19).
22. Wilhelm Dilthey, *Einleitung in die Geisteswissenschaften* (Leipzig: Duncker and Humboldt, 1883).
23. F. Meinecke, *Cosmopolitanism and the National State*, trans. Robert B. Kimber (New Jersey: Princeton University Press, 1970).
24. Karl Lamprecht, *Krieg und Kultur* (Leipzig: S. Hirzel, 1914); idem, *Deutsche Geschichte* (Berlin: Weidmann, 1912–1913); idem, *What is History?*, trans. E. A. Andrews (New York: Macmillan, 1905); Otto Hintze, *The Historical Essays of Otto Hintze*, ed. Felix Gilbert (New York: Oxford University Press, 1975); Kurt Breysig, *Forschungen zur Geschichte- und Gesellschaftslehre* (Stuttgart: Cotta, 1929–1932); Karl Kautsky, see chapter 11.
25. Claude Welch, "A Social History of Christianity," *Protestant Thought in the Nineteenth Century*, vol. 2, 1870–1914 (New Haven, CT: Yale University Press, 1985), 292.
26. Michael Pye, "Troeltsch and the Science of Religion," *Ernst Troeltsch: Writings on Theology and Religion*, eds. Robert Morgan and Michael Pye (Atlanta, GA: John Knox Press, 1977), 246.
27. Gustav Schmoller, *Die Soziale Frage: Klassenbildung, Arbeiterfrage, Klassenkampf* (Munich: Duncker, 1918); idem, *Grundriss der Allgemeinen Volkswirtschaftslehre* (Leipzig: Duncker, 1900–1904); Adolf Wagner, *Grundlegung der Politischen Ökonomie* (Leipzig: C. Winter, 1892–94); Lujo Brentano, *Hours and Wages in Relation to Production*, trans. Mrs. William Arnold (New York: Scribners, 1894); idem, *Mein Leben im Kampf um die soziale Entwicklung Deutschlands* (Jena: E. Diederichs, 1931); idem, *The Relation of Labor to the Law of Today*, trans. Porter Sherman (New York: G. P. Putnam, 1891).
28. Wilhelm Wundt, *Elements of Folk Psychology*, trans. Edward L. Schaub (New York: Macmillan, 1928); idem, *Outlines of Psychology*, trans. Charles Judd (New York: G. E. Stechert, 1902); idem, *Principles of Physiological Psychology*, trans. Edward Titchener (New York: Macmillan, 1904).
29. Ferdinand Tönnies, *Community and Society*, trans. Charles P. Loomis (New York: Harper and Row, 1963).
30. Georg Simmel, *The Conflict in Modern Culture and Other Essays*, trans. K. Peter Etzkorn (New York: Teachers College, 1968); idem, *On Individuality and Social Forms*, ed. and trans. D. N. Levine (Chicago: University of Chicago Press, 1971).
31. See Edwards, Paul, ed., *The Encyclopedia of Philosophy*, Vol. 8 (New York: Macmillan and Free Press, 1967), s.v. "Max Weber," by Peter Winch, 283.
32. Gustav Freytag, *Die verlorene Handschrift*, bk. V, ch. 1 (Leipzig: Hirzel, 1865). Also cited in *Craig, Germany, 1866–1945*, 198.
33. Craig, *Germany: 1866–1945*, 198–99.
34. Ringer, *Decline of the German Mandarins*, 8–10.
35. Meinecke, *Die Idee der Staatsräson in der neueren Geschichte* (Munich and Berlin: Oldenbourg, 1924). Also quoted in Lukes, *Individualism*, 20. Luke's translation is used here.
36. Ibid., 17–18.
37. Ernst Troeltsch, "The Ideas of Natural Law and Humanity in World Politics," *Natural Law and the Theory of Society: 1500 to 1800*, ed. Otto Gierke, trans.

Ernest Barker (Boston: Beacon Press, 1957), 211. Both Ringer and Lukes use this essay by Troeltsch, originally published in 1922, to illustrate the meaning of German individualism. See Ringer, *Decline of the German Mandarins*, 100–1; see Lukes, *Individualism*, 20.

38. Ibid.

39. Ibid.

40. For example, Max Weber argued that a well-governed state was ruled by a small number of gifted, educated men, led by a strong, charismatic leader. He believed that such men are imbued with rationality and freed from the passions of the "masses." Although Weber felt that mass democracy could never really be implemented, he still pointedly warned against it.

    As a German liberal, Weber did believe in "the democracy of personnel selection," in other words, that the nation's ruling elite should be comprised of the best and the brightest, determined by an open selection process based on merit. But he was opposed to democratic decision making processes. Walter Struve, *Elites Against Democracy: Leadership Ideals in Bourgeois Political Thought in Germany, 1890–1933* (Princeton, NJ: Princeton University Press, 1973), 122–23, 125.

41. Ibid., 211–212.

42. Ringer, *Decline of the German Mandarins*, 97.

43. Ringer, *Decline of the German Mandarins*, 102.

44. Ernst Troeltsch, *Die Absolutheit des Christentums und die Religionsgeschichte* (Tübingen: J.C.B. Mohr [Paul Siebeck], 1902; idem, *Der Historismus und seine Probleme, Gesammelte Schriften*, vol. 3 (Tübingen: J.C.B. Mohr [Paul Siebeck], 1922).

45. Ernst Troeltsch, "My Books," *Religion in History*, trans. James Luther Adams and Walter F. Bense (Minneapolis, MN: Fortress Press, 1922, 1991), 370.

46. Ibid., 374.

47. Ibid., 371; Troeltsch, "Meine Bücher," 10.

48. Thus, while Troeltsch was more contextual and historical in his interpretation of early Christianity than Ritschl and Harnack, he did not depart from the idealist approach to history as such, described above. A recent study discusses "Troeltsch's critical retrieval of Hegel." George J. Yamin, Jr., *In the Absence of Fantasia: Troeltsch's Relation to Hegel* (Gainesville: University Press of Florida, 1993), 146.

49. Karl Kautsky, *The Materialist Conception of History*, edited by John H. Kautsky (New Haven, CT: Yale University Press, 1988), 169.

50. Ibid., p. 170.

51. Ringer, *Decline of the German Mandarins*, 119.

52. Ibid., 446–47.

53. Ibid., 3, 10–13. Rubanowice, a leading interpreter of Troeltsch, utilizes Ringer's typology of the German mandarin. However, he fails to address the main thrust of Ringer's analysis, which uncovers the sociological origin and ideological function of the mandarins' "crisis of culture." Rubanowice, *Crisis in Consciousness*, with a foreword by James Luther Adams, 131–32.

54. Much has been written on the decline of academic freedom in the Second Reich. The best treatments include R. H. Samuel and R. Hinton Thomas, *Education and Society in Modern Germany* (London: Routledge and Kegan Paul, 1949); Friedrich Paulsen, *The German Universities and University Study* (New York, 1906); Lujo Brentano, *Mein Leben im Kampf um die soziale Entwicklung Deutschlands* (Jena, E. Diederichs, 1931); and Ringer, *The Decline of the Ger-*

man Mandarins, 141–43. Gordon Craig provides a compact summary of this literature. Craig, *Germany 1866–1945*, 198–206.

55. Ringer, *Decline of the German Mandarins*, 141–43.

56. Craig, *Germany, 1866–1945*, 202.

57. Fritz Stern, *The Politics of Cultural Despair: A Study in the Rise of the Germanic Ideology* (Berkeley: University of California Press, 1961), 71–81; Robert W. Lougee, *Paul de Lagarde, 1827–1891: A Study of Radical Conservatism in Germany* (Cambridge, MA: Harvard University Press, 1962), 203ff.

58. Craig, *Germany 1866–1945*, 487; Ringer, *The Decline of the German Mandarins*, 258.

59. In his autobiographical statement of 1922, Troeltsch appeals to the authority of "my teacher Paul de Lagarde" to support his own statement that at present "there is nothing remotely resembling the great systems of antiquity or of the seventeenth, the end of the eighteenth, and the beginning of the nineteenth centuries. In this sense, everything that we do today is the work of followers [*Epigonenwerk*]...." Ernst Troeltsch, "My Books," 377.

60. Brentano, *Mein Leben*, 200–5.

61. Craig, *Germany: 1866–1945*, 205.

5

"Catechism, Bayonet, and Scepter": The Protestant Churches and the State

Relations between church and state in Germany had a complex history. Martin Luther had unleashed a cultural revolution that shook all of Europe, liberating many regions from Roman domination. At the same time, however, he depended on the northern German princes for protection from Rome, and embraced their authority even more fervently when confronted with peasant rebellions inspired by his own example. Nor was Luther a champion of religious freedom for Anabaptists, Calvinists, or Jews. He both reflected and contributed to centuries of intolerance and anti-Semitism that culminated in the Holocaust.

When the Catholic rulers of the Holy Roman Empire realized they could not crush Lutheranism, they accepted its legitimacy in the 1555 Peace of Augsburg, which permitted individual princes to officially institute the new church in their territories. By then, most rulers in northern Germany were Lutheran, while most in the south remained Catholic. After nearly a century of further religious conflict in Europe, John Calvin's form of Protestantism gained legitimacy and became the official religion of some German states.

Prussia, which increasingly dominated and eventually united the German states in 1871, was Lutheran. The Catholicism of the south had been a barrier to this unification, which Bismarck could only overcome by launching a major foreign war—against Catholic France. His subsequent attempt to crush Catholicism in Germany—the *Kulturkampf*—proved ineffectual and was abandoned in 1879. Meanwhile, the Lutheran and Calvinist (Reformed) churches in Germany had become associated and adopted the common name "Evangelical." This Evangelical Church of Germany was funded by tax revenues in Troeltsch's day and still is today.

Out of a population of some 50 million Germans in 1890, about 31 million belonged to the Evangelical Church of Germany, 18 million were Catholic, nearly 600,000 were orthodox Jews, and 150,000 were Christian sectarians.[1] While still occupying their privileged, state-sponsored position, the Protestant Evangelical churches were steadily losing members. The mass movement of population from rural to urban settings because of industrialization ruptured ties with the home parish, ties that were often not reestablished. The loss of members also partly reflected the displacement of traditional religious outlooks by modern science, including the natural and social sciences as well as the application of scientific philology and historiography in biblical studies and church history. Nineteenth-century modernist theologians such as Albrecht Ritschl sought to reformulate Christian doctrine in accordance with the new knowledge, but it nevertheless undermined the pieties of traditional believers, many of whom then left Christianity altogether.

Even more important than the rise of science in undermining Christianity was the challenge of socialism. Peasants who joined the urban ranks of the proletariat often left their religion behind them. In 1906, Max Weber remarked that only a minority of working-class people leaving the churches were leaving because of modern science. Most were leaving because of the injustice of the social order and their desire for revolutionary change in this world. Most people viewed the churches as aligned with the establishment of the time.[2] This popular perception is consistent with the findings of Fritz Fischer and other recent historians regarding the role of nineteenth-century German Protestantism in legitimizing the state.[3]

In the 1860s, for example, the issue of whether parliamentary government would be adopted in Prussia was hotly debated.[4] Some liberal Protestants and Catholics supported the expansion of parliamentary powers against the crown and the mainstream Protestant churches. An address of orthodox pastors to the king in 1863 clearly upheld the patriarchal conception of the state going back to Luther's Catechism, that the relationship of government to subject is that of father to child. The state minister of public worship and education at this time, Bethmann-Hollweg, was politically a liberal-conservative and theologically a strict Pietist who supported the conservative wing of the Protestant churches. He was succeeded by Mühler, a conservative orthodox believer.

In fact, from 1840 until 1918 there was an uninterrupted succession of conservative ministers overseeing ecclesiastical affairs except for the brief six-year liberal era of Adalbert Falk. The influence of the churches on the elementary schools was sweeping and provided the foundation for its social influence. Within this arena it did its best to instill obedience to the crown.[5]

Bismarck himself was highly influenced by his Lutheranism although later in life he turned to Pietism. He subordinated his own will to the needs of the state and its divinely ordained monarch. He frankly confessed to a split between power and conscience (*Macht und Gewissen*), between means and ends (*Mittel und Zweck*), and believed in the need to surrender to the perceived inevitabilities of history. The state was central for Bismarck, and he believed that Prussia was destined for preeminence among nations. He considered it his divine calling to uphold and ensure its independence through forcible external expansion and maintenance of a stable internal order. His was a Lutheran anthropology, with its rejection of progressive optimism and its intrinsic suspicion of "the masses."[6]

With Bismarck's unification, the Protestant National Liberals increasingly engaged in dynastic territorial thinking while the Protestant Conservatives spoke of obedience to God and king. With the Franco-Prussian War came the slogan: "With God for King and Fatherland." The annexations including the French provinces of Alsace and Lorraine seemed justified to both liberals and conservatives, since the divinely ordained king had achieved them. Theologian Martin Kähler applauded the military discipline of the soldiers as an instance of virtuous obedience in accord with Lutheran teaching.[7]

Bismarck's *Kulturkampf* against Roman Catholicism, which forced many Jesuits and other Catholic clergy into exile, also had the enthusiastic support of both liberal and conservative Protestants. The idea of a Protestant Empire gained wide currency even among the most educated classes. As Fritz Fischer remarks,

> It is astonishing the degree to which German Protestantism, from individual (free) churches to far into the confessional camp, gave assent to the beginnings of the *Kulturkampf*.[8]

Konstantin Frantz was a contemporary Protestant critic of the National Liberals, the party that led the way in this persecution of Roman Catholics. He saw in Imperial Germany under Bismarck the realization of the Hegelian state which dominates all of life and which demands a religious devotion. In his book, *The Religion of National Liberalism* (1872), he critiqued this new civil religion.[9] Furthermore, he criticized

ecclesiastical circles for being unable to challenge this "liberal" deifi-
cation of the state, because their own cult centered around the monarchy. In Frantz' view, true religion must separate itself from the state.[10]

Frantz's lone critique was far eclipsed in popularity by the replies of
people like Danish Lutheran bishop, Hans Martensen who argued that
the German principles of monarchy, authority, and order were superior
to the French principles of the plebiscite, popular sovereignty, and
democracy.

Martin Kähler, a strict Bible-believing Pietist, also responded that
Prussia conformed to the Protestant ideals of duty, service, and incor-
ruptibility.[11] In fact, ethics is rooted in obedience. A person is to unre-
servedly perform his or her duty to the state without expecting anything
in return.

Kähler rejects the principle of "eudaemonism," the right to pursue
happiness, as found in the American Declaration of Independence. He
explains that renouncing the selfish claim to happiness and embracing
obedience to country accounts for the discipline of the Prussian army.[12]

Who gets the credit for instilling the virtues of obedience and duty
into the German people? The Protestant churches, through their gover-
nance over religious training at the earliest ages, argues Kähler. In fact,
German educational practices down through the centuries show what
Protestantism has achieved for the country: it has instilled the desire
for obedience. So exclusively does Kähler focus on this ethic of obedience to the state that the discourse of constitutionality or of freedom
does not appear in his writing.

It becomes abundantly clear that whatever progressive impulses might
have briefly surfaced during the Revolution of 1848 had been largely
suppressed by the time of the Bismarckian empire. German Protestantism, once aligned with the old Germany ruled by feudal princes, simply transferred its allegiance to the new authoritarian state. It continued
to be a voice against the enemies of God and country.

As mentioned in chapter 2, the Union of German Students, which
was formed in 1881, included many future theologians. The liberal and
democratic values of past student organizations were emphatically dis-
carded. Lectures by the popular Berlin historian Treitschke that were
aimed at Mommsen and the Progressive Party, and rising anti-Semitism
pushed the student organizations in a conservative direction. The mood
of the time was captured by the famous speech of the court preacher,
Adolf Stöcker, "The Awakening of German Youth." The nation was at
a crossroads; what would the decision be? Would Prussia take the low

road into modern theorizing or the high road that returned to the values which had made her great, namely, "catechism, bayonet and scepter"?[13]

Many a festival sermon referred to the Revolution of 1848 as a fall from grace, "when the sun set on God's wrath," when "the genius of our people was untrue to itself," or when "the people stood up against their king." It was also the period "which with tears we gladly erased from the history of Prussia."[14]

It is clear that the student fraternities of the 1880s provided an incubator for the strong nationalism of pastor and social activist Friedrich Naumann.[15] Presumably the same can be said for his contemporaries, Weber and Troeltsch. The fraternities also supported the Protestant clergy's theological petition of 1887 challenging the Center Party's proposal for the exemption of theologians from military service.

In summary, the Evangelical churches overwhelmingly rejected the liberal Revolution of 1848, based on popular sovereignty, in favor of the authoritarian nation state.[16]

Albrecht Ritschl (1822–1889) was perhaps the most representative theologian of this authoritarian Bismarckian era. Professor of systematic theology at Göttingen from 1864 to 1889, Ritschl was the teacher of an entire generation of clergy and theologians, including Troeltsch, and was, according to Harnack, the last of the church fathers. He was to defend and uphold the relation of church and state which had developed historically in Prussia.

The historical Jesus for Ritschl was the archetypal hero who trusted completely in God's love and power to give him victory over the blind, mechanistic, impersonal forces of nature. This heroic Jesus is the unique revelation of God. His work makes possible the transcendence of Darwinian nature. Through Jesus, God imparts value or worth to the individual, and it is on this basis that Ritschl built his theology of "value-judgments." Those who are delivered from the threat of nature by the work of Jesus form a community of believers which will gradually usher in the Kingdom of God that will ethically transform society.[17]

Ritschl's work represented a conscious break from that of his mentor, Ferdinand Christian Baur, the Tübingen church historian who applied a Hegelian philosophy of history to early church history.[18] Baur saw early Christianity caught up in the struggles between Jewish and Gentile Christians; between the followers of Peter and Paul respectively. Early Catholicism of the late second century was a Jewish-Gentile synthesis arising from this conflict, he believed.

By contrast, Ritschl embraced a neo-Kantian philosophy of history, rejecting this Hegelian "conflict model" as "too speculative."[19] In his view the differences that existed between Jewish and Gentile Christians were not decisive and the emergence of early Catholicism was a predominantly Gentile phenomenon with the Jewish elements strained out.[20] We shall see that Troeltsch in *The Social Teaching* followed Ritschl's interpretation.

During the founding and consolidation of the Second Empire under Bismarck, Ritschl published two monumental works which established him internationally as the leading Protestant systematic theologian of the period: *The Christian Doctrine of Justification and Reconciliation* (1870–74) and *History of Pietism* (1880–86).[21] While Bismarck set about to complete the German Empire, Ritschl set about to complete the Protestant Reformation which, he argued, had been left unfinished.

Ritschl believed that the Reformers had recovered the essential New Testament gospel of justification and reconciliation, but that they had failed to adequately comprehend the biblical Kingdom of God. Their religion of personal redemption, he believed, neglected the corporate and social dimension of Christianity. Furthermore, post-Reformation Protestantism had degenerated either into mysticism, Pietistic sectarianism and otherworldliness, or into Enlightenment rationalism and eudaemonism.

According to Ritschl's theological and ethical system, the individual's relationship with God the Father is restored for the sake of Jesus through justification and reconciliation. This results in the religious qualities of trust in the providence of God, and of patience, humility and prayer. It results also in the ethical qualities of loyalty to one's calling (*Beruf*) and love of neighbor which would include a moral community of nations. Ultimately, the Christian life holds out hope of the spiritual domination over the world (*Herrschaft über die Welt*) and entrance into an order of persons above the order of nature.[22]

Fischer observes that Ritschl's emphasis upon providence provided a way of accommodating Christianity to the status quo. Further, his conception of the calling as the foundation for ethical action insured that all would keep their assigned place in society, in contrast, for example, with Mommsen's call to active citizenship. In other words, Ritschl emphasized the moral duty of the individual within a given social framework. He did not entertain the notion of democratically shared responsibility for society as a whole.[23]

As prorektor during the 150th anniversary of the University of Göttingen in 1887, Ritschl articulated the official position when he attacked the Progressive, Center and Socialist Parties, which had defeated the government's Military Appropriations bill. He argued that the opposition had succumbed to the fallacy of natural law, which was an assault upon the historically grounded rights of the state.[24] These principles of natural law upheld a state based upon consensus and the common weal and found their roots in the Stoics, Aristotle, Gratian, Aquinas, Bellarmin, Grotius and Rousseau. Ritschl accused Bellarmin of teaching the conception of popular sovereignty and of providing legitimation for the masses to shape the state and appropriate governmental power (*Herrschaftsgewalt*). Similarly, he found fault with Aquinas and the Roman Catholic theory of the state, because they justified the overthrow of a tyrannical king by the people.

Ritschl viewed conceptions of natural law as a relapse into medieval thinking, in contrast with historical justifications for positive law, which were modern.[25] He invoked Luther against the Aristotelian Aquinas, against Erasmus, against the Anabaptists and Spiritualists with their embracal of natural law. Interestingly, he said nothing about the Calvinist conception of king-making nor even mentioned the German Althusius. This omission underscores his continuance of the longstanding Lutheran disparagement of the Reformed tradition with its "mistaken ethos" (*Irrgeist*).[26]

In summary, Ritschl's efforts to complete the Protestant Reformation contributed legitimation to the Bismarckian Empire. While clearly conservative, however, his thought was not proto-fascist. That ideological niche was occupied by Ritschl's fierce antagonist on the Göttingen faculty, Biblical scholar and moralist Paul de Lagarde (1827–1891). Lagarde deplored Ritschl's systematizing efforts in theology; he had little use for his Lutheran confessionalism. He also totally disagreed with Ritschl on the subject of mysticism, which Ritschl rejected and Lagarde embraced. On these points of disagreement, Troeltsch, who was influenced by both men, broke with Ritschl to follow Lagarde (see "Mysticism" in chapter 12). Indeed, so admiring was Troeltsch of the latter that in 1913, one year after *The Social Teaching* was published, he dedicated the second volume of his collected works "to the memory of Paul de Lagarde" and praised Lagarde's *Deutsche Schriften* (*German Writings*).[27] Yet comparatively little is known of Lagarde by most Anglo-American interpreters of Troeltsch. In light of this hiatus, it is particularly appropriate to take a closer look at this shadowy figure.[28]

As a child, Lagarde grew up in the Berlin household of a strict gymnasium teacher.[29] For a while it was a religiously observant household.

The family enthusiastically took the boy to hear the great German liberal theologian Friedrich Schleiermacher preach every Sunday. But after Schleiermacher's death they and others stopped attending church altogether. This discrepancy suggested to Lagarde that perhaps the theologian's personality, rather than the substance of his ideas, had been the attraction. Coupled with his explorations in biblical higher criticism, this experience led to Lagarde's eventual rejection of organized Christianity.

But Lagarde remained very religious, and his religious views—drawn from Pietistic and romantic impulses—became irrevocably linked with his political views. In the *Deutsche Schriften*, he prophesied that a new Germanic religion would develop from the pure "folk" (*Volk*).[30]

Thus, Lagarde could aptly be called a mystical nationalist. He understood God to be the Creator and Redeemer who had designed a special purpose for every man and nation. The greatest purpose for which men had been created was the achievement of mystical union with God. This drive to achieve union with the divine Father provided the foundation for all human searching for excellence.[31] Like other German mandarins, Lagarde emphasized a dualism between spiritual and material needs, viewing the former as much more important.[32] History was the human unfolding of the purpose that God has planned for men and nations; it was also the arena in which the spirits of light and darkness vied for dominance.[33]

Lagarde did indeed find plenty of evil spirits to war against, beginning with the boredom and mediocrity of modern middle-class existance. Like the preacher in Ecclesiastes, he argued that the popular habits of frequenting theaters and bars, light reading, gardening, and smoking were futile and a chasing after the wind; vain attempts to stave off the lack of meaning in modern city life.[34]

In the *Deutsche Schriften*, which Troeltsch praised highly,[35] Lagarde continues his invective against soulless modernity: "Better to chop wood than to go on with this worthless life of civilization and education. We must return to our origins, on lonely mountain tops, where we are not heirs, but rather ancestors."[36] The spirits that dragged Germany into the valleys of spiritual darkness had concrete form: Jews, liberals, Eastern Europeans, and professors.

Lagarde's belief that evil was conspiring against the nation helps explain the brutality of his proposed solutions.[37] For example, his virulent anti-Semitism was unmatched in his generation.[38] Some of his most brutal diatribes against the Jews are found in the *Deutsche Schriften*, which Troeltsch specifically lauded.[39] It is here that Lagarde propounds his extreme view that Judaism was a nationalistic religion that had completely broken with Old Testament religion. Here, too, he argues that the Jewish community possessed a cohesiveness that the German community lacked. Therefore, the Jews in Europe had become the dominant people. Echoing Treitschke, he exclaimed, "The Jews as Jews are a terrible misfortune for all Europeans."[40] In fact, contained in the *Deutsche Schriften* is a torrent of anti-Semitic invective that utilized the metaphors of disease, pollution and decay:

> Moreover, we Germans are made of much too soft material to be able to withstand these hard-bitten Jews with their Talmudic discipline. It is acknowledged, how little our youth, who are studying and serving in the army, have the moral power to withstand the corruptive monetary offers of the Israelites; how Jewish merchants of fashion apparel impregnate with vanity the unborn generation which the mother carries; how Jewish money changers in the country offer to the farmer and the day laborer money and baubles on credit for awhile, until in the wink of an eye, the careless borrower is evicted from house and yard.
> ⁻ Because I know the Germans, I do not want the Jews to be allowed to be together with them.[41]

If nothing were done, Germany would eventually become *verjudet*, or overrun by Jews. This word, which Lagarde popularized if not actually coined, would later be adopted by the National Socialists.[42]

Not content to prophesy merely the destruction of Germany at the hands of the evil enemy, Lagarde goes further in the *Deutsche Schriften*:

> The *Alliance Israelite* is nothing but an international conspiracy, like Freemasonry, to achieve Jewish world domination; it is to the Jewish realm what the Jesuit order is to the Catholic: it confirms its sheer existence, that the Jews living in Germany, France and England are not German, French or English, but rather are Jews.[43]

After describing a worldwide Jewish conspiracy, Lagarde called for the forcible removal of the Jews to Palestine in the *Deutsche Schriften*.[44]

By the time he published the *Ausgewälte Schriften* (*Selected Writings*), Lagarde was calling for nothing less than their extermination.

> [The Jew had] a heart as tough as crocodile skin in order to feel no sympathy for the poor Germans who are bled dry…out of humanity!—the word addresses these Jews, or else they are too treacherous, this proliferous vermin, to stamp out. One does not bargain with trichinae and bacilli, nor are trichinae and bacilli educated; they are destroyed as quickly and as thoroughly as possible."[45]

The biological imagery of this statement and its genocidal thrust anticipated both the theory and the practice of the Final Solution by half a century.

Lagarde also developed what later became known as the *Lebensraum* or "living space" argument. A believer in the need to extend Bismarck's unification project to "greater Germany," so as to relieve Germany's crowded living conditions, Lagarde argued for the German colonization of Eastern Europe and for the deportation of all non-Germans. This would stop the flow of German immigrants to the United States where pure Germans were becoming contaminated Americans.[46]

Needless to say, "Lagarde was the patron saint of the emergent anti-Semitic or *völkische* movement."[47] It was Lagarde who provided the religious foundation for modern German racism.

In 1934 the National Socialists republished Lagarde's *Deutsche Schriften* and *Ausgewählte Schriften* as a two-volume work entitled, *Schriften für das deutsche Volk (Writings for the German Folk)*. In 1944, while carrying out the Final Solution, they issued to their soldiers copies of Lagarde's work calling for the extermination of the Jews.[48] As Alfred Rosenberg was to say to Adolf Hitler, "'You, mein Führer, have rescued from oblivion, the works of Nietzsche, Wagner, Lagarde, and Dühring—works which foretold the doom of the old culture.'"[49]

Although Lagarde was a cultural pessimist with respect to his own generation, he hoped for a day when the German "folk" (*Volk*) would rise again. Despite his idealization of the *Volk* and espousal of "individualism," Lagarde saw no role for democracy in his vision of a transformed nation. Rather he envisioned the rise of a *Führer* and a purified aristocracy embodying the *Volk* ideal. Further, the ideal society was one in which all were of one mind and spirit. What he meant was that cultural homogeneity should prevail and dissent abolished.[50] Thus, "individualism" was for him a transpersonal concept (as discussed in chapter 4) projected onto the mystical nation. "Central to his political thought," wrote Rosenberg, "was a dualism which he posited between 'state' and 'nation,' a dualism meant to correspond to that between body and soul."[51] The primary purpose of both "soul" and "nation" was to fulfill the destiny set forth by a transcendent God.

Central to reaching such a destiny was the education of youth.[52] Higher education should be reserved for elite young men. It should involve a Spartan regimen in a rural setting, away from the indulgence of families and corrosive effects of city life. It should offer training in the development of mind and soul, and the discipline of body, to produce men of quality. Peasant men and all women should be content with elementary education; women who aspired to more should look to their husbands for it.[53]

Thus, Lagarde's fierce attack on the social "cancers" of his time was the negative side of his heroic understanding of society.[54] In fact, he thought of himself as the fearless warrior fighting modern-day dragons to recover timeless values and transcendental ideals. An Old Testament scholar, he viewed himself as less like a political scientist and more like a prophet.[55] Above all, his brutal vision for the future arose—not out of a conviction of Germany's greatness—but out of a deep sense of Germany's spiritual and cultural crisis. Herein lay the magnetism of Lagarde's ideas for his contemporaries. He sought war and destruction as the necessary medicine for healing and restoring an ailing German nation.[56]

Adolf von Harnack (1851–1930), like Troeltsch, was influenced by both Ritschl and Lagarde and admired the latter.[57] He was widely considered to be the preeminent historian of early Christianity and, with Troeltsch, the foremost spokesperson of liberal Protestantism of his generation. While Ritschl had focused on the gradual removal of Jewish influences from early Christianity, Harnack in his monumental *History of Dogma* (1885–90) preferred to focus on the progressive Hellenization of Christianity, which he viewed as detrimental.[58] According to Harnack, the doctrines of the Trinity and the Incarnation were not solely later accretions, but were very much products of a Greek-inspired intellectualism.

In *What is Christianity* (1900), Harnack attempted to distinguish between the timeless "kernel" of Christianity and its culturally relative "husks." The essence of the faith included the gospel as Jesus had originally preached it and which surfaced repeatedly throughout the course of Christian history. Appropriating themes from Ritschl, Harnack included the ideas of divine fatherhood of God, the holy God who rules the trusting heart and confers value, the universal brotherhood of man and duty of neighborly love.

For Ritschl and Harnack, the gospel did include a social ethical component. However, this had little in common with a socialist interpretation that challenged the status quo.[59] I shall return to the question of Harnack's interpretation of the Christian ethic in chapter 7.

Thus, for Harnack, the gospel, though proclaimed within the relativity of history, was essentially timeless and speaks to human nature which is also unchanging at its spiritual core as it yearns to find the eternal, that of ultimate value, within time.[60]

While Harnack remained controversial all his life in the eyes of the many orthodox clergy of the Evangelical churches, he managed to remain on the best of terms with the Emperor and his government as Ritschl had done. As mentioned in chapter 3, Harnack was brought in by Reich Chancellor Bülow at the opportune time to counsel the emperor on how to make his 1903 military spending bill palatable to the Reichstag.[61] He was elected to the Prussian Academy of Sciences and was the director general of the Royal Library in Berlin from 1905 to 1921. He was the first president of the Kaiser Wilhelm Institute for the Advancement of the Sciences from 1911–1930 (now known as the Max Planck Institute).

Harnack accepted the title of "von" from the emperor in 1914, which meant being raised to the level of hereditary nobility. This acceptance of ennoblement illustrates the relinquishment of "political emancipation" on the part of some church and university professors for the traditional values of "classical education and property" (*Bildung und Besitz*).[62] Harnack was also one of the founders and first presidents (1903–1911) of the Evangelical Social Congress which was the Protestant establishment's response to Social Democracy as we shall see in chapter 7.

In summary, the Protestant leadership of the time, both orthodox and liberal, stood with a coalition of Conservatives and National Liberals who together uncritically supported the political and social order of Imperial Germany. The enemies of the throne were also seen as enemies of the altar and included such "undesirables" as socialists, progressives, Jesuits, and Jews. The most accepted voice of dissent to the existing regime, that of Paul de Lagarde, was positioned on the far right.[63]

Even in the aftermath of World War I and the overthrow of Imperial institutions, loyalty to the crown on the part of clergy was passionate and steadfast. Thus, the president of the first German Evangelical annual conference (*Kirchentag*) of the Weimar period stood up and with great emotion and anguish addressed the congregants:

> The pride of every German lies in the splendor of the German Empire, the dream of our fathers and with it the chief bearer of German might, the monarch and the royal house which we as standard bearers of German greatness so intimately loved and honored....
>
> The Evangelical Church of the German Reformation deeply identifies with their collapse....
>
> We can do nothing other than declare solemnly in deep pain how the Church of our Fatherland which became bound up with their royal patronage, with their lineage over the course of many centuries of history, owe them deep gratitude. This deeply felt gratitude will live on unforgotten in the Evangelical people.[64]

Notes

1. Craig, *Germany: 1866–1945*, 181.
2. Max Weber, *Gesammelte Aufsätze zur Religionssoziologie*, vol. 1 (Tübingen: J.C.B. Mohr, 1920–21), 247.
3. Fritz Fischer, "Der deutsche Protestantismus und die Politik im 19. Jahrhundert," *Probleme der Reichsgründungszeit 1848–79*, edited by Helmut Böhme (Cologne and Berlin: Kiepenheuer & Witsch, 1968), 49–71.
4. Although Troeltsch wrote during the Second Reich, the pattern of church/state relations he experienced had been significantly shaped by earlier developments in Prussia. After German unification in 1871, Imperial values and practices were largely modeled on and merged with those of Prussia. In this chapter, I therefore follow Fritz Fischer in reconstructing the Prussian roots of church/state relations in the Second Reich.
5. Fischer, "Der deutsche Protestantismus," 63.
6. Ibid.
7. Ibid., 64.
8. Ibid., 65.
9. Konstantin Frantz, *Die Religion des Nationalliberalismus* (Leipzig: Rossberg, 1872).
10. Fischer, "Der deutsche Protestantismus," 65–66.
11. Kähler is best-known in the English-speaking world for his book, *The So-called Historical Jesus and the Historic Biblical Christ*, trans. and ed. Carl E. Braaten, with a foreword by Paul J. Tillich (Philadelphia, PA: Fortress Press, 1988). His writings on the German state are far less known.
12. Martin Kähler, *Die starken Wurzeln unserer Kraft. Betrachtungen über das deutsche Kaiserreich in seiner ersten Krise* (Gotha: F.A. Perthes, 1872), 66.
13. Fischer, "Der Deutsche Protestantismus," 67. See also Adolf Stöcker, *Christlich-sozial Reden und Aufsätze* (Bielefeld and Leipzig: Velhagan, 1885); idem, *Sozialdemokratie und Sozialmonarchie* (Leipzig: Velhagen, 1891).
14. Fischer, "Der deutsche Protestantismus," 67.
15. Friedrich Naumann, *Central Europe*, trans. Christabel M. Meredith (New York: Alfred A. Knopf, 1917); idem, *Demokratie und Kaisertum*, 4th ed. (Berlin: Schoenberg, 1905).
16. Fischer, "Der deutsche Protestantismus," 67.
17. James Richmond, *Ritschl: A Reappraisal* (London: Collins, 1978), 168–93 passim; David W. Lotz, *Ritschl and Luther* (New York: Abingdon Press, 1974), 42f., 89–93.
18. Ferdinand Christian Baur, *The Church History of the First Three Centuries*, 3rd ed., trans. A. Menzies (London: Williams and Norgate, 1878–1879); idem, *Paul, the Apostle of Jesus Christ, his Life and Work, his Epistles and his Doctrine. A Contribution to a Critical History of Primitive Christianity*, trans. E. Zeller (London: Williams and Norgate, 1875–1876).
19. Albrecht Ritschl, *Die Entstehung der altkatholischen Kirche*, 2nd ed. (Bonn: Adolph Marcus, 1857).
20. I am here using "neo-Kantian" in a broad sense; in a different context, Richmond distinguishes between Ritschl's philosophy of history and that of Windelband, who was "neo-Kantian" in a stricter sense. James Richmond, *Ritschl: A Reappraisal*, 20–24.
21. Albrecht Ritschl, *The Christian Doctrine of Justification and Reconciliation*, ed. and trans. H. R. Mackintosh and A. B. Macaulay (New York: Scribner, 1900); idem, *Geschichte des Pietismus* (Bonn: A. Marcus, 1880–1886).

22. Richmond, *Ritschl: A Reappraisal*, 220f.; David W. Lotz, "Albrecht Ritschl and the Unfinished Reformation," *Harvard Theological Review* 73:3–4 (July-October 1980): 342–44.
23. Fischer, "Der deutsche Protestantismus," 68.
24. Ibid.
25. According to Fischer, Ritschl appropriated Hegelian political theory (*Staatslehre*). Ibid., 69.
26. Ibid.
27. *"Dem Gedächtnis Paul de Lagardes gewidmet."* Troeltsch also concluded the first essay of this collection with a two-page eulogy to Lagarde, describing at length his mentor's inspiring influence. By the time Troeltsch made this dedication, Lagarde had been dead for over twenty years. Everything Lagarde had to say had been published, and his notoriety well established. Ernst Troeltsch, *Gesammelte Schriften*, vol. 2, *Zur religiösen Lage, Religionsphilosophie und Ethik* (Tübingen: J. C. B. Mohr, 1913), v; idem, "Die theologische und religiöse Lage der Gegenwart," *GS*, 2, 19–21.
28. Virtually the only work within the Troeltsch literature that links Lagarde to Troeltsch is that of Hans-Georg Drescher, *Ernst Troeltsch: His Life and Work* (Minneapolis, MN: Fortress Press, 1993) 21, 45, 349 note 82, 350 note 85. See also Drescher, "Ernst Troeltsch und Paul de Lagarde," *Mitteilungen der Ernst-Troeltsch-Gesellschaft* III, (Augsburg, 1984), 95–115.
29. Lagarde's mother died at his birth and he had very poor relations with his harsh, grieving father. Fritz Stern draws a connection between the misery of his childhood and who he later became. Fritz Stern, "Paul de Lagarde and a Germanic Religion," *The Politics of Cultural Despair* (Berkeley: University of California Press, 1963), 4. For a psycho-historical study of childrearing practices in Germany and their contribution to Nazism, see Alice Miller, *For Your Own Good: Hidden Cruelty in Childrearing and the Roots of Violence*, trans. Hildegarde and Hunter Hannum (New York: Farrar, Straus and Giroux, 1983).
30. Paul de Lagarde, "Die Religion der Zukunft," *Deutsche Schriften*, 4th ed. (Göttingen: Lüder Horstmann, 1903), 217–47.
31. Stern, *Politics of Cultural Despair*, 39.
32. Ibid., 28.
33. Ibid., 39.
34. Anna de Lagarde, *Paul de Lagarde. Erinnerungen aus seinem Leben für die Freunde zusammengestellt* (Göttingen: Kästner, 1894), 164.
35. E. Troeltsch, "Die theologische und religiöse Lage der Gegenwart," *GS* II, 19–20.
36. Lagarde, "Die Reorganisation des Adels," *Deutsche Schriften*, 290.
37. Stern, *Politics of Cultural Despair*, 33.
38. According to Stern, "The brutality of Lagarde's utterances far exceeded the modern anti-Semitism that was then common among German conservative critics." Ibid., 63.
39. Stern documents Lagarde's anti-Semitism primarily from portions of the *Deutsche Schriften*. Ibid., 61–64; 307–8n.
40. Lagarde, "Programm für die konservative Partei Preussens," *Deutsche Schriften*, 366.
41. Lagarde, "Über die gegenwärtigen Aufgaben der deutschen Politik," *Deutsche Schriften*, 34.
42. Stern, *Politics of Cultural Despair*, 62.
43. Lagarde, "Die Stellung der Religionsgesellschaften im Staate," *Deutsche Schriften*, 255.

44. Ibid., 34.
45. Lagarde, "Juden und Indogermanen," *Ausgewählte Schriften*, ed. Paul Fischer, 2nd ed. (München: Lehmanns, 1934), 239.
46. Stern, *Politics of Cultural Despair*, 68–9.
47. Ibid., 90.
48. Ibid., 63n.
49. Alfred Rosenberg, *Parteitag*, 1934; quoted in Stern, 82.
50. Ibid., 56–8.
51. Ibid., 56.
52. Ibid., 71–81.
53. Ibid., 74, 77.
54. Ibid., 33.
55. Ibid., 70.
56. Ibid. In his biography on Troeltsch, Drescher makes no reference to Lagarde's extreme anti-Semitism or German nationalism and what bearing they might have had on Troeltsch's thought. Rather, Drescher dignifies him by writing, "Lagarde was a deeply pious person." Drescher, *Ernst Troeltsch: His Life and Work*, 350 note 84. Ibid, 21, 45, 349 note 82, 350 note 85.
57. In a letter to Lagarde written June 20, 1890, Harnack expressed his sympathy with respect to Lagarde's long battle with Ritschl. He was so impressed with Lagarde's semi-autobiographical, *Über einige Berliner Theologen und was von ihnen zu lernen ist*, that he said he acquired the other volumes of Lagarde's *Mitteilungen*. (The Harnack letter is to be found in Lagarde's correspondence contained in the State and University Lagarde Collection in Göttingen, vol. XXVI, no. 216.) Robert W. Lougee, *Paul de Lagarde, 1827–1891: A Study of Radical Conservatism*, 223, 343n.
58. Harnack, *History of Dogma*, trans. Neil Buchanan (New York: Russell and Russell, 1958).
59. Harnack explicitly challenges socialist interpretations of the Christian ethic in *What is Christianity*, trans. Thomas B. Saunders (Glouster, MA: Peter Smith, 1978), 110–11.
60. G. Wayne Glick, *The Reality of Christianity: A Study of Adolf von Harnack as Historian and Theologian* (New York: Harper and Row, 1967), 268–72.
61. Brose, *Christian Labor and the Politics of Frustration in Imperial Germany*, 187.
62. Mayer, *The Persistence of the Old Regime*, 101.
63. Fischer, "Der deutsche Protestantismus," 69; Craig, *Germany: 1866–1945*, 186. Lagarde, it should be noted, eventually received a senior faculty position at a major German university, a status unthinkable for socialists such as Karl Kautsky.
64. D. Möller, "Kirche und Monarchie," *Quellen zur Geschichte des deutschen Protestantismus (1871–1945)*, Karl Kupisch, ed. (Göttingen: Musterschmidt Verlag, 1960), 143–44.

6

The Challenge of Social Democracy

While university students were returning to the traditions of catechism, bayonet, and scepter, the urban working classes in their toil and crowded rooming houses looked elsewhere for inspiration. The liberal-democratic League of Workers' Clubs that arose in Saxony, southwest Germany and Bavaria, worked to preserve the ideals of the Revolution of 1848. Led by August Bebel and Wilhelm Liebknecht, this group opposed the forced annexation of Alsace-Lorraine and supported the Paris Commune, in coalition with the General German Workers' Union, founded in 1863 by Ferdinand Lassalle. When they were branded as unpatriotic and the Bavarian police began to round up some of their southern members, the two groups united and formed the German Social Democratic party in 1875.[1]

By the 1877 elections, socialists polled 500 percent more than in 1871, giving them twelve seats in the Reichstag. Although this was still a tiny minority within a relatively weak legislative body, Bismarck viewed the trend with alarm. He had the foresight to see that the Social Democrats' strength in the cities and industrial areas, precisely where the future of the country lay, could grow into a major threat to the Empire's ruling classes. Two years earlier the Socialists had succeeded in blocking a law that the Chancellor had proposed to strengthen the existing class structure, the family and private property.

An assassination attempt on the emperor by a plumber's apprentice gave Bismarck the opening he needed to call for a ban of the Social Democratic party, even though the party could not actually be linked to the crime. Just one week after the attempt, Bismarck proposed a law to the Reichstag which would outlaw the socialists. Since this legislation jeopardized the independence of all political parties, however, the Progressive and National Liberal parties refused to support it.

But a second attempt on the emperor's life just a few weeks later by a Dr. Karl Nobiling, who shot and severely wounded him while he was riding down the streets of Berlin, provided Bismarck with the conservative reaction he needed. Although again the Social Democratic party could not be implicated in the crime, that didn't matter given the hysterical public reaction. In the days that followed, mass round-ups occurred of people who merely voiced opinions considered disrespectful of the emperor. For example, one woman was sentenced to a year and a half in prison for saying, "The Emperor is not a poor man; he can have himself treated."[2]

Bismarck capitalized on the hysteria by disbanding the Reichstag and calling for new elections in which the Conservative parties gained at the expense of the National Liberals and Progressives. (The Social Democrats dropped from twelve to nine deputies, a comparatively minor loss.) With the new composition of the Reichstag, the Socialist Ban was passed, annulling their party's rights of assembly and publication.

Meanwhile, being called enemies of the Empire did not sit well with the National Liberals, who saw themselves as *the* national party. Chastened also by electoral defeat, they gave in and voted for the law. This acquiesence to the crown over the abrogation of civil liberties established a pattern for the National Liberals that would last as long as the Empire itself. Lujo Brentano was among a mere handful of dissenters in condemning this betrayal of liberal principle as a step toward state-controlled barbarism. These dissenters were to leave the National Liberals in 1880 to form the Progressive Party; Troeltsch eventually joined the majority faction who continued to call themselves National Liberals, while accommodating to Bismarck's repressive policies.[3]

The effects of the Socialist Law were draconian. As soon as it went into effect in October 1878, Social Democratic party newspapers were suppressed, and the police forcibly disbanded workers' clubs and trade unions. The labor movement in Germany practically disappeared until the end of the 1880s. As if dismantling the party apparatus weren't enough, the police began to round up, evict, and deport leaders and rank-and-file members who would not give up their memberships.

The growing realization that the chancellor was determined not only to destroy the new party, but also to personally ruin its members first caused panic, then a growing determination to fight back. From places of exile such as London and Zurich, socialist newspapers continued to be printed, smuggled into Germany and circulated through an efficient system of underground networks.

Meanwhile, the socialist leadership continued meeting on foreign soil. Their first major conference after the Socialist Ban was held in

August, 1880 at Schloss Wyden, Switzerland. There, they took an important, principled stand in agreeing not to use counter-tactics of anarchism and terrorism, but to maintain their electoral, parliamentary approach as the road to power.

Bismarck not only used a big stick against the socialists, but dangled a surrogate socialist carrot before the laboring class. During the 1880s he developed a social insurance program initially covering sickness and accidents, and eventually including old age and disability.

These social programs were bolstered by the activities of Adolf Stöcker, an Evangelical pastor who became court and cathedral chaplain in 1874 and head of the Berlin City Mission in 1877. Challenged by the social activism of the Roman Catholic Center party as well as by "godless" socialism, Stöcker took over direction of the Mission with great enthusiasm and from this base tried to organize a Protestant Christian and patriotic workers' party.

In a speech during the 1878 election campaign, he made a vitriolic attack on the Social Democrats for their alleged hatred of the German state. His defense of God and country did not play well with his working-class audience, however, and his Christian Social Workers' party received only 1,421 votes in Berlin. Realizing the need to modify his approach, Stöcker continued to preach his brand of Christian state socialism, but now combined with anti-Semitism. He began to portray the Jews as aliens who worship only "idols of gold": "The Jews are and remain a people within a people, a state within a state, a tribe among a foreign race. All immigrants eventually assimilate into the people among whom they live; the Jews do not."[4]

The Jew-baiting worked; Stöcker's Christian Social Workers' party began to gain at the polls. The temptation for religious leaders and politicians to use anti-Semitic slogans became so great that socialist leaders felt they had to issue warnings to their members not to give in to it.[5] Karl Kautsky, the leading German socialist thinker at this time, wrote a short book and several articles criticizing the rising sea of anti-Semitism.[6]

When the time came for new Reichstag elections in 1881, Bismarck stepped up the imprisonment and deportation of socialists so that in the last weeks of the campaign more than 600 of them were incarcerated. Given the fact that most of the socialist leadership had already fled the country, one would think they did not stand much of a chance in the elections. Yet they ran candidates in absentia, often the same slate of candidates in district after district, publicizing the slate through the underground communications system. The election results surprised everyone, even the socialists themselves: the party in exile actually *gained* three seats in the Reichstag, bringing their total number to twelve! Meanwhile the Conservative parties lost a considerable block of seats, enough to cost Bismarck control of the Reichstag.

With the loss of his governing majority and the backfiring of his Socialist Ban, the chancellor began to look for ways to limit further the power of the Reichstag while strengthening the state bureaucracy and the army—the major pillars of the Prussian-dominated Empire.[7]

Given its continued climb with every succeeding election, the Social Democratic Party was the thorn in Bismarck's side that ultimately proved to be fatal. The young Emperor William II did not approve of his hardline policy, and asked for the Chancellor's resignation in 1890. This happened during the Emperor's brief "liberal" period when he took an interest in the Social Problem and in Stöcker's work with the Inner Mission. He had met with a gathering of notables in 1887 to discuss financial support for the Berlin Mission and had upheld Christian social principles in a widely publicized speech.

When the emperor's repeal of the Socialist Law and other conciliatory gestures failed to elicit the gratitude and loyalty from the working class that he felt he deserved, the young William soon reversed himself. With all the impetuousness he was known for, he publicly denounced the working class as untrustworthy, disloyal, and traitorous—a fifth column undermining the nation. Predictably, the emperor's ravings only drove the common people further into the embrace of the Social Democrats.

By the time the Socialist Ban was lifted in 1890, the Social Democrats had acquired thirty-five seats in the Reichstag. Despite the ban, they had succeeded in becoming a mass party, a force to be reckoned with. Though they suffered severe losses in the "Hottentot election" of 1907, by 1912 the SPD came back with a vengeance to win a plurality of seats in the Reichstag bringing their number to 110, nearly one-third of the total number of seats. And they achieved this in spite of electoral districting that severely underrepresented their urban social base.

Thus, in the entire period before and during Troeltsch's writing of *The Social Teaching*, the Social Democrats were riding a groundswell of popular opinion, at the expense of the other parties. The time was ripe for a major social revolution in Germany entirely through electoral methods. But the revolution never materialized, partly because of political developments within the SPD itself.

After Bismarck's resignation and the lifting of the Socialist Ban, the Lassallian wing of the party gained ascendancy. This was the period of the Second International or of what later became known as revisionism. The independent labor unions were the strongest force within the Social Democratic party. Planning for the revolution had no meaning to a number of labor leaders, and so they succeeded in forcing the party to modify its traditional conception of class struggle. By 1905, the unions also forced the party to give up the weapon of the political mass strike. Bavarian socialist Georg Vollmar, in a speech delivered in Munich in 1891, argued for "*gradual* socialization" as the practical road to transformation of the country.[8] Later in the decade socialist theorist Eduard Bernstein would expand upon Vollmar's arguments.

A notable example of this shift to revisionism was the temporary coalition between the socialists and more progressive liberals (probably members of the Progressive Party) in the Badenese lower house (Landtag). During the time Troeltsch wrote *The Social Teaching*, he represented the University of Heidelberg in the upper house of the Baden legislature.[9] Unlike some Progressive leaders, however, Troeltsch's National Liberal Party never entertained coalition politics with the SPD.

The Social Democrats occasionally found themselves cooperating with the Catholic Center Party. As mentioned in chapter 2, both parties voted against military spending increases in 1905. Matthias Erzberger, a Center Party leader, denounced government and corporate brutality in Germany's African colonies. Chancellor Bülow responded by forming a coalition of Progressive, National Liberal, and Conservative Parties. He built this coalition by calling for new elections and appealing during the campaign to patriotism on the one hand, and to antisocialism and anti-Catholicism on the other.

In the face of this challenge to the Imperial war machine, those in power either failed or refused to recognize the moderate tendencies within German socialism and persisted in portraying the threat of socialism as Bismarck had done. For the Conservative, Progressive, or National Liberal Parties, no compromise was possible even with a reformist socialism. While refusing to share power with the Social Democrats politically, members of the German elite also continued to bar them from teaching posts in universities, as discussed in chapter 4.

Karl Kautsky was the leading socialist intellectual during the period in which Troeltsch was writing *The Social Teaching*.[10] His historical works on Christianity, first published in the 1890s, were of particular interest to Troeltsch. Kautsky fought attempts by Bernstein and the revisionists to make fundamental alterations to Marxist socialism.[11] Like the revisionists, Kautsky believed socialism could be realized only through parliamentary democracy, but unlike them he insisted on a "revolutionary" or oppositional strategy, because he believed accommodation to the junker and bourgeois parties would undermine labor's solidarity.[12]

As an advocate of parliamentary democracy, Kautsky was also struggling with forces within the Social Democratic party to his left and therefore occupied the center of the party's political spectrum.[13] In 1910, Kautsky criticized Rosa Luxemburg's strategy of a revolutionary general strike as a reckless abandonment of parliamentary politics. Later he denounced the Bolshevik revolution as a betrayal of Marxism and democracy. It would result in dictatorship and eventual failure, he believed.[14]

Socialist unity dissolved with the onset of World War I. While the Social Democratic Party officially supported the war effort, Rosa Luxemburg never did and Karl Kautsky withdrew his support soon after hostilities broke out. His refusal to support the war caused him to lose the editorship of *Neue Zeit* in 1917 and his influence to wane.[15]

In addition to opposing militarism and supporting democracy, Kautsky championed religious tolerance. About the time Chancellor Bülow tried to revive Bismarck's *Kulturkampf*, Kautsky published his pamphlet, "Social Democracy and the Catholic Church," in which he vehemently opposed such persecution on grounds that it violated basic principles of civil liberty. Troeltsch dismissed this pamphlet in *The Social Teaching*, as we shall see.

The Social Democrats supported religious equality, which meant abolishing the state privileges of Protestants vis-à-vis Catholics and Jews. They advocated separation of church and state such as found in the United States. As Kautsky declared:

> German Social Democracy has always adhered to the principle upheld in the time of the "Kulturkampf" and its program says: "Religion is a private affair. No public money is to be spent for ecclesiastical or religious purposes. The ecclesiastical and religious communities are private institutions which manage their affairs as they please."[16]

While poles apart in many other respects, the Social Democratic and Catholic Center parties shared one principle that would account for their persecution in Imperial Germany: their internationalism. Each refused to place the state at the center of their political theories. While the Catholics gave their first allegiance to the Pope, the Socialists gave it to the international working class and viewed history in terms of class conflict.

From a German nationalist perspective, the fact that Social Democracy eschewed the methods of violent insurrection was not decisive. Rather, it was revolutionary because it fundamentally undermined the Bismarckian state. To Imperial elites, the rise of Social Democracy was a political problem of the first order.

As if confronting class oppression, colonial imperialism, anti-Semitism, and Protestant privilege were not enough, the Social Democrats also dissented from the mainstream on the sensitive issue of women's equality. Suffragette leader Elisabeth Lüders was admitted to their national executive committee. Inspired by August Bebel's book, *The Woman and Socialism* (1883), a bestseller that went through fifty printings before World War I, socialist women's associations began to spread. By contrast, even the Progressive Party gave only lukewarm support for women's suffrage and formulated no strategy for implementation.

In summary, the Social Democratic Party advocated nothing less than a sweeping cultural and economic transformation of the German Empire. Its growing popularity caused members of the ruling elite of every major social institution to mount a serious campaign of opposition. For them the "Social Problem" ultimately *was* the Social Democratic Party.

Notes

1. Craig, *Germany: 1866–1945*, 93f.
2. Franz Mehring, *Geschichte der deutschen Sozialdemokratie*, vol. 2 (Berlin: Dietz Verlag, 1960), 500.
3. Lujo Brentano, *Mein Leben im Kampf um die soziale Entwicklung Deutschlands* (Jena, 1931), 96f.; see also Walter W. Goetz, ed., "Der Briefwechsel Gustav Schmollers mit Lujo Brentano," *Archiv für Kulturgeschichte*, vol. 30 (Weimar: Hermann Böhlaus Nachfolgen, 1941), 204.
4. Adolf Stöcker, "Unsere Forderungen an das moderne Judentum (19. September 1879)," *Quellen zur Geschichte des deutschen Protestantismus (1871–1945)*, Karl Kupisch, ed. (Göttingen: Musterschmidt Verlag, 1960), 73, 74.
5. Mehring, *Geschichte des Deutschen Sozial-Demokratie*, 546.
6. I concur with Jack Jacobs who argues that Kautsky was not anti-Semitic. Jacobs writes, "Karl Kautsky—who was not of Jewish origin—fought consistently against anti-Semitism throughout his career, and was unusually concerned with the fate of European Jewry." Kautsky first wrote on the subject of anti-Semitism in 1885, at a time when such bigotry was on the rise. He declared that even though its proponents used socialist discourse, anti-Semitism was unequivo-

cally reactionary and a deadly enemy to socialism. See Kautsky, "Der Antisemitismus," *Oesterreichischer Arbeiter-Kalender für das Jahr 1885*. Jack Jacobs, "Karl Kautsky and the 'Jewish Question,'" Collected Papers Presented at the Internationale Wissenschaftliche Konferenz "Karl Kautskys Bedeutung in der Geschichte der Sozialistischen Arbeiterbewegung," (Bremen, 1988), 312–13; idem, "Marxism and Anti-Semitism: Kautsky's Perspective," *International Review of Social History*, 30:3 (1985), 400–30.

7. Mehring, *Geschichte der deutschen Sozialdemokratie*, 541–49; August Bebel, *Aus meinem Leben*, vol. 3 (Stuttgart: J. H. W. Dietz, 1914), 189.

8. Georg Vollmar, *Über die nächsten Aufgaben der Sozialdemokratie* (München: M. Ernst, 1891).

9. Pauck, "Ernst Troeltsch," 121.

10. For twenty years, "from 1895 to 1914, Karl Kautsky was the most important theorist of Marxism in the world." Gary P. Steenson, *Karl Kautsky 1854–1938: Marxism in the Classical Years* (Pittsburgh, PA: University of Pittsburgh Press, 1978), 3.

11. "Revisionism" is, after all, a relative term. Today it is often used to refer to anyone associated with the Second International positioned to the "right" of Rosa Luxemburg. The fact that there were important differences between Bernstein and Kautsky is often overlooked.

12. John H. Kautsky, *Karl Kautsky: Marxism, Revolution & Democracy* (New Brunswick: Transaction Pupblishers, 1994), 1–2.

13. Massimo Salvadori, *Karl Kautsky and the Socialist Revolution 1880–1938* (London: NLB, 1979), 133f.

14. Ibid. Kautsky is often criticized as becoming a revisionist in 1910, based on his debate with Rosa Luxemburg and his later rejection of the Bolshevik revolution. But this view does not take into account the fact that Kautsky poured more energy into criticizing the right-wing of the SPD during these same years. Steenson, *Karl Kautsky*, 6.

15. Steenson, *Karl Kautsky*, 4.

16. Karl Kautsky, "Die Sozialdemokratie und die katholische Kirche," 2nd ed. (Berlin: Buchhandlung Vorwärts, 1906), 25; idem, "Social Democracy and the Catholic Church," *The Social Democrat*, vol. VII (London, 1903), 362.

7

"Thy Kingdom Come! Thy Will be Done on Earth!" The Challenge of Christian Socialism

"Render therefore unto Caesar the things which are Caesar's; and unto God the things that are God's" (Matt. 22:21 KJV). To Germans living in the Second Reich, these words of Jesus had a special relevance, since their own ruler was called "Caesar" (*Kaiser*). But the historical context of Christianity had been transformed.

Jesus had originally used these words to differentiate his movement from Zealot insurrection on the one hand and Jewish collaboration with Rome on the other. He taught that his disciples should be in the Roman world, but not of it, and that Rome was <u>irrelevant</u> to their true purpose: building God's Kingdom of love and justice "on earth, as it is in heaven" (Matt. 6:10). In the end, Rome crucified Jesus on political charges, underscoring for all time how subversive of existing power relations his agenda really was, however much he eschewed armed revolution.

By the time of Imperial Germany, however, Christianity had for centuries been the state religion of the Roman and Holy Roman Empires. In this fundamentally different context, the words "Render unto Caesar" took on a new and conservative meaning. According to Kaiser Wilhelm I, *summus episcopus* of the Prussian Evangelical churches, this dictum of Jesus meant that clergy should not take positions on social issues, except to encourage patriotism and compliance with Imperial law and policies. This conservative view was endorsed by the Evangelical Church Council in 1878, which warned pastors that the Gospel does not address social injustice.

To be sure, the Catholics exhibited more independence from the emperor's wishes, especially through the leadership of Wilhelm Emmanuel von Ketteler, archbishop of Mainz, who helped establish German Social Catholicism with its Catholic trade union movement and worker cooperative societies. Under Ketteler's influence, the Catholic Center party supported legislation for improvement of working conditions, the shortened work day, factory safety inspection, restriction on child labor and labor-management arbitration. In his widely read book, *The Labor Question and Christianity* (1864),[1] Ketteler argued that the Christian was obligated to help the working class organize against the oppressive aspects of capitalism. His ideas provided the foundation for Pope Leo XIII's encyclical *Rerum novarum* of 1891.[2]

However, the bishop's extensive social activism was meant to be an alternative to cooperation with or membership in the Social Democratic Party. Ketteler wanted to ameliorate the effects of class inequality, not to challenge the class structure itself and its associated system of property and privilege.[3]

As restrained as the Catholic social agenda was, it far outstripped that of the Evangelical churches, except during Emperor William II's short-lived experiment with liberalism. This brief liberal phase occurred after Paul Göhre's publication of *Three Months in a Workshop*, which, as mentioned in chapter 2, took the cultured classes by surprise. The shocking account by this theology student of life and working conditions in industrial Saxony stimulated a response from members of the German elite.

With the blessing of the young emperor, the Evangelical Church Council admonished the clergy to study the "labor question" (*Arbeiterfrage*). This led to the founding in 1890 of the Evangelical Social Congress by Paul Göhre, Friedrich Naumann, Adolf Stöcker, Adolf von Harnack and others. Göhre was made general secretary during the early years of the Congress, which was to be an academic forum of Protestant theologians and laity to address the Social Problem. The Congress offered a nationalist Christian socialism as an alternative to international Marxist socialism.[4]

In two addresses delivered to the Evangelical Social Congress in 1894 and 1902, as well as in his famous 1899 series of Berlin lectures, *What is Christianity?*, Harnack laid forth his "social Gospel," one that was thoroughly nonpolitical.[5] He explicitly caricatures the Social Democratic interpretation of Christianity developed by Kautsky:

> Finally, the latest critics that have come into the field assure us that the whole history of religion, morality and philosophy is nothing but [p. 3] wrapping and ornament; that what at all times underlies them, as the only real motive power, is the history of economics; that, accordingly, Christianity, too, was in its origin nothing more than a social movement and Christ a social deliverer, the deliverer of the oppressed lower classes.[6]

Harnack criticizes the socialists for two doctrines: (1) that religion is "nothing but" an epiphenomenon of economics and (2) that Christ came to do "nothing more than" deliver the poor from class exploitation. Harnack then argues in favor of the opposite view, that Christianity was not a class-based movement of any kind. Rather, the gospel operated within a sphere of purely inward faith, against which social concerns "sink into the background."[7] In another rebuttal to the socialists he writes, "Jesus never had anyone but the individual in mind."[8]

While the New Testament provided no concrete social or economic program, according to Harnack, its ethic of living for one's neighbor was a call to form associations for performing acts of charity. This mandate included ministry directed at what Harnack considered to be the paramount social and moral ills of prostitution and dueling. However, he thought it was beyond the scope of the churches to address economic questions or questions of property, length of the work day, taxation, or land reform.

While Harnack admitted that the churches had generally supported conservative positions on such issues, he felt that additional philanthropic activity could correct this imbalance. Indeed, if the churches never took a progressive stand on economic questions, this would not be a reason for criticism. Christianity provided a salvation of souls, not a solution to the problem of poverty.[9]

Harnack criticized as utopian the Catholic religious orders with their continuing practice of the early Christian communion of goods. He also dismissed Social Democracy as a vulgar pursuit of material well-being of the individual, self-preservation, and the universal right of suffrage.[10] While attacking both communitarians and Social Democrats, however, Harnack tried to co-opt their discourse for his own purposes, because socialism was so popular among the people.

Harnack argued that Christianity in a spiritual sense is "profoundly socialistic, just as it is also profoundly individualistic because it establishes the infinite and independent [p. 100] value of every human soul." In fact, the goal of the gospel is to provide a new, improved socialism: "its object is to transform the socialism which rests on the basis of conflicting interests into the socialism which rests on the consciousness of a spiritual unity."[11] With this Harnack explicitly rejects a material or political dimension to Christian socialism as well as the concept of class struggle. For Harnack, "Christian socialism" is completely spiritualized.

As mentioned in chapter 5, Harnack followed his teacher Ritschl in taking existing socioeconomic and political structures as a given, and in restricting social reform to action within the existing framework of vocations and charitable institutions. Like Ritschl, Harnack was friend to the friends of the existing state and enemy to its enemies.[12]

Another founder of the Evangelical Social Congress was Adolf Stöcker (1835–1909), the court chaplain under Emperor William I and guiding light of the Berlin Inner Mission in the 1880s. As we saw in chapter 6, he tried to organize a Christian workers' party as an alternative to the Social Democratic Party. An orthodox Christian, Stöcker resorted to anti-Semitic sloganeering to compensate for his otherwise complete failure to appeal to the working classes.

Friedrich Naumann (1860–1919) was a close associate of Paul Göhre and a liberal Christian. Like Göhre, he came up through the neoconservative student movements of the 1880s and Stöcker's Inner Mission. He went a step beyond Harnack in recognizing that charity was not adequate to deal with the social problems of the time. He was also more nuanced than Stöcker in his opposition to the Social Democrats, viewing them as a "modern heresy" in relation to Christian ethics, rather than an alien enemy.

Like Stöcker, Naumann counterposed a nationalist Christian socialism to the secular internationalism of the Social Democrats. But where Stöcker looked back with nostalgia to the old monarchical and purely feudal, agricultural order, Naumann looked forward to the new imperialist industrial state for his ideal. Naumann, like Stöcker, outlined a moderate program of social reform which included restrictions on the accumulation of capital, greater social security benefits, and full employment guarantees. His vision of Christian socialism remained the dominant view for the Evangelical Social Congress throughout the emperor's liberal period in the early 1890s.

Even with the emperor's support, Naumann received criticism from the governing council of the Frankfort Evangelical churches in 1893 for participating in a meeting sponsored by Theodor von Wächter, a Christian socialist who had joined the Social Democrats. The Church Council issued a new policy statement in December 1895, which criticized the "social pastor" who plays the role of advocate for one class.[13] The following year, William II abandoned his liberal course and at the urging of industrialist Stumm-Halberg issued a telegram which read: "Political pastors are nonsense [*Politische Pastoren sind ein Un-Ding*]. Anyone who is a Christian is social too, but Christian-Social[ism] is nonsense."[14] It was clear to all concerned that this telegram was aimed especially at Naumann.

Soon thereafter, Naumann and Göhre left the Evangelical Social Congress to organize the National Social Union. Stöcker also left and went his own way to found the exclusively orthodox Church Social Conference. This left the Evangelical Social Congress in the hands of conservatives such as Harnack who became its president from 1903 to 1911, the years during which Troeltsch wrote *The Social Teaching*. It was during this conservative phase, in 1904, that Troeltsch made a programmatic address to the Congress, subsequently published under the title, "Political Ethics and Christianity."[15] We will examine the contents of this address in detail in chapter 10.

In 1914, on the eve of World War I, Troeltsch's friend Otto Baumgarten delivered a speech to the Congress entitled, "The Influence of Social Relations on the Development of Piety and Organized Religiosity." He relied heavily on Troeltsch's recently published *Social Teaching* to argue that the Congress could not hope to achieve significant social reform, but should content itself with humanizing and palliative actions.[16]

At this point the Evangelical Social Congress functioned only as a forum for the liberal Protestant academic community. Under Harnack's guidance, it concerned itself with the promotion of private philanthropy and minor reform measures rather than with analysis of social structures. The emperor's telegram of 1896 marked the end of the Second Reich's short-lived flirtation with Christian socialism.

Secular historians are not alone in regarding the Protestantism of this period, both orthodox and liberal, as a civil religion. Church historian Claude Welch remarked that following the emperor's 1896 telegram, "essentially, an incipient social gospel had vanished in the smoke of national religion."[17]

Of course, even before this rightward shift, the Evangelical Social Congress—like the Inner Mission before it—was intended as an alternative to Social Democracy. Therefore, the handful of individual pastors who chose to cooperate with or actually join the Social Democrats stood apart and deserve mention. Many of them dared to argue that joining the Social Democratic Party was not only compatible with their beliefs—it was a moral imperative for them as Christians.

Paul Göhre, author of *Three Months in a Workshop*, again appears. After leaving the Evangelical Social Congress with Naumann and establishing with him the National Social Union, Göhre eventually took the radical step of joining the Social Democrats in 1899. If his book had dropped like a bombshell into the awareness of polite society ten years earlier, surely his decision to go "red" had comparable impact. The Evangelical churches wasted no time launching an intensive disciplinary proceeding against Göhre with intent to defrock him. Rather than submit, he chose to break with the official churches.

Soon Göhre was using his literary talents on behalf of the Social Democrats. Half a million copies of his pamphlet, "How I became a Social Democratic Pastor," were printed and circulated through the party membership. He argued for a "religion of Jesus," which emphasized Jesus' commandment to love one's neighbor and to make solidarity with the oppressed. The continuing opposition he received from the organized churches, however, caused Göhre to eventually break with Christianity altogether. His precipitous fall from grace, from being general secretary of the Evangelical Social Congress to coming under discipline, was undoubtedly a shock from which he never recovered.

Meanwhile, the Social Democrats apparently had little difficulty accepting a religious socialist into their midst, for they supported Göhre's successful bid to become a Social Democratic deputy to the Reichstag in 1903. He united with the revisionist Bernstein wing of the party and like his mentor, Naumann, was a strong nationalist and supporter of Imperial Germany. His nationalism became more extreme with age. During the years leading up to World War I, Göhre became a supporter of Germany's imperial aims. In 1918, he was named undersecretary in the Prussian War Ministry. He made his final political career change by breaking with Social Democracy to join the newly formed National Socialist German Worker's party (NSDAP). In 1928, Göhre died a Nazi, having returned full circle to the virulent anti-Semitism of his youth, when he was influenced by Treitschke, Stöcker, and the student movements of the 1880s.[18]

Göhre was not the first Christian leader to join the Social Democrats. Theology student Theodor von Wächter, mentioned above, had forfeited a career as a pastor by joining the Social Democrats. True Christianity, according to Wächter, does not teach that the present social order of throne and altar is divinely ordained. He understood the gospel to inaugurate a freedom movement:

> The teacher of true Christianity must therefore show Christian people how they came to hear the voice of God out of their need and slavery, which will awaken them to struggle; how to gather together for the common struggle for freedom, to bring about needed structures for a new time.[19]

For Wächter there can be no Christian reconciliation until class domination is overcome through political struggle. Yet, he was not inclined to accept a purely materialist definition of religion. Though he lacked the philosophical tools to elaborate his intuition, he felt the spiritual and material dimensions of reality were inextricably bound together. With a socialist revolution, false, alienated religion would disappear, making room for the breakthrough of true religion.

Wächter cited Kautsky's Erfurt Program in a pamphlet entitled, *The Place of Social Democracy for Religion* (1894). He argued that since the party officially declared religion to be a private matter about which the individual is free to decide, there is nothing to prevent Christians and non-Christians from working together as socialists to bring about social justice. Wächter sharply criticized Stöcker, Naumann, and other "Christian socialist" clergy, who argued for separate Christian worker unions. If the churches have a problem with Christians and atheists belonging to the same organization, then why don't they object to the union of Christian and non-Christian employers in the Rhenish-Westphalian Coal Syndicate? Wächter concluded:

> Just as the Christian, Jewish and secular supporters of the present dominant order are able to work together for their ideological and worldly dominance, so also should the religious and secular proletariat…be able to stand together in a common universal struggle for the economic, political and spiritual freedom of humankind![20]

There were three other German Lutheran pastors during this period who dared to join or speak on behalf of the Social Democratic Party. One, writing under the pseudonym of Dr. G. Carring, declared that Christianity requires a commitment to socialism and demanded in 1902 that the churches stop fighting the socialist movement, which is helping to usher in the kingdom of God.[21]

Albert Kalthoff (1850–1906) wrote in 1904 that the early churches had given the world "the widest communist manifesto that was ever framed."[22] His book influenced Karl Kautsky's *Foundations of Christianity* (1908).[23] Kalthoff took the rather extreme view that there was no historical Jesus, that Christianity arose as a purely socioeconomic phenomenon, as a response of the Roman urban proletariat to their condition.[24]

Swabian pastor Christoph Blumhardt (1842–1919) joined the Social Democrats in 1899.[25] Like Göhre, Blumhardt was soon forced to resign his pastorate. At a Social Democratic Party assembly he declared: "Christ was a socialist. He made twelve proletarians his apostles." As a disciple of Christ, he wanted to dedicate himself to the cause of the poor, which for him meant working within a political party for the working class. Normal pastoral duties just didn't seem to address the larger social issues.[26]

Blumhardt viewed Social Democracy as a call for the churches to repent of their social paralysis, and criticized their condemnation of the party. Socialists showed more faith in the Kingdom of God than the clergy, he believed, and Social Democracy was a more authentic vehicle of God's purpose than the contemporary churches. Against the Lutheran concept of two separate kingdoms—eternal and temporal, Blumhardt argued that the Kingdom of God was being concretely ushered in on the very streets where the poor were to be found. The coming of the Kingdom was not expressed in alternative Christian social parties, nor was it completely expressed in the Social Democratic party. Rather, it was an eschatological reality which Social Democracy approximated to the extent that it worked on behalf of the lower classes, for where the poor are, there is Christ. God's promised Kingdom means world transformation on behalf of justice, freedom and peace, a transformation which is actively being brought about in history.[27]

Blumhardt began to develop the notion of the anonymous Christian, which resurfaces again in twentieth century thinkers such as Emil Brunner and Karl Rahner. For Blumhardt, the true Christian is not necessarily the one who says, "Lord, Lord," but the one who through deed places the values of human life and justice above profits and possessions:

> The heart of a man who denies God with his reason more often contains God in spirit and in truth than does that of one who confesses with the mouth.... If then today socialism has its eye on the goal that specifies an equal right to bread for everyone, which necessitates that property relationships assume such a form that the life of man, rather than money and possessions, has the highest value—why is that an objectionable desire? I am certain that it is based on the spirit of Christ...and that there will be uprisings until it is reached.[28]

Blumhardt did more than pay lip service to his ideals. He publicly supported striking picketers in Württemberg in 1899, despite a law which imposed severe penalties on picketers. From 1900 to 1906 he also served as principal spokesperson for the Social Democratic deputies in the Württemberg Lower House (Landtag). At the Lübeck Party Congress of 1901, he supported Bebel over Bernstein. Unlike Göhre, he took a leftist or nonnationalistic position within the Social Democratic Party.

Another influential figure in prewar Germany was Swiss religious socialist Hermann Kutter (1863–1931). His work *They Must!* (*Sie Müssen!*) of 1903 is, according to Claude Welch, one of the most important declarations to appear in the history of European Christian so-cialism.[29] Kutter argued that through their energetic commitment to the transformation of social life, the Social Democrats have a "must" that the churches do not have. He viewed Social Democracy as unintention-ally doing God's work in the struggle against evil, while the churches wallow in sin as if Christ had never overcome it. Rather than attacking Social Democracy, he argued, the churches ought to be constructively formulating their own "must."

Kutter exposed the irony of the institutional churches' reactions to Social Democracy. While condemning the Social Democrats for their atheism, the churches believe in a dead God and recast the gospel of Jesus into an irrelevant inwardness. While criticizing the Social Demo-cratic call for revolution, the churches ignore the revolutionary mes-sage of the New Testament. While criticizing the Social Democrats for their materialism, the churches bow down to Mammon.

The Social Democrats do not encourage nationalism, Kutter argued, because their internationalism holds out the possibility of peace among all peoples. What could be more Christian?

Therefore, Kutter saw the future belonging to the international So-cial Democratic workers' movement, rather than to national Christian social parties. God the Revolutionary was upholding their cause. "They must go forward because God's Kingdom must go forward. They are men of disturbance because God is the great Disturber."[30]

Troeltsch himself singles out a contemporary living outside of Ger-many as one of the strongest representatives of the Christian socialism of this period: the German Swiss theologian Leonhard Ragaz.[31] We shall see in chapter 12 that Troeltsch classifies Ragaz as an "aggressive sectarian" and argues against his position. It is therefore of some inter-est to take a brief look at him.

Leonhard Ragaz (1868–1945) was pastor at the Münster Cathedral in Basel between 1902 and 1908. Whereas Kutter remained only a fellow traveler of the Social Democrats in Switzerland, Ragaz took the big step of actually becoming a member. He saw the Social Problem as the cen-tral question of theology and the socialist movement as a sign of the coming of the Kingdom.[32] Having received his theological education at the Universities of Basel, Jena, and Berlin, Ragaz was trained in theo-logical liberalism, but the writings of Blumhardt and Kutter also left their imprint on him. It should be added that Ragaz's student days in Berlin caused him to become a severe critic of the Prussian-inspired mili-tary, the trappings of which were highly visible in the German capital.[33]

England's victory in the Boer War (1899–1902), an unjust outcome in Ragaz's mind, gave him a new understanding of the meaning of the cross and drove home to him the fact that historical progress is not necessarily linear. Also, as he witnessed the labor struggles of his own day, he became convinced that the churches must take the side of the poor and wholeheartedly support the Social Democratic movement.[34]

On the occasion of the Basel bricklayers' strike of 1903, Ragaz preached a sermon supporting the strike and interpreting it as a sign of the coming Kingdom. Three years later in his definitive statement, "The Gospel and the Social Struggle of the Present," presented to the Swiss pastors' association, Ragaz set forth his understanding of Christian socialism, a position he consistently maintained until his death.

Ragaz contrasted a stagnant Christianity with one that was actively working toward the realization of the Kingdom of God. Influenced by Kutter, he also argued that the socialists had in some ways better understood the will of God than most pious Christians. He viewed the struggle of the present as between capitalism with its concern to make profits and socialism with its concern to meet human needs.

Ragaz also observed that traditional Christian ethics was wedded to patriarchal structures. Historically, Christianity has been both regressive and progressive. Its regressive form looks to the past for a salvation that occurred with Christ. It focuses upon maintaining individual piety, correct doctrine, and the institutional churches. Its progressive form emphasizes practicing Jesus' teachings, rather than correct belief. It focuses on building the Kingdom of God rather than on building ecclesiastical empires. It is a Christianity that is activist and revolutionary.

According to Ragaz, when the Christian is serving humanity, he is serving God. When the Christian hopes for the Kingdom of God, she is praising God. While capitalism has enslaved a whole class of people, socialism has ushered in the struggle for freedom. This struggle is a sign of God's intervention in history. Only by joining it can the churches hope to be renewed.

Thus, Ragaz was calling the churches to decision, to hope for the Kingdom and to struggle with the poor: "The social movement is revealed as the true way to God for our generation."[35] Indeed, some have seen in Ragaz' message a precursor to the theologies of hope of our own time.[36]

Around the time that Ragaz delivered this address, a circle of religious socialists began to form and publish *New Ways* (*Neue Wege*). Ragaz served as its editor until his death in 1945.

In summary, the voices of Emperor William II and Adolf von Harnack demanding that churches stay out of politics (i.e., the Social Democratic Party) represented the dominant response to the "Social Problem" in the Evangelical churches of Imperial Germany. Harnack argued that the Gospel had to do with a purely inward sphere, above the vicissitudes of timebound concerns, and that philanthropy can address whatever social need may exist.

But dissent was being voiced from within Christianity. German Catholics took a more critical view of the status quo, at least on economic and foreign policy questions. Protestant socialists such as Ragaz interpreted Jesus' prayer, "Thy Kingdom Come! Thy Will be done on Earth as it is in Heaven!" as a call for palpable, material relief for the poor. For Kutter, God was the great "Disturber." These precursors of twentieth-century liberation theology were catalysts of popular disaffection with the liaison between throne and altar. They illustrate that the "Social Problem" of Troelstch's day was very much a religious as well as a social and political problem.

Notes

1. Wilhelm Emmanuel von Ketteler, *Die Arbeiterfrage und das Christentum*, 3rd ed. (Mainz: F. Kirchheim, 1864).
2. Eric Dorn Brose, *Christian Labor and the Politics of Frustration in Imperial Germany* (Washington, DC: The Catholic University of America Press, 1985), 28–35.
3. Ketteler favored a socialism of producer cooperatives, and allowed individual Catholics to join the party of Ferdinand Lassalle before it merged into the Social Democratic Party in 1875. However, he could not bring himself to cooperate with the Social Democratic Party itself. John Cort argues that his reason was mainly the "militant atheism" of the Social Democratic leadership. Cort, *Christian Socialism* (New York: Orbis, 1988), 64, 194–95. However, this fails to explain how Christian clergy were able to gain full acceptance into the SPD and even attain positions of high leadership, as described later in this chapter. Cort's argument that the Marxist wing of the SPD was uniformly hostile to religion is contradicted by the case of Karl Kautsky, the leading Marxist intellectual, who actively built bridges to people of faith through his extensive writings on religion. Although at one point he refers to Kautsky's classic work on Thomas More and quotes his high praise of More, Cort contradicts himself by dismissing Kautsky as a militant atheist.
4. Richard Sorg, *Marxismus und Protestantismus in Deutschland* (Cologne: Pahl-Rugenstein, 1974), 87.
5. In *The Social Teaching* as part of a rebuttal to the socialists, Troeltsch refers specifically to Harnack's address of 1894: "Die ev.-soziale Aufgabe im Lichte der Kirche," later published in *Reden und Aufsätze* (1904). Troeltsch, *The Social Teaching*, 165.
6. Adolf Harnack, *What is Christianity*, trans. Thomas Bailey Saunders (New York: Harper and Brothers, 1957; reprnt. ed., 1978), 2–3.

7. Harnack, *What is Christianity*, 17; idem, "Das doppelte Evangelium in dem Neuen Testament," *Aus Wissenschaft und Leben*, vol. 2 (Giessen: A. Töpelmann, 1911), 215.
8. Harnack, *What is Christianity*, 111.
9. M. A. Canney, ed., *Essays on the Social Gospel*, trans. G. M. Craik (London and New York: 1907), 18–19.
10. Ibid., 64.
11. Harnack, *What is Christianity*, 99–100.
12. Welch, *Protestant Thought in the Nineteenth Century*, 240.
13. Craig, *Germany: 1866–1945*, 184.
14. Theodor Heuss, *Friedrich Naumann, der Mann, das Werk, die Zeit* (Stuttgart: Deutsche Verlag, 1937), 134; Welch, *Protestant Thought in the Nineteenth Century*, 244.
15. Ernst Troeltsch, *Politische Ethik und Christentum* (Göttingen: Vandenhöck und Ruprecht, 1904).
16. Harry Liebersohn, *Religion and Industrial Society: the Protestant Social Congress in Wilhelmine Germany* (Philadelphia, PA: American Philosophical Society, 1986), 55–57.
17. Welch, *Protestant Thought in the Nineteenth Century*, 244.
18. Sorg, *Marxismus und Protestantismus in Deutschland*, 92–4.
19. Theodor von Wächter, *Die Stellung der Sozialdemokratie zur Religion* (Stuttgart, 1894), 21.
20. Ibid., 31.
21. Sorg, *Marxismus und Protestantismus in Deutschland*, 96.
22. Albert Kalthoff, *The Rise of Christianity*, trans. Joseph McCabe (London: Watts & Co., 1907), 181.
23. Karl Kautsky, *The Foundations of Christianity* (New York: International Publishers, 1925), 26.
24. Kalthoff, *The Rise of Christianity*, 158.
25. Christoph Blumhardt, *Eine Auswahl aus seinen Predigten, Andachten und Schriften*, ed. R. Lejeune (Zürich: Erlenbach, 1925).
26. Sorg, *Marxismus und Protestantismus in Deutschland*, 95.
27. Welch, *Protestant Thought in the Nineteenth Century*, 245.
28. Christoph Blumhardt, *Metanoia* (September 1971), 6.
29. Welch, *Protestant Thought in the Nineteenth Century*, 247–48.
30. Hermann Kutter, *They Must; or God and the Social Democracy; a Frank Word to Christian Men and Women*, ed. and trans. Rufus W. Weeks (Chicago: Co-operative Prints Co., 1908), 93.
31. Troeltsch, *The Social Teaching*, 803.
32. Leonhard Ragaz, *Dein Reich Komme* (Zürich: Rotapfel, 1922, 3rd ed.)
33. M. Douglas Meeks, Foreword to *Signs of the Kingdom: A Ragaz Reader*, ed. and trans. Paul Bock (Grand Rapids, MI: Eerdmans, 1984), xi.
34. Paul Bock, Introduction to *Signs of the Kingdom: A Ragaz Reader*, ed. Paul Bock (Grand Rapids, MI: Eerdmans, 1984), xii, xiii.
35. Leonhard Ragaz, *Das Evangelium und der soziale Kampf der Gegenwart* (Basel, 1906), 3; cf. also his *Dein Reich Komme*; Markus Mattmüller, *Leonhard Ragaz—Religiöser Sozialist, Pazifist und Theologe des Reiches Gottes* (Darmstadt: Lingbach, 1986), 7–30; Welch, *Protestant Thought in the Nineteenth Century*, 249–50.
36. Bock, Introduction to *Signs of the Kingdom*, 18.

8

A Quest for the Historical Troeltsch

Ernst Peter Wilhelm Troeltsch was born in Haunstetten, a village just outside of Augsburg on February 17, 1865, during the period when Bismarck was carving out the Second Reich. Augsburg, named after the Roman Emperor Augustus who helped found it, lies on the Roman road on the way to the Alps, about a half-hour's drive west of Munich.[1] In 1985, this small city with a population of 400,000 celebrated its 2,000th anniversary. It is the oldest city in Bavaria.

By the tenth century, Augsburg had become an international trading center, and by the fifteenth and sixteenth centuries it had become the home of the banking families Fugger and Welser, and the richest city in all of Europe. In both wealth and notoriety the Fuggers were comparable to the Medicis of Florence. They helped finance the wars of the Holy Roman Empire among other enterprises. A Welser, at one point, was to own what later became Venezuela.

During this Renaissance period, Augsburg was also a center of the Anabaptist movement, a reminder of the lower classes' potential for revolution that Troeltsch himself noted.[2] The city had a special religious importance as the place where Lutherans and Catholics signed their famous peace treaty in 1555. In addition to being a leading cultural center of the medieval and Renaissance worlds, Augsburg maintained its prominence with the advent of industrialization, becoming the largest textile producer in southern Germany.

Son of a wealthy physician and descendant of a line of South German burghers, Troeltsch was sent to the famous prep school or Gymnasium of Saint Anna in this museum of a town. There he received a classical humanistic education that was modernized to some degree by the influence of the natural sciences. Given its importance in Troeltsch's development, the gymnasium, its social location, and its culture warrant a few remarks.

During this period, the gymnasium, with its emphasis on the classics, was hailed as representing German idealism. In the aftermath of the French Revolution, the *Realschulen*— or grammar schools emphasizing modern languages—sprang up along with technical schools. These were frowned upon as "French" by members of the educational elite and dismissed as *Nützlichkeitkramschulen* or "schools of utilitarian rubbish." The sages of the time warned that a curriculum focusing on concrete, utilitarian subjects would lead to philosophical materialism, thereby undermining throne and altar. Fritz Ringer summarizes the situation:

> Since the Revolution of 1848, there had been a steady increase in the hostility of gymnasium supporters for the realschulen. The [p. 29] attacks on the modern curriculum, which became ever more frequent toward the end of the century, showed how thoroughly the classical ideal had become entangled with political conservatism and social snobbery.[3]

To understand just how exclusive the gymnasium was in Troeltsch's day, consider that only three out of a thousand Germans attended a gymnasium in 1885. Of this select group, only five percent actually received an *Abitur* or official diploma, which was the prerequisite for higher education. Thus, only about one out of 6,700 Germans were qualified to enter a university.[4]

By the 1870s and 1880s, increased competition for careers in the professions and the civil service greatly heightened the conflict between the gymnasium and the realschulen.[5] It was a war that the classical gymnasium consistently won throughout this period. Max Weber was to remark that finding a career in government or the free professions had less to do with specific qualifications involving specialized knowledge and more to do with general refinement. Indeed the whole school and university system, especially the teaching of the humanities, was aimed at producing the man of good breeding.[6]

With his material needs fully provided for and the best of opportunities opened to him, the young Troeltsch chose to turn his attention to intellectual and theological concerns. Far removed from Augsburg's textile mills, Saint Anna's provided the finest of traditional upper-class educations with a traditional religious training. Neo-orthodox Lutheranism, a blend of orthodox confessionalism, Pietism and romanticism, permeated his world through family, school, and pulpit.

Theological neo-orthodoxy was one aspect of his background Troeltsch was to rebel against. After one year of theological study at

Erlangen where neo-orthodox Lutheranism also prevailed, he transferred to Berlin. One year later in 1886 he transferred again to Göttingen, where he found a cultural and intellectual climate to his liking. There he began to study under Albrecht Ritschl who impressed him with his "utterly unromantic and bourgeois but deeply moral integrity."[7]

At Göttingen in 1890, Troeltsch joined a group of young scholars involved in biblical investigations from a history-of-religions perspective including Albert Eichhorn, Hermann Günkel, Alfred Rahlfs, William Wrede, Heinrich Hackmann, and Wilhelm Bousset. Troeltsch became the "systematician" of this circle.[8] Paul de Lagarde was a major influence on the group in the area of methodology. Through Alfred Rahlfs, Troeltsch came to have a deep appreciation for Lagarde's work.[9]

In 1894, Troeltsch was given the chair of systematic theology in Heidelberg where he was to remain for twenty-one years. It was here that he completed *The Social Teaching* in 1912.

In 1915 he took a chair of philosophy at the University of Berlin. After World War I, Troeltsch published *Der Historismus*, his other major work, which was an analysis of historicism. According to Harnack, who delivered Troeltsch's funeral address on February 3, 1923, Troeltsch was "indisputably *the* German philosopher of history of our time."[10]

Troeltsch was remembered for his captivating personality no less than his academic achievement. A few tales of the young professor as *Wunderkind* are worth recounting.

Not long after Troeltsch's arrival in Heidelberg, heads were wagging over this southern German "force of nature" who loved to frolic in the waters of the Neckar.[11] But not everyone was charmed by his Bavarian exuberance. When Troeltsch first arrived, he visited each of his faculty colleagues in their offices as custom would have it. Entering the office of Kuno Fischer, the eminent historian of philosophy, Troeltsch exclaimed: "'My dear colleague, I am so glad finally to make your personal acquaintance!'" Fischer replied coldly, "'Address me as "Your Excellency," please!'" Fischer then conducted a purely formal exchange with Troeltsch for the traditional seven minutes before terminating the visit.

As soon as he left the office, Troeltsch went to the railroad station, called together the porters and hired them to each stand by a lamp post along the route that Fischer walked every morning from home to this office. When the professor passed by, each was to doff his hat, bow ceremoniously and greet him with, "'Good morning, Your Excellency!'" The next morning all went according to plan. Apparently, Fischer nodded back to each porter as if everything were normal.[12]

Everyone fell in love with the dynamic young professor. Gertrud von le Fort, who later became a writer, remembers the sensation created by his Heidelberg lectures:

> It is impossible for me to report on the impressions this lecture made upon me, for it went above my head. Intellectually, I understood only very little. And yet the impact as such was overwhelming. For the first time in my life, I found myself exposed to and under the disturbing sway of the power of an enormous eloquence, the power of something *elemental*—say the power of the sea or of a storm—but yet very clearly with the distinctive awareness that this elemental power was the bearer or wing of something spiritual.[13]

Another incident illustrates this "elemental quality" ascribed to Troeltsch. Two years after he came to Heidelberg, Troeltsch attended a gathering of theologians in Eisenach where a well-respected theologian had just completed a learned, but conventional lecture. During the following discussion, Troeltsch took the floor and began his statement with the words: "'Gentlemen, everything is tottering!'" Appalled, a spokesman for the older scholars got up and made a dismissive reply. At this, Troeltsch got up and walked out, slamming the door behind him. While the old guard of German theology were happy to see him go, the younger members began to pay attention to the young dissident.[14]

The historian Friedrich Meinecke, one of Troeltsch's closest friends during his Berlin years, said this about him:

> One had to hear him talk in order to completely understand him. Then the hasty and bold but energetically conceived abstract thought-complexes, which he loved almost cyclopedically to pile up in enormous sentence structures, took on at once an inner liveliness and an enthralling vividness. Then there appeared behind the great thinker a great human being for whom all knowledge and perception was transformed into personal and spiritual vitality.[15]

In his eulogy to Troeltsch, Harnack said:

> His manner of lecturing and speaking was unique and at the same time captivating. He did not aim to formulate his ideas sharply and concisely but with repeated efforts and with an overflowing eloquence which was amply, even overabundantly at his command, he tossed an observation or an idea to and fro, assailing it from all sides and putting it in different contexts until it appeared purified and clear.[16]

While it may be hard for readers today to understand the appeal of Troeltsch's unwieldy prose, these accounts capture the alchemy by which it was transformed into something else: Troeltsch's charismatic effect on his audience.

After his death, Troeltsch's stature continued to grow until his thought became "a veritable gospel."[17] Hugh Ross Mackintosh remarked about Troeltsch's writing style:

> His books now and then leave the impression that the author has emptied out the contents of his notebooks into the printed page without too much regard for form or clarity.... Especially in his later years, the gain would have been immense had more time been spent on the shaping of his materials, in obedience to Goethe's never-to-be-forgotten maxim: "The artist is known by selection."[18]

But, Mackintosh concluded, this weakness only serves to disguise a greater strength: "Encyclopaedic in learning, [Troeltsch] often appears to know too much."[19] Robert Rubanowice agrees, and adds more. Although Troeltsch was "eminently eclectic," this is because he eschewed the "uncomplicated and easy." Troeltsch never achieved a "durable synthesis;" nevertheless, "he ranks with pivotal thinkers of the past such as Schleiermacher, Hegel and Ritschl."[20] At a Göttingen University celebration of the 100th anniversary of his birth, Troeltsch's work was hailed as immortal.[21]

H. Stuart Hughes took the sharply dissenting view that Troeltsch's charisma and popularity outstripped his actual intellectual achievement. Troeltsch was overly dependent upon ideas borrowed from Weber and Meinecke, he argued. Echoing Mackintosh's observation concerning Troeltsch's compositional style, Hughes drew a different conclusion: Troeltsch's exuberance left him with no patience to clarify his thinking.[22] Before continuing with the present narration of Troeltsch's life, it will be helpful to examine Hughes's assessment in more detail. The following reexamination of Troeltsch's intellectual stature draws upon and supplements Hughes's essay.

Troeltsch is portrayed by leading interpreters as the man who replaced the dogmatic method in theology with the historical method.[23] In fact, Troeltsch was by no means the first theologian to apply the historical critical method to the discipline. Modern German historicism began with Hegel and influenced the work of nearly all major German intellectuals of the nineteenth century. After Leopold von Ranke, who, as we have seen, developed the method within the discipline of political history, no mainstream German intellectual would seriously consider *not* using the historical critical method.

In fact, Ferdinand Christian Baur was probably the first to apply the historical method to the discipline of theology.[24] As was mentioned above, he was more appreciative of the Jewish antecedents of early

Christianity than was Ritschl or Troeltsch. Ritschl substituted a neo-Kantian form of historical criticism for the Hegelian model of his teacher and combined it with a more neo-orthodox confessionalism. Troeltsch simply took up his teacher's neo-Kantian historical method while rejecting his neo-orthodoxy. He also used Weberian sociological methods. Therefore, to say that Troeltsch was the first to place early Christianity within an historical developmental framework is incorrect. Baur had done this half a century earlier.

One factor contributing to this misconception has been the ascendancy of Karl Barth and the neo-orthodox school in the twentieth century, with Barth's emphasis on Christian revelation as transcending history. Insofar as Troeltsch came to be perceived as the "historical" alternative to Barth, he also came to eclipse earlier historical interpreters of Christianity.[25]

It is also commonly said that Troeltsch was influenced by Dilthey, but the implications of this fact are not generally understood. Dilthey made a sharp distinction between the human or historical sciences and the natural sciences, and argued that the psychological factor operative in history created novelty in a way that was not possible for natural phenomena. It was mentioned in chapter 4 that Dilthey was critical of Ranke's historiography for allegedly failing to place more emphasis on intellectual history (*Geistesgeschichte*). This was the method that both Troeltsch and his friend Meinecke took up. Intellectual history marked a departure from the concrete realities of political historiography and complemented the prevailing idealist bias against the "material."

It was also noted that during the Second Empire a school of social historiography had come into being that went virtually unrecognized in its own time in part because of prevailing German idealist assumptions. Kautsky's work on Christianity certainly represented this approach. Like most of his contemporaries, Troeltsch had little use for it. It is therefore simply not accurate to say that Troeltsch pioneered the "historical" or "social" approach to theology.

It is also a misconception to suggest that Troeltsch made a decisive break with the past by regarding Christianity as nonabsolute and equal to other religions. He may have had a lower Christology than Ritschl, but so did Baur—and even Hegel. Just as Hegel considered Christianity to be the most evolved religion in history, so also Troeltsch never transcended such ethnocentrism.

Troeltsch considered Christianity to be the highest point of religious development for the West and surely higher than the religions of "primitive" races. He does not repudiate this position even in his later essay, "The Place of Christianity among the World Religions" (1923).[26] Here he opens the door to the "possibility that other racial groups, living under entirely different cultural conditions, may experience their contact with the Divine Life in quite a different way." But then he nearly closes it again by stating that "we shall, of course, assume something of this kind only among nations which have reached a relatively high stage of civilization.... We shall not assume it among the less developed races."[27]

In this same essay, Troeltsch insists that "Christianity has become the religion of all Europe."[28] Also, Christianity is "of such a highly developed racial group" that in its "progress towards a kingdom of the Spirit" it has become "deorientalised," that is, has ceased to be "a Jewish sect." Thus, his oft quoted words—that Christianity is *a truth for us*"[29]—refer not just to professing Christians, but to persons of a European "racial group."

His analysis of world religions based on race and nation ("race" appears at least twelve times; "culture" only a few times) bears an ominous ring, coming just months before Hitler's Beer Hall Putsch of November 8, 1923. Indeed, no recognition of Judaism is given in the latter half of this essay where he presents his modifications of earlier views. Nor does Troeltsch acknowledge a legitimate role for European Jewry in any part of his essay. Rather in the second half, he recognizes only three other "world" religions: Buddhism, Hinduism, and Islam.

These religions are perceived as valid only for their own "races" within their own geographic locales. Smaller cults of "primitive" races are dismissed as inferior; in fact, Troeltsch encourages traditional missionary activity among the latter.[30] Troeltsch said this at a time when European colonialism still prevailed in Africa and parts of Asia.

The only question Troeltsch poses that might possibly be innovative is whether "objective" historical manifestations of an underlying "Spirit" may not be more widespread than previously thought.[31] He still holds the hierarchical assumption of higher and lower forms of spiritual manifestations.

Troeltsch closely links this spiritual hierarchy with the concepts of nation and race. The religion of the European colonizers is clearly higher than the religions of the colonized peoples.

Further, if Christianity is "the religion of all Europe," then no room is left for a European-based Judaism, precisely the religion under attack in Troeltsch's home country.[32] It is significant that the reactionary

Paul de Lagarde exerted his greatest influence upon Troeltsch precisely in developing a methodology for the history of religions, according to Troeltsch's official biographer.[33]

Another intellectual achievement commonly attributed to Troeltsch was his revitalization of academic ethics with real world experience. According to this view, Troeltsch became actively involved in the current events of his day and in shaping their historical direction out of a sense that academic and ethical reflection had to be grounded in concrete events. Most notably, Troeltsch represented the University of Heidelberg in the upper house of Parliament in the Grand Duchy of Baden. As mentioned, he was an active member of the National Liberal Party.

While this may be true, Troeltsch political involvement was by no means unusual among his social peers. In fact, it was common for the German intelligentsia of this period to be involved in public affairs, as we have seen from the political involvements of the student fraternities of the 1880s, for example.

Nor should we overestimate the impact of concrete experience on the thought of Troeltsch and others in the philosophical idealist tradition. Such thinkers tended to transform experience into theoretical abstractions, and deal with the world and its problems from a seemingly lofty perspective. To the extent that Troeltsch dealt with history and culture it was on the level of intellectual history (*Geistesgeschichte*), not material history (*Historie*).

A final misconception about Troeltsch regards the extent of his indebtedness to Albrecht Ritschl. In fact, he was equally, if not more indebted to another professor at Göttingen, Ritschl's bitter foe, the archconservative Paul de Lagarde.[34] Lagarde's approach to the study of the history of religions was foundational for Troeltsch and his theological companions at Göttingen. It was through this circle that Lagarde came to have a major impact on Troeltsch in the following ways:[35]

Though he was more philosophically sophisticated than Lagarde, who was trained as a Biblical scholar, Troeltsch found him to be "one of the most inspiring and most important, although at the same time one of the most peculiar theological thinkers."[36] Further, "his *Deutsche Schriften*, written in powerful prose, has finally had the impact of which his great and important thought is worthy."[37] It was this work—full of virulent anti-Semitism—that set forth Lagarde's vision for a new Germanic religion of the pure *Volk* (folk).[38] Troeltsch's admiration is also attested to by his 1913 book dedication to Lagarde.[39]

Though Troeltsch did offer a disclaimer regarding Lagarde's anti-Semitism, he quickly adds that this feature does nothing to lower his great respect for Lagarde and his allegedly profound religious and political insights.[40] His disclaimer is also contradicted by the racialist and anti-Semitic elements in Troeltsch's own thought.[41]

Lagarde broke with organized Christianity while Troeltsch sought to reform it from within; nevertheless, the latter viewed Lagarde as expressing an authentic religious longing, which contained the seeds for such reform:

> [Lagarde's] longing inspiring us again for power and life, [his] aversion toward hollow scepticism, toward mere utilitarianism, toward the merely physical scientific [*naturwissenschaftliche*] and merely historical [*historische*] developments promises an integration of all the striving and work...of theology of the nineteenth century.[42]

Thus, Troeltsch felt that Lagarde's thought, although incomplete, contained the decisive ingredient that could achieve theological "integration." Indeed, Lagarde introduced Troeltsch to the romantic and Pietistic impulses that would inform his own philosophy of religion.[43] For example, it was through Lagarde that Troeltsch developed a sharp distinction between "religion" and its ecclesiastical embodiment. Lagarde influenced Troeltsch to contrast living, effervescent religion with the fixed, immovable Church.[44]

It was Lagarde who caused Troeltsch to discern a new kind of Protestantism emerging after the eighteenth century—a blend of the Reformation and Renaissance and open to modern influences.[45] Also, in *The Social Teaching*, Troeltsch broke with Ritschl to adopt Lagarde's understanding of mysticism.[46]

Troeltsch's social and political views, indeed his whole approach to the history of religions, were influenced by Lagarde. Troeltsch accepted Lagarde's state—nation dualism which paralleled that of body—soul; that religion was bound up with the living nation (*Volk*) rather than the state.[47] He agreed with Lagarde that the Kingdom of God makes its appearance in racially defined, national religion, and that the Spirit of God is manifested in the pure German *Volk*.[48]

Troeltsch also concurred with Lagarde that Germans needed to reject a politics based on class division; that the remedy for this was the cultivation of a specifically Germanic spirituality.[49] Troeltsch followed Lagarde in emphasizing the "sacred heritage" of the German spirit (*Geist*) as opposed to the materialism, atomism and egalitarianism of the Anglo-French tradition. Lagarde's influence can be seen in the following statement by Troeltsch:

> You abandon a world where men are always seeking, on the basis of equality and by a mere process of incessant climbing, to increase [p. 212] the range of reason, well-being, liberty and purposive organisation, until they attain the goal of the unity of mankind. You enter a world in which there is a hierarchy of qualitatively different cultures—a world in which the people that from time to time enjoys the hegemony hands on the torch to the next.[50]

It was precisely by engaging in this competition for dominance that religion, politics and education come together for both Lagarde and Troeltsch. Like Lagarde, Troeltsch argued on behalf of the classical training of the gymnasium exclusively dedicated to Germanic cultural traditions. He also spoke in favor of the restoration of "family values"—code words for an anti-suffragette agenda, as mentioned in chapter 2. Further, both Lagarde and Troeltsch were involved in national politics and social criticism.[51] In summary, Troeltsch had many reasons to emphasize his indebtedness to Lagarde.[52]

In the volume which he dedicated to Lagarde, Troeltsch concludes his introductory essay with a lengthy quote from the radical right-winger, which reads in part: "We are not to be human, but rather children of God; not liberal, but rather free; not conservative, but rather German."[53]

Despite certain shared views, Troeltsch possessed a personal smoothness and charm that Lagarde lacked; he also chose to locate himself more within the mainstream. Indeed, Troeltsch mediated Lagarde's extreme ideas to the academic mainstream and helped make them respectable there.[54]

During his years at Heidelberg, Troeltsch also began his study of sociology and formed a strong friendship with Max Weber, a professor of sociology at the university. In fact, he utilized Weberian sociological typology in *The Social Teaching*. Weber was a very intense personality who took solid, principled positions, and who subbornly fought for his chosen causes and his reputation. Troeltsch was more compromising, humorous, and tolerant of the foibles of others. As different as they were, they grew close and travelled together to the United States in 1905 and in 1909. With their families, Troeltsch and Weber shared an elegant estate on the shore of the Neckar River, which became a meeting place for the Heidelberg intellectual community. By then, Troeltsch was completing the last section of *The Social Teaching*.

However, differences between the two men eventually surfaced in a political context and brought their friendship to an end. Even though this happened three or four years after *The Social Teaching* was published, it is worth noting for the insight it gives into their differences of character.

During World War I, Weber, a reserve military officer, was put in charge of several military hospitals. Troeltsch, a civilian, administered one of them. It so happened that Weber and other hospital directors adopted a policy of allowing German civilians to visit relatives among the convalescing French prisoners of war. Conservatives marshalled public opinion against this policy, accusing the hospital directors of a lack of patriotism. Troeltsch responded to this right-wing pressure by requiring a military officer to be present during the visits.

At this, Weber angrily accused Troeltsch of cowardice in bending to inhumane public opinion. Although he later apologized for his rage, Weber could never accept Troeltsch's accommodationism. Only after the elapse of five years (through the negotiations of their wives) was something like a reconciliation achieved. By then, they had physically separated, with Troeltsch teaching in Berlin and Weber, in Munich. The closeness of the original friendship was never restored.[55]

On June 12, 1917, Troeltsch wrote a letter about Weber to Paul Honigsheim, a former classmate and friend:

> During the war, Max Weber has developed such a radical outlook and he judges the whole situation with such pessimism and hostility that he has become totally isolated and is on bad terms with most people, including me. Older differences concerning politics and matters of principle burst through in him, so that he broke off relations with me in the most harsh manner without any particular reason. Fundamentally, his life is a constant duel with everything that he views as corruption, and above all with the person of the Emperor whom he holds accountable for just about everything. An argument with him is impossible. You can imagine how sorry I am over this and how very much I did not want this to happen.[56]

Troeltsch tried to attribute his falling out with Weber primarily to personality differences, in particular, to Weber's apparently neurotic behavior.[57] However, it seems to have involved a genuine ethical conflict.

This conflict is of particular interest, since Troeltsch and Weber otherwise had so much in common. They were both National Liberals, both supported the war, but both also signed the Delbrueck petition repudiating imperialist war aims, as we will see in the next chapter. They also shared a common ethical framework. Both agreed theoretically in distinguishing between an ethic of ultimate ends versus an ethic of responsibility and the need to compromise between these two poles. Yet they strongly disagreed in this concrete instance as to where compromise must leave off and a stand on principle be taken. In this case, Weber took his stand while Troeltsch compromised. Weber found Troeltsch's compromise ethically unacceptable.[58]

While playing down the reasons for the break with Weber, Troeltsch did admit in his letter that "older differences concerning politics and matters of principle burst through in him."[59] Indeed, Gerth and Mills, in the context of discussing the relation of Weber's views to fascism, specifically make a point to disassociate Weber from Troeltsch:

> It is, of course, quite vain to speculate whether Weber with his Machiavellian attitude might ever have turned Nazi. To be sure, his philosophy of charisma—his skepticism and his pragmatic view of democratic sentiment—might have given him such affinities. But his humanism, his love for the underdog, his hatred of sham and lies, and his unceasing campaign against racism and anti-Semitic demagoguery would have made him at least as sharp a 'critic,' if not a sharper one, of Hitler than his brother Alfred has been.

> Weber was far from following Troeltsch, who felt it necessary to speak of the 'most basic dispositions and volitional tendencies' ultimately underlying the social institutions, and ideological structures of history: 'We have no words for this and, in this case, speak of races, of plastic, historical forces, or of primeval impulses.' Weber was far from this quest for a metaphysical anchorage in 'blind nature.' One may sum up Weber's dispersed and repeated disclaimers of racial arguments in the words of John Stuart Mill: 'Of all vulgar modes of escaping from the consideration of the effect of social and moral influences on the human mind, the most vulgar is that of attributing the diversities of conduct and character to inherent natural differences.'[60]

Critics of Troeltsch, such as Gerth and Mills, are not the only ones who see racialist elements in his thought. Manfred Wichelhaus, a member of the Ernst Troeltsch Society and a sympathetic interpreter, summarizes how Troeltsch appropriated modern sociology to an essentially racialist worldview:

> And for the expansion and illumination of the horizon of historiography [p. 82] he employed the help which sociology, as a science of the formal structures and conditions of community, offered. Climate [Klima] and race [Rasse] were valid for him as the final and unconditional motivations of sociological phenomena.[61]

Wichelhaus clearly states that racialist categories were foundational to Troeltsch's understanding of social phenomena. In his programmatic essay, "Political Ethics and Christianity" (1904), to which we will turn in chapter 10, Troeltsch focuses on the alleged natural differences and inequalities of class, race, and gender. He held these views throughout his life, as indicated by his essay cited above, "The Place of Christianity among the World Religions," written just before his death in 1923.[62]

This evidence fundamentally calls into question the conventional wisdom, held by American liberals such as the Niebuhrs and James Luther Adams, that Troeltsch was a liberal in the Anglo-French sense, such as John Stuart Mill.

In summary, as one reviewer put it, "Troeltsch was conservative in politics," and was caught up in the German nationalism that was sweeping the country during Imperial Germany.[63] Both as a member of the National Liberal Party before the Great War, and the German Democratic party after it, he stood to the right of the political center (see figures 8.1 and 8.2).[64] As mentioned, he was highly involved in the political arena, sitting in the Baden upper house for a number of years before the war and in the Prussian lower house from 1919 to 1921. During the Weimar period he also served as undersecretary of state for public worship.[65]

Troeltsch argued against the socialist party agendas that were sweeping public opinion before and after World War I (note the election trends for 1912 and 1919 in figures 8.1 and 8.2). At the same time, he appropriated the discourse of socialism for his own purposes (see chapter 12, "Christianity and Socialism").

Some interpreters incorrectly infer from this use of socialist discourse that Troeltsch was moving to the left. It is common for members of an elite that is losing legitimacy, however, to co-opt the discourse of its competition in an attempt to recover lost ground. According to McCann, Troeltsch's purpose in his essay, "Socialism" (1920), was to achieve "an accommodation with socialist demands."[66] This becomes understandable when one realizes that by 1919 there were *three* socialist parties, and the Majority Socialist Party with 163 seats led a coalition of parties to form the government (see figure 8.2). According to O'Dea,

> Troeltsch...urged that the Republic be accepted whole-heartedly, despite its alien character (its basis in Anglo-French eighteenth century values) and the inferior quality of its office holders. The true conservatism required to restore balance to German life could be brought about, he declared, only by the acceptance of the Weimar Republic.[67]

Thus, it was in a context of Anglo-French military control and a socialist-led governing coalition that Troeltsch counselled a policy of accommodationism with the Republic. It was the best way to keep alive his own neoconservative agenda.[68]

Not only did Troeltsch have no affinity with Social Democracy, he also "took no satisfaction in the various social gospels of recent times."[69] Indeed, the Emperor's pronouncement in 1896 against "political pas-

FIGURE 8.1
National Parliament Party Representation, 1912

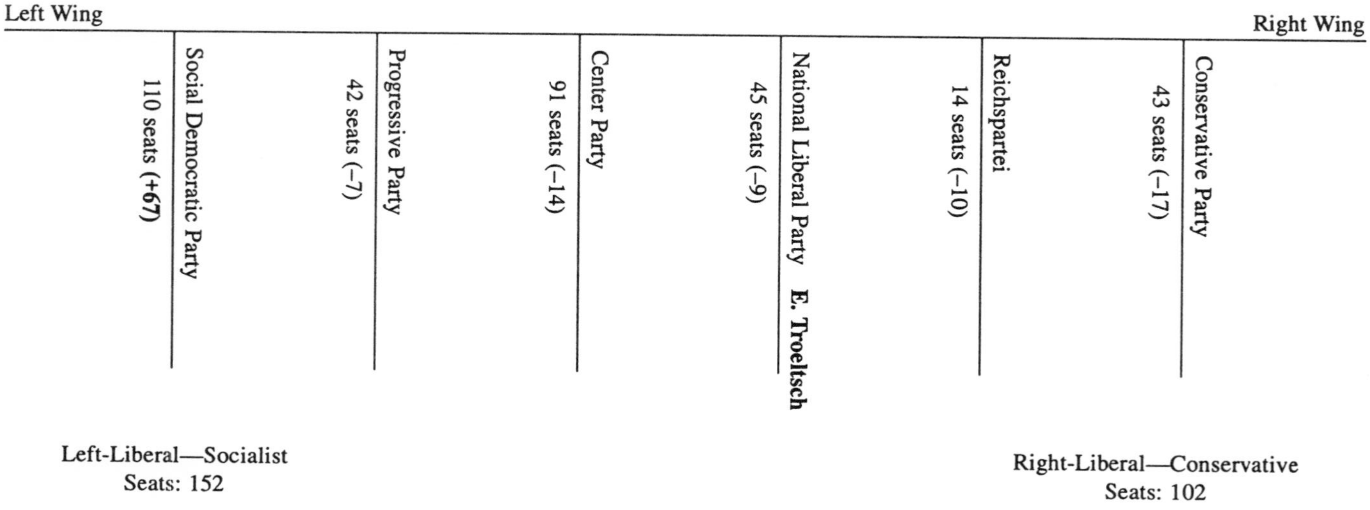

Right Wing

Conservative Party
43 seats (−17)

Reichspartei
14 seats (−10)

National Liberal Party   **E. Troeltsch**
45 seats (−9)

Center Party
91 seats (−14)

Progressive Party
42 seats (−7)

Social Democratic Party
110 seats **(+67)**

Left Wing

Left-Liberal—Socialist
Seats: 152

Right-Liberal—Conservative
Seats: 102

In the 1912 election the Social Democratic Party gained 67 seats to take the lead; the other parties all lost seats (cf. numbers in parentheses). Troeltsch was a member of the National Liberal Party which lost nearly 17 percent of its seats.

Source: Craig, *Germany, 1866–1945,* 292.

FIGURE 8.2
National Assembly Party Representation, 1919

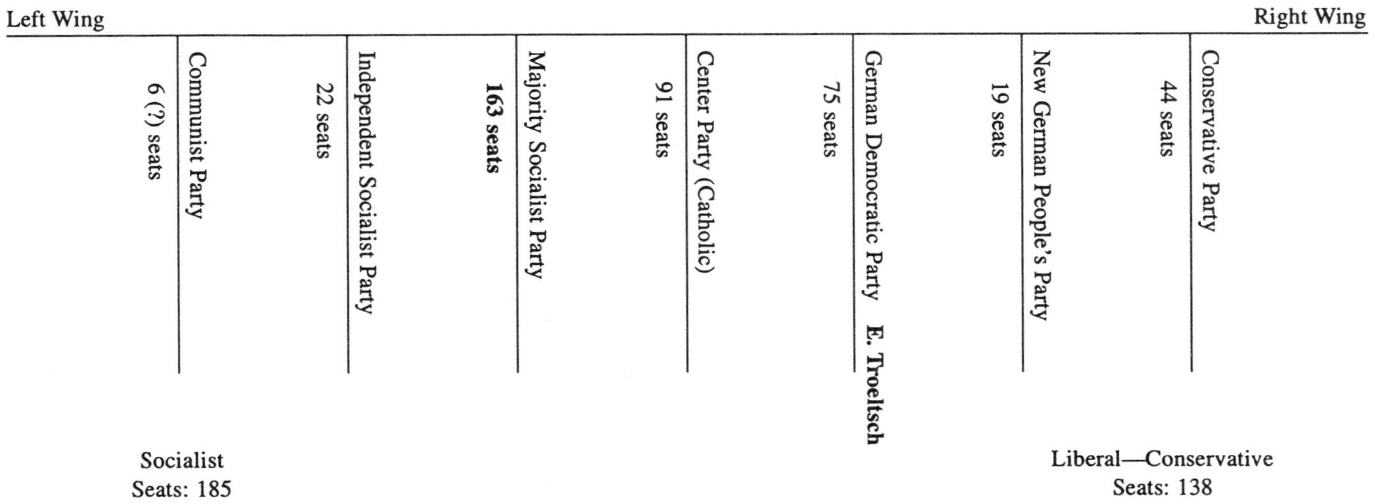

Right Wing

Conservative Party

44 seats

⎫
⎪
⎪ Liberal—Conservative
⎬ Seats: 138
⎪
⎪

New German People's Party

19 seats

German Democratic Party   **E. Troeltsch**

75 seats

Center Party (Catholic)

91 seats

Majority Socialist Party

163 seats

⎫
⎪
⎪ Socialist
⎬ Seats: 185
⎪

Independent Socialist Party

22 seats

Communist Party

6 (?) seats

Left Wing

After the war, three socialist parties emerged with the Majority Socialist Party holding the reins of power. As in 1912, Troeltsch's party occupied a minority position to the right of the political center.

Source: Craig, *Germany, 1866–1945*, 412–13.

FIGURE 8.3
Leadership of the Evangelical Social Congress before 1896

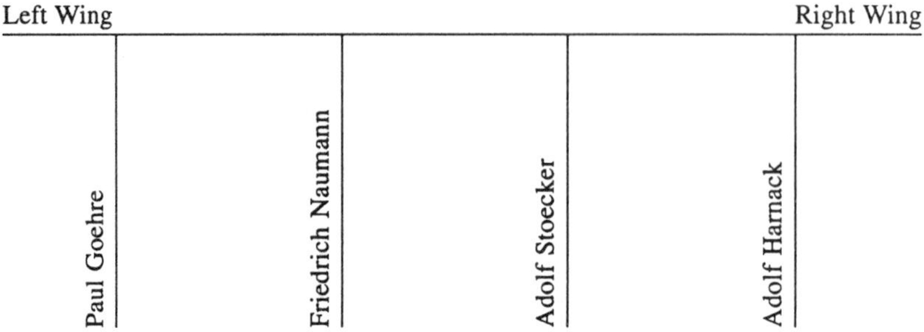

Left Wing   Right Wing

```
Paul Goehre    |    Friedrich Naumann    |    Adolf Stoecker    |    Adolf Harnack
```

To the left stood Goehre and Naumann who advocated social welfare policies and curbs on capital accumulation. To the right stood Harnack who advocated private charity.

Source: Sorg, *Marxismus und Protestantismus in Deutschland*, 87f.

FIGURE 8.4
Leadership of the Evangelical Social Congress after 1896

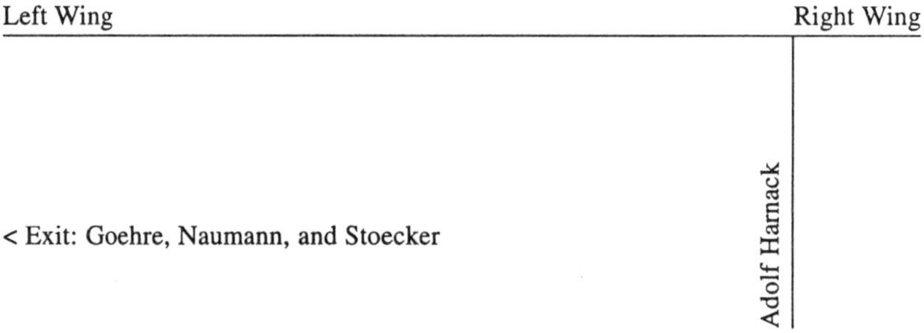

Left Wing   Right Wing

```
< Exit: Goehre, Naumann, and Stoecker                    |    Adolf Harnack
```

E. Troeltsch (1904)

After the emperor's declaration against "political pastors" in 1896, Goehre, Naumann, and Stoecker were forced out of power. All left the organization, which now had Harnack as head. Troeltsch delivered his 1904 address to this conservative remnant.

tors" had caused a shake-up in the leadership of the Evangelical Social Congress, forcing out liberals and moderates (see figures 8.3 and 8.4). With this event, what had been "an incipient social gospel had vanished in the smoke of national religion."[70] What was Troeltsch's relation to this purge? He explicitly stated his approval of the emperor's edict in "Political Ethics and Christianity," (1904) which he delivered to the Congress under Harnack's conservative leadership (see chapter 10).[71] Far from having ties with socialism or the social gospel movements, Troeltsch had certain affinities with the ideologies of the radical right as his racialist theories and his admiration for Paul de Lagarde attest. Even after the war, Troeltsch's own ideology prevented him from taking a clear stand against the ultra-right pan-Germanists, as summarized by Fritz Ringer:

> [Troeltsch] felt the need for a 'new immediacy and inwardness, for a new intellectual and spiritual aristocracy, which counterbalances the rationalism and the leveling tendencies of democracy...[and the] spiritual barrenness of Marxism...with a more organically synthetic mentality.' In short, Troeltsch wanted to make use of the spiritual revolution [in which the Pan-Germanists played a role], without allowing it to get out of control.[72]

Troeltsch's "use of the spiritual revolution," is illustrated in his appropriation of the mystical theories of Paul de Lagarde. Troeltsch, along with others of the educated classes, was highly influenced by Lagarde, even though Lagarde wanted to destroy liberalism and exterminate the Jewish people.[73] Instead, Troeltsch hailed Lagarde as the man who most successfully synthesized a century of reflection in the fields of philosophy of religion, theology and ethics. Lagarde's "inspiring" vision of a Germanic religion of the pure *Volk* would lead Germany into the future.

Troeltsch's life roughly coincided with the rise and fall of Imperial Germany. Born six years before its inception, he died in 1923, just five years after its demise. This survey of Troeltsch's historical context would not be complete, however, without a brief examination of the Great War which brought the regime to a catastrophic end. If everything was tottering in 1896 as Troeltsch claimed, it came crashing down in a much more concrete way than he expected, when the cannons began to fire in August, 1914.

Notes

1. Mircea Eliade, ed., *Encyclopedia of Religion* (New York: Macmillan and Free Press, 1987), s.v. "Ernst Troeltsch," by Friedrich Wilhelm Graf, 58.

2. Troeltsch, *The Social Teaching*, 704.
3. Ringer, *The Decline of the German Mandarins*, 28–29.
4. Ibid., 39, 32–33.
5. Ibid., 29.
6. Women were not yet allowed into the universities or the gymnasiums. Upper-class women attended finishing schools instead. Ibid., 25–35.
7. Wilhelm Pauck, *Harnack and Troeltsch: Two Historical Theologians* (New York: Oxford University Press, 1968), 55.
8. E. Troeltsch, *Gesammelte Schriften*, vol. 4 (Tübingen: J.C.B. Mohr, 1923), 5.
9. Hans-Georg Drescher, *Ernst Troeltsch: His Life and Work*, (Minneapolis, MN: Fortress Press, 1993), 45, 349 note 82.
10. Adolph von Harnack, "Ernst Troeltsch: A Funeral Address delivered on February 3, 1923," *Harnack and Troeltsch: Two Historical Theologians*, Wilhelm Pauck, ed. and trans. (New York: Oxford University Press, 1968), 122.
11. H. Stuart Hughes, *Consciousness and Society: The Reorientation of European Social Thought 1890–1930* (New York: Alfred A. Knopf, 1961), 230.
12. Pauck, *Harnack and Troeltsch*, 54–55.
13. Emphasis mine. Gertrud von le Fort quoted in Pauck, *Harnack and Troeltsch*, 47.
14. Hughes gives this anecdote as an example of Troeltsch's charisma. Hughes, *Consciousness and Society*, 229–30.
15. Friedrich Meinecke, "Ernst Troeltsch: 1. Nachruf," *Werke*, IV (Stuttgart: Koehler Verlag, 1965), 364.
16. Harnack, "Ernst Troeltsch," 122.
17. See chapter one; Bainton, "Ernst Troeltsch—Thirty Years Later," 71.
18. Hugh Ross Mackintosh, *Types of Modern Theology: Schleiermacher to Barth* (London: Nisbet and Co., 1937), 188–89.
19. Ibid., 188.
20. Rubanowice, *Crisis in Consciousness*, 136–37.
21. Heinz Eduard Tödt, "Ernst Troeltschs Bedeutung für die evangelische Sozialethik," *Zeitschrift für Evangelische Ethik*, 10 (1966), 228.
22. Hughes departs from the general consensus despite Antoni's earlier endorsement. H. Stuart Hughes, *Consciousness and Society*, 230–39; Carlo Antoni, *From History to Sociology*, trans. Hayden V. White (Detroit, MI: Wayne State University Press, 1959), 39f.
23. Bainton, Pauck, Reist, Rubanowice and Drescher take this view. Bainton is critical of the canonization of Troeltsch that has evolved, as mentioned in chapter one. Nevertheless, he still believes his work "should be canonized…for its methodology." Bainton, "Ernst Troeltsch—Thirty Years Later," 72. In his official Troeltsch biography, Drescher has recourse to Troeltsch's own assessment of *The Social Teaching* as launching a new discipline. Drescher, *Ernst Troeltsch*, 222; Pauck, *Harnack and Troeltsch*, 55–57; Rubanowice, *Crisis in Consciousness*, 44; Reist, *Toward a Theology of Involvement*, 39.
24. Peter C. Hodgson, *The Formation of Historical Theology, A Study of Ferdinand Christian Bauer* (New York: Harper and Row, 1966).
25. For example, Bainton's call for the "canonization" of Troeltsch's method follows his recounting of the history of twentieth century neo-orthodox opposition to Troeltsch. Bainton does not reconstruct the history of interpretation prior to and contemporaneous with Troeltsch. Bainton, "Ernst Troeltsch—Thirty Years Later," 70–72.
26. Ernst Troeltsch, "The Place of Christianity among the World Religions," *Christian Thought: Its History and Application*, edited by Baron F. von Hügel (Lon-

don: University of London Press, 1923), 1–35. The racist aspects of Troeltsch's thought are examined further in Constance L. Benson, "The Role of Race in Ernst Troeltsch's Analysis of World Religions," paper presented to the American Academy of Religion, Mid-Atlantic Region, March 4–5, 1993, Temple University, Philadelphia, PA.

27. Troeltsch, "The Place of Christianity," 26–27.

28. Ibid., 24–25.

29. Emphasis his. Ibid., 34.

30. "We have a missionary duty towards these races." Ibid., 29.

31. Ibid., 10–11.

32. This raises questions about the exchange between Troeltsch and the Marburg moral philosopher Hermann Cohen. Each produced proposals for monotheistic religion with the other in mind: Cohen, for Judaism and Troeltsch, for Christianity. While they conducted a respectful conversation, they disagreed over fundamental issues. Troeltsch made it clear to Cohen that Christianity had to play the principal religious role within the Western world. He also strongly disagreed with Cohen that the Hebrew prophets provided an ethical foundation for the modern world, dismissing them as "utopian." I do not understand how such ethnocentrism can be reconciled with Dietrich's claim that Troeltsch laid a foundation for Jewish-Christian dialogue. Wendell S. Dietrich, *Cohen and Troeltsch: Ethical Monotheistic Religion and Theory of Culture* (Atlanta, GA: Scholars Press, 1986), 1, 2, 5.

33. "Paul de Lagarde...pointed the way forward for the history-of-religions school in the question of methodology.... What attracted Troeltsch to Lagarde was the way in which Lagarde gave religious phenomena a place in history." Drescher, *Ernst Troeltsch*, 45.

34. The following description draws largely from Lougee, who devoted several pages to drawing the parallels between the thinking of Lagarde and Troeltsch. Robert W. Lougee, *Paul de Lagarde 1827–1891: A Study of Radical Conservatism in Germany* (Cambridge, MA: Harvard University Press, 1962), 280–83.

35. Virtually nothing in the Troeltsch literature addresses the issue of Lagarde's influence on Troeltsch. One exception is Drescher's work. In his biography of Troeltsch, however, Drescher makes no mention of Lagarde's extreme anti-Semitism or German nationalism and what effect it might have had on Troeltsch's thought. Instead, Drescher writes, "Lagarde was a deeply pious person." Drescher, *Ernst Troeltsch*, 350 note 84; also 21, 45, 349 note 82, 350 note 85; idem, "Ernst Troeltsch und Paul de Lagarde," *Mitteilungen der Ernst-Troeltsch-Gesellschaft* III, (Augsburg, 1984), 95–115. Another exception is Sarah Coakley's discussion of Troeltsch's "disengagement from 'Ritschlianism,'" where she describes Troeltsch's break from Ritschl as the result of Lagarde's influence. In a cryptic footnote, Coakley does touch on Lagarde's anti-Semitism, merely stating that Troeltsch disavowed it in the process of dedicating a book to him. She does not develop her point, nor does she address the fact that Troeltsch highly praised Lagarde's *Deutsche Schriften*, a work that equals Hitler's *Mein Kampf* for anti-Semitic venom, and which envisioned a new Germanic religion developing from the pure "folk," as I discussed in chapter 5. Sarah Coakley, *Christ Without Absolutes: A Study of the Christology of Ernst Troeltsch* (Oxford: Clarendon Press, 1988), 48.

36. Troeltsch, "The Theological and Religious Situation of the Present," *Gesammelte Schriften* II, 19.

37. Troeltsch, *GS* II, 20. Stern singles out Troeltsch's dedication to Lagarde as being "a most impressive testimony to [his] influence...." Stern, *The Politics of Cultural Despair*, 35n.

38. Paul de Lagarde, "Die Religion der Zukunft," *Deutsche Schriften* (Göttingen: Lüder Horstmann, 1903), 217–47.
39. See chapter 5 for a profile of Lagarde and reference to Troeltsch's dedication to Lagarde of the second volume of his *Gesammelte Schriften*.
40. "Particularly, I want nothing to do with [Lagarde's] anti-Semitism, his low assessment of Paul and Luther, his Catholicizing romanticism, and his misunderstanding of the great social upheavals of our time. But none of that changes the fact that the breadth of his historical vision, his essentially historical, rather than speculative, approach to religions, his strongly self-assured piety, his relating of religions to the general conditions of life, especially to politics, gave me at the time an almost shocking stimulation." Troeltsch, *GS* II, 8.
41. Discussed elsewhere in this chapter; also, see chapters 10 and 12 of this book.
42. Troeltsch, *GS* II, 21.
43. Lougee, *Paul de Lagarde*, 281.
44. Troeltsch, "Die Christliche Weltanschauung und die Wissenschaftliche Gegenströmung," *Zeitschrift für Theologie und Kirche*, 4 (1894), 176.
45. Stern, *The Politics of Cultural Despair*, 44n.
46. Troeltsch, *The Social Teaching*, 801; see "Mysticism," in chapter 12.
47. See chapter five for a description of Lagarde's state—nation dualism; also Stern, *The Politics of Cultural Despair*, 56; Drescher explains that Lagarde was the inspiration behind the methodology of the history-of-religions school of which Troeltsch was an important member. Drescher, *Ernst Troeltsch*, 45.
48. Lougee, *Paul de Lagarde*, 281.
49. Troeltsch, *GS* II, 20, 21, 150, 151.
50. Ernst Troeltsch, "The Ideas of Natural Law and Humanity in World Politics," *Natural Law and the Theory of Society: 1500 to 1800*, edited by Otto Gierke, translated by Ernest Barker (Boston: Beacon Press, 1957), 211–212. Lougee, Ringer and Lukes each cite this essay by Troeltsch, originally published in 1923. Ringer cites it as representative of the German mandarins; Lukes cites it to distinguish German "individualism" from its Anglo-French counterpart; Lougee cites it to indicate a further link to Lagarde. E. Troeltsch, "Naturrecht und Humanität in der Weltpolitik," quoted in Ringer, *Decline of the German Mandarins*, 100–101; Lukes, *Individualism*, 20; Lougee, *Paul de Lagarde*, 282; also discussed in chapter 4.
51. Lougee, *Paul de Lagarde*, 282–83, 349n.
52. Stern also observed that Troeltsch was "deeply moved by Lagarde's earnest faith, his national ethos, his individualism, his scorn for German education." Stern, *The Politics of Cultural Despair*, 85.
53. Troeltsch, "The Theological and Religious Situation of the Present," GS II (1913), 21.
54. See Constance L. Benson, "Mainstreaming the Radical Right: Ernst Troeltsch's Appropriation of Paul de Lagarde," paper presented to the American Academy of Religion, Mid-Atlantic Region, March 4–5, 1993, Temple University, Philadelphia, PA.
55. Pauck, *Troeltsch and Harnack*, 70–74.
56. Eduard Baumgarten, *Max Weber: Werk und Person* (Tübingen: J.C.B. Mohr, 1964), 489.
57. Earlier Weber had suffered from a nervous condition that had forced him to take leaves of absence from his teaching post. However, by 1904 he had returned to a light teaching load and "his productivity was in full swing again and rising steeply." His days of nervous collapse were behind him. H. H. Gerth and C.

Wright Mills, "Introduction: The Man and His Work," *From Max Weber: Essays in Sociology* (New York: Oxford University Press, 1958), 14.

58. Gerth and Mills give the following description of Weber's character: "Being personally characterized by an extremely stern conscience, Weber was often quite ready to forgive others but was quite rigid with himself." Ibid., 20. In the case described above, Weber could not bring himself to forgive Troeltsch. Perhaps this had to do with the political realities of the case: with his decision to allow hospital prisoners of war private visiting rights, Weber was incurring the wrath of the public caught up in the war hysteria. When his close friend, Troeltsch, who was an ethicist, bowed to public opinion, this left him completely isolated. Therefore, our focus might well rest, not on the alleged neurotic aspects of Weber's personality, but on the mass neurosis gripping the public at this time, to which Troeltsch acquiesced.

59. In writing about the friendship between Troeltsch and her husband Max, Marianne Weber observed that Troeltsch was a wonderful, charismatic presence. However, there were important differences between the two men: "To be sure, in many things—especially politics—Weber and Troeltsch had different ideas. Troeltsch's views at that time made him part of the older National Liberal generation; social and democratic ideals were alien to his strongly bourgeois instincts. He did not believe in many things that the Webers were striving for—neither in the intellectual and political development of the working classes nor in the intellectual development of women. Their temperaments were different, too. For Troeltsch it was enough that he had to fight for intellectual freedom and tolerance within theology. Otherwise, he was not a fighter but was oriented toward reconciliation, adjustment, and acceptance of human weakness." Marianne Weber, *Max Weber: A Biography*, translated by Harry Zohn (New York: John Wiley & Sons, 1975), 228.

60. "Wir haben dafür keine Worte und sprechen in diesem Falle von Rassen, von plastischen Bildkräften der Geschichte oder von ursprünglichen Antrieben." Ernst Troeltsch, "Das logische Problem der Geschichts-philosophie," *Gesammelte Schriften*, (Tübingen: J.C.B. Mohr, 1922), vol. 3: *Der Historismus und seine Probleme*, 754; and John Stuart Mill, *Principles of Political Economy* (Boston, 1848), vol. I, 379, the English version quoted in Gerth and Mills, *From Max Weber*, 43.

61. To support this, Wichelhaus cites in a footnote Troeltsch's *Gesammelte Schriften* III, 165 and also 754, which Gerth and Mills quote above. He also mentions *Gesammelte Schriften* III, 706: "'Humankind does not exist in all circumstances as a unified historical subject.'" Wichelhaus concludes that for Troeltsch, "there is therefore no unified goal of religion; universal religions are religions of race." Wichelhaus also refers to Troeltsch's *Uberwindung*, 8 and to *Gesammelte Schriften* II, 828 (1913). Softer variations of Troeltsch's racialist views are found in *Die Absolutheit des Christentums und die Religionsgeschichte* (Tübingen: J. C. B. Mohr, 1902), 69f. and *Gesammelte Schriften* II, 794 (1906). Manfred Wichelhaus, *Kirchengeschichtsschreibung und Soziologie im neunzehnten Jahrhundert und bei Ernst Troeltsch* (Heidelberg: Universitätsverlag, 1965), 81–82, 82n.

62. A recent study of Troeltsch's ethics states, "Troeltsch's ruminations about ethics nevertheless show little substantive change from at least 1902 onwards." Bryce A. Gayhart, *The Ethics of Ernst Troeltsch: A Commitment to Relevancy* (Lewiston, NY: The Edwin Mellen Press, 1990), 168.

63. David L. Sills, ed., *International Encyclopedia of the Social Sciences* (New York:

Macmillan and Free Press, 1969), s.v. "Ernst Troeltsch," by Thomas F. O'Dea, 151.

64. This generalization regarding Troeltsch's location on the political spectrum would hold even if it were assumed that Troeltsch's parties had been to the left of the Catholic Center party. On that assumption, there still would have been more seats in the National Parliament to the left of Troeltsch's parties than to their right, both in 1912 and in 1919.

65. Ibid.

66. Dennis P. McCann, "Ernst Troeltsch's Essay on 'Socialism,'" *Journal of Religious Ethics* 4 (Spring, 1976), 160.

67. O'Dea, "Ernst Troeltsch," 152.

68. McCann further supports this interpretation of accommodationism by observing that Troeltsch attempted to bring together elements from both socialism and conservatism. McCann, "Ernst Troeltsch's Essay on 'Socialism,'" 159f. Rubanowice concurs, describing Troeltsch's prescription for the new Weimar regime as including "social forces as old as aristocracy and as new as socialism." Rubanowice, *Crisis in Consciousness*, 120.

    Donald E. Miller's discussion of Troeltsch's critique of Marx in *Der Historismus und seine Probleme* (1922) also supports this interpretation. While claiming to be indebted to Marx, Troeltsch criticized him for failing to do justice to "value, philosophy and religion." Troeltsch also argued that Marx's thought was obscured in a "naive dogmatism." Here we find the catch words of German mandarin ideology that Ringer described (see chapter four). Donald E. Miller, "Troeltsch's Critique of Karl Marx," *Journal for the Scientific Study of Religion*, 1 (October, 1961), 121.

69. Welch cites *The Social Teaching*, 20, 33–34, 1012, to support this assessment. Welch, *Protestant Thought in the Nineteenth Century*, 296.

70. Ibid., 244.

71. McCann also observes that Troeltsch's politics is to be distinguished from that of Paul Tillich. While the latter was critical of "scientific socialism," he did adopt the concept of class struggle. "It is difficult to imagine Troeltsch ever advocating such a leap of faith." McCann, "Ernst Troeltsch's Essay on 'Socialism,'" 161–62.

72. Ringer, *Decline of the German Mandarins*, 346–47. Ringer quotes from Troeltsch's "Die geistige Revolution," *Kunstwart und Kulturwart*, 34 (1921), 232–33.

73. Fritz Stern also wrote about how Troeltsch was influenced by "the 'soft' Lagarde" but "remained unperturbed by his brutal side, by his immense capacity to hate, by his desire to destroy Jews, liberals, *literati*, and, if need be, the non-German peoples of Central Europe. Stern, *The Politics of Cultural Despair*, 88.

9

On Earth as It is in Hell

In his conclusion to *The Social Teaching* Troeltsch wrote, "Faith is the source of energy in the struggle of life, but life still remains a battle which is continually renewed upon ever new fronts."[1] His words proved to be more timely in a literal sense than he could have imagined. Just two years after his book appeared a war broke out that raised the meaning of battle to a completely new level.

None of Troeltsch's generation, least of all the German high command who in August 1914 sent troops into Belgium, were prepared for the carnage that resulted. Many greeted the war as the solution to the decline of traditional ideals and the bitterness of party strife. In 1912, the Social Democrats had won their biggest electoral victory ever, emerging as the largest party in the Reichstag. With no other parties willing to enter a coalition government with them, a political stalemate resulted.

The Social Problem seemed solved with the outbreak of foreign hostilities. Almost as quickly as he declared war, the emperor proudly proclaimed that partisan politics had given way to German patriotism.[2] Meinecke agreed that the war would solve many recalcitrant problems.[3] Every political party supported the war. Even the revisionist wing of the Social Democratic party that included the trade union movement was swept up in the war fever.[4] For members of the ruling elite the choice was clearly war over social revolution.

In Ernst Gläser's war novel, *Jahrgang 1902*, many Germans viewed the war in Wagnerian terms. It took on religious dimensions; it was seen as a purification ritual, "the providential lightning flash that would clear the air" and cleanse humanity, a salvific path that transcended "the trading and shopkeeping spirit," leading back to older precapitalist, presocialist ideals of loyalty, patriotism, and altruism. The war awakened the Lagardian hope in the birth of "a new world guided by a race of noble souls who would root out all signs of corruption and lead humanity back to the deserted heights of the eternal ideals." So there was almost an unspoken prayer for war to come.[5]

In all fairness it should be noted that the French, British, and Russians had their own nationalistic hopes pinned on the war. Although the Germans fired the first shot, it was within the framework of a multilateral spiral of escalating hostilities. Because the English, French and Russians had formed an alliance against them and had rapidly strengthened their position in the arms race, the Germans felt they needed the advantage of a first strike.

Russian war mobilization in the wake of the assassination of the Austrian Archduke Franz Ferdinand by a Serbian nationalist caused the Germans to put the first-strike Schlieffen Plan into effect. They strategized that they had to make quick work of Russia's allies to their west before tackling the Russian troops that were mobilizing to their east. To accomplish this the element of surprise, which a first strike provides, was considered essential.

An argument could be made that the outbreak of the Great War was in large measure the result of an arms race that the major European countries had run for the latter part of the nineteenth century and which by 1908 was completely out of control. After the resignation of Bismarck in 1890, the German leadership made one diplomatic blunder after another while accelerating its naval and other arms build-up.

The officer corps with roots in feudal knighthood dominated every European country at the time. This venerated institution placed a premium on the arts of warfare as the path to honor, greatness, and manliness. A great power has been traditionally defined by its capacity to wage war and not by its life-supporting capacities. The emperor for his part was never seen in public except in a military uniform bedecked with rows of medals. It is said that he had a whole wardrobe of uniforms representing every conceivable military tradition.

To summarize, the outbreak of the war reflected not only a desire to deflect from internal social unrest, but also a religious yearning for redemption, the triumph of the traditional values of the officer corps which helped legitimize an arms race, and geopolitical competition.

The mass hallucination of soldiers marching off to war in clouds of glory was soon laid to rest on battlefields more bloody than Genghis Khan could have imagined. Just as the machine had come to dominate the workplace, so munitions now dominated war.

The French army had 5,000 cannon and the German, 4,000. Some were extremely large and all highly mobile. But none compared to "Big Bertha," the massive seventeen-inch mortar nicknamed after the wife of its maker, Gustav Krupp. This giant cannon fired projectiles a distance of nine miles and packed a force comparable to the power of five 250-ton express trains travelling sixty-five miles per hour.[6] In the opening days of the war, the German troops rolled in Big Bertha and demolished the hitherto impregnable Belgium fortresses in front of Liege as the first step in their move toward Paris.

The German people were so euphoric over the success and power of this big gun that the Emperor bestowed the Iron Cross on Gustav Krupp, while the University of Bonn gave him an honorary Doctor of Philosophy.

The euphoria over Big Bertha was premature. The Germans soon fell behind their timetable for advancing through Belgium due to stiff concerted resistance from the inhabitants. Meanwhile, a bloody standoff between the Germans and French in Alsace-Lorraine was taking place. Throwing mass armies fighting in open fields against machine guns resulted in an unprecedented slaughter on both sides. The battle at Ypres in Flanders came to be known as the Massacre of the Innocents. The German units sent here were comprised of gymnasium and university students who had enthusiastically volunteered for the front. They were torn to pieces—as were the French. This battle and others simply ended because there were no ammunition and no men left.

No one had foreseen or planned for the losses that would take place. By December 1914, just five months into the war, nearly 1,000,000 French and 1,000,000 German men were killed. The British lost over 100,000, more than from an entire century of imperial warfare. These fatality figures were not made public at the time, and the few survivors were so traumatized they often suffered partial amnesia.

As wartime hospital administrators, Weber and Troeltsch had box seats overlooking the horror. This perspective would help explain Weber's intense anger toward the Emperor during this time.

We will see that Troeltsch was inclined to remind people of "brutal reality" when he wished to call into question the practical wisdom of pacifists, socialists, and other seeming idealists.[7] Ironically it was the "realist" leaders behind the scenes who seemed incapable of grasping the realities of what was happening on the front lines. The battle plans of each side were soon in shambles, yet the men back home in the planning rooms remained locked into the obsolete ways of the Franco-Prussian war.

With no one to give them intelligent guidance, the troops in the field took it upon themselves to dig trenches in a desperate attempt to survive. With the winter of 1914, hell moved underground. Young men, three-quarters of whom had never seen battle before, tried to survive in a labyrinth of hastily dug ditches that quickly turned into sewers filled with rats, lice, excrement, the dead, the injured and the crazed.

Erich Maria Remarque's great war novel, *All Quiet on the Western Front* (*Im Westen Nichts Neues*), portrays how the values of work, duty, culture, and progress disintegrated under the bombardment in the trenches. His protagonist, Paul Bäumer, a German volunteer who went from the classroom to the front, summarized: "I am young, I am twenty years old; yet I know nothing of life but despair, death, fear, and fatuous superficiality cast over an abyss of sorrow."[8] In the insanity and horror, Paul finds one meaningful value to cling to. He vows to fight against the senseless hatred that pits young men of the same age but different uniforms against each other, if only he can come out of the war alive.

The Great War not only swallowed up—with a whole generation of young men—the national liberal values Troeltsch stood for; it was also a catastrophe for the socialist values of Kautsky. The realities of the trenches shattered both conservative fantasies that war would mobilize humanity's "highest ethical powers"[9] and socialist dreams of international working-class solidarity. Neither Troeltsch nor Kautsky understood the social, economic, and psychological underpinnings of militarism. The same can be said of many social theorists today.

Unlike the National Liberals, the Social Democrats had a consistent record of voting against the arms race and arguing against nationalism and militarism. Intellectuals like Kautsky were pressured by the revisionist trade unionists within the party to support the war credits.

Though they finally supported the war, the Social Democrats were the only party that refused to support the annexation of new territories; they insisted that the war be purely defensive.

There was a Petition of the Intellectuals circulated by the Berlin theologian Reinhold Seeberg and signed by 1,347 theologians, school teachers, professors, artists, and writers which supported a war fought for ultra-right, extreme imperialist objectives. A counter-petition circulated by military historian Hans Delbrück and Adolf von Harnack was signed by 141 professors and other intellectuals. This petition also supported the war but with a more moderate plan of territorial acquisition. The latter petition was signed by both Max Weber and Ernst

Troeltsch. The political agenda of the time provided a choice between German imperialism and ultra or pan-German imperialism.[10]

Once the terrible reality of the war began to set in, the initial euphoria evaporated. Two months into the war Meinecke's tone changed remarkably. He saw greedy forces that would destroy everything good in Germany. Yet at the same time he felt there was little that he or anyone else could do, since fate would determine the outcome. A similar fatalism towards war is suggested by the aforementioned statement by Troeltsch, that life is inherently a battle renewed on ever new fronts. Some observers argue that this fatalism was as much of a problem for German thinkers of this period as their glorification of the nation and its military might.[11]

Notes

1. Troeltsch, *The Social Teaching*, 1013.
2. Craig, *Germany: 1866–1945*, 340.
3. Ibid., 341.
4. Tenfelde finds it astonishing how the mood swung in the German labor movement from a sense of crisis in July to the approval of the war credits in August, 1914. The labor leaders within the Social Democratic party had the desire to prove that they were not "enemies of the fatherland" by supporting the war. Therefore, just when the party reached its peak of success, it betrayed its basic principle of solidarity with the international working class by approving the German war credits. Tenfelde, "Germany," 268.
5. Ernst Gläser, *Jahrgang 1902* (Berlin: G. Kiepenheuer, 1929), 188–9. See also the account in Richard Aldington, *Death of a Hero* (New York: Covici, Friede, 1929), 225f., 252f.
6. Peter Batty, *The House of Krupp* (New York: Dorset Press, 1966), 131–32.
7. Troeltsch, *The Social Teaching*, 1012.
8. Erich Maria Remarque, *All Quiet on the Western Front*, trans. A. W. Wheen (New York: Ballantine Books, 1987), 263.
9. Ernst Troeltsch, *Politische Ethik und Christentum* (Göttingen: Vandehök & Ruprecht, 1904), 20–21.
10. Ringer, *Decline of the German Mandarins*, 190; Fischer, *Griff nach der Weltmacht* (Düsseldorf: Droste Verlag, 1961), 199f.
11. F. Meinecke, *The German Catastrophe*, trans. Sidney B. Fay (Boston: Beacon Press, 1963); E. R. Curtius focuses on the ideology of fatalism that pervaded German culture. Curtius, *Deutscher Geist in Gefahr* (Stuttgart: Deutsche Verlagsanstalt, 1932).

10

Troeltsch's "Political Ethics and Christianity": The Case for Hierarchy[1]

In 1904 Troeltsch set forth his political ethics in a programmatic essay entitled, "Political Ethics and Christianity."[2] It was based on an address he made to the fifteenth Evangelical Social Congress. By this time, the Evangelical Social Congress had taken a more conservative turn, as discussed in chapter 7. Harnack was now the president. Troeltsch's essay reflects the new conservatism, for in it he recalls approvingly the Emperor's pronouncement, "Political pastors are nonsense!" (PE, 39), which signalled the monarch's shift to the right in 1896.

This essay is particularly important to a proper understanding of *The Social Teaching* for here Troeltsch makes explicit what in the longer work are only implicit presuppositions.

While Troeltsch begins his essay by surveying four general types of ethics concerning the state, he identifies only the last two, namely, democracy and conservatism, as penetrating the essence of the state and arising out of Christianity (PE, 37). The first type, namely what Troeltsch calls "the ethic of the constitutional state" (e.g., the Lockean negative theory of the state), does not succeed in tapping the essence of the state itself and certainly does not arise out of Christianity (PE, 10). The second type, namely nationalism, has greater significance in Troeltsch's mind for a political ethic. It likewise does not arise out of Christianity, but rather out of the nature of the state (PE, 12).

Therefore, Troeltsch focuses on his third and fourth types, and views Christianity as a synthesis of the two, arguing that the Christian political ethic contains both a democratic and a conservative or aristocratic thrust.[3] By "conservative" Troeltsch actually means "aristocratic" and often interchanges the terms. The democratic values are based on the Christian concept of personalism (*Personalismus*). The aristocratic, on the concept of redemption (*Erlösung*).

Troeltsch describes his third type, the "democratic principle," (*das demokratische Prinzip*) as

> *the great conception of human rights.* Human rights means the moral right of the personality (*Persönlichkeit*), to have its own independent value in and of itself, or in Kant's formulation, the right to qualify not merely as means but rather also as an end in oneself. (PE, 13)

He goes on to tell how this principle came into its own in the American and French revolutions which he describes as the most ethically significant events in modern history.

Even as he hails the Anglo-French conception of democracy, Troeltsch gives it a decisive shift of meaning. His choice of the word "personality" (*Persönlichkeit*) contrasts with the classical meaning of "rule by the *people*." A faithful rendering of "people" in German would lead to the usage of *Volk*. For Troeltsch the principle of democracy does not lead to rule by the people, but rather to rule by "personality" or "character." By declaring that the "personality" has ultimate worth, Troeltsch has transformed the principle of democracy to mean something "inward."

Something else of importance is missing from Troeltsch's description of democracy. In his "great conception of human rights" the notion of equality of rights, opportunity and treatment is not mentioned. Indeed, the concept of equality used in a political and social sense is one that Troeltsch explicitly opposes as we shall see (PE, 27–28).

Along with his professed belief in democracy, Troeltsch argues on behalf of the modern state and nationalism. He disagrees with those who believe that democracy leads to a diminishing of the conception of the "Fatherland." Rather, a compromise must be achieved with "the realistic conditions of the life of national power" (PE, 13–15).

Troeltsch argues that his conception of democracy is supported by Christianity as the religion of "personalism." In Christianity the human being becomes "a personality of incomparable worth through devotion to God" (PE, 26). Christians also become equal "before God." However, in "external relations...freedom and equality" can be realized only "in a sinless condition" (PE, 28). The closest approximation in Christianity to the Enlightenment values of liberty, equality and fraternity is found in feelings of compassion and love for the neighbor (PE, 27–8). The implicit subject of this ethic is the middle or upper class Christian who is called to respect the equality of the lower classes "before God" and to extend charitable feelings towards them. This is posed as an alternative to active solidarity with them as potential revolutionary subjects capable of transforming the "external relations."

Troeltsch's fourth type, the aristocratic principle, is based in Christianity upon the doctrine of redemption. The essence of this principle can be summarized in a simple formula: *"Authority, not majority!"* (*Autorität, nicht Majorität!*) (Troeltsch's emphasis, PE, 17). While democracy is said to rest upon the equality of inner personalities before God, conservatism rests upon the principle of the natural inequality of persons in the world (PE, 17). Conservatism or aristocracy is also rooted in age-old customs having to do with "possession of the land" (*Grundbesitze*), "patriarchy" (*Patriarchalismus*) and "the immobility of Mother Earth" (*die Unbeweglichkeit der Mutter Erde*) (PE, 18–19).

Upon these conceptual foundations is developed the conservative or aristocratic (*aristokratische*) ethic. This involves two kinds of morality, one for those whose vocation is to serve and one for those in authority over them. Subordinates are to develop the qualities of devotion, piety, loyalty, and moderation in relation to persons in authority. Authority figures are to develop the qualities of loving care, responsibility and sacrifice toward inferiors. Subordinates are to exhibit joy and proficiency in their services; their superiors are to exhibit civic duty and good character. These depend on one another and are mutually complementary. The whole comprises the national character (PE, 19).

Clearly, Troeltsch is not describing here the values of early republicans or the bourgeoisie. These values derive from feudalism and uphold the virtue of *noblesse oblige*. This ethic presupposes a large servant class over which presides a small ruling class comprised of those who have acquired the proper accoutrements of learning and cultivation.

The ethic of conservatism or aristocracy, according to Troeltsch, also includes nationalism and the use of war-making to resolve power struggles on the international level. It recognizes that the "small states" ought to be ruled by the "large ones" and the "lower races" to be ruled by the "white race":

It [the national character of conservatism] will therefore hold war to be an inevitable result of power struggles which lie in the nature of things and will see in the discipline and authority, which are necessary for the guidance of war, an establishment of the highest ethical powers. Furthermore, it will also transfer its aristocratic conception to relations among different peoples. It will assent to the leadership of the *small states* by the *large ones*, to the subjection of *lower races* by those more capable of ruling and more culturally rich, and will hold the conception of rule by the *white race* to be the natural consequence of the place of the *white race* which was won in history.[4]

Such rule (*Herrschaft*) comes about as the result of natural inequalities (PE, 20–21). That is, natural inequality is the foundation of aristocratic rule and justifies it.

Troeltsch finds these aristocratic values to be rooted in the Christian concept of redemption. Redemption is described as "an elevation (to God) of the personality established in God and...a prevailing over the world by a higher, morally more perfect world."[5] Here we see that redemption is also inward, indeed, mystical. It involves the inner individual personality transcending the flawed external world. The formulation "prevailing over the world" (*Überwindung der Welt*) provides the key. It is the solution to the struggle with sin and presupposes a fallen world in need of redemption (PE, 29). It indicates the need for various forms of rule to be exercised in the form of hierarchical levels of authority so as to bring about this victory:

> The *natural inequality of the situation* creates thousands of differences of rank, of possession, of position, of gender, of social conditions. So the powers and conditions as they are formed in this *natural process* are to be accepted by believers as divine tolerance and order and to be endured as the external latitude, within which the inner religious and moral power of everyone in his place is to be practiced.[6]

Thus the conservative not only invokes the phrase, "prevailing over the world," but also the concepts, "natural inequality of the situation" and "natural process." Unlike the Social Democrats, unlike the Jews and Catholics pushing against the German social structures for greater social equality, unlike the women suffragettes of his time, the conservative assumes that the various kinds of social inequalities arise out of natural conditions rather than out of social relations. These inequalities are therefore to be accepted as being from God. This position is never explicitly justified, but is rather a foundational presupposition.

Further, unlike more progressive liberals (such as Lujo Brentano of the Progressive Party), the conservative takes a relatively pessimistic view of the "natural process" and human nature. The social inequalities that characterize the status quo are here to stay. The possibilities for improvement are minimal.

For his part, Troeltsch argues that the Christian ethic accords absolute value to the personality, yet it surrenders to a divinely sanctioned hierarchical world order which is full of natural inequalities. The fact that these differences may stem from property, position, gender, or other social conditions does not lessen their legitimacy.

Troeltsch explicitly addresses the contradiction that normally arises in trying to mesh democratic and aristocratic values. He concedes that

"in the world" these two value systems split "into a polarity" (PE, 36).
Yet he points out that democratic and aristocratic values can be unified
in the Christian ethic as long as it remains an inward idea: "pure inwardness in itself."[7] Again Troeltsch makes it quite clear that the Christian ethic is really a private matter of the heart of an individual.

Indeed, he emphasizes repeatedly that the Christian ethic is above
all personal and not political (PE, 32, 39). Here he begins to outline his
reconstruction of church history which he will develop in *The Social
Teaching*. He views the original gospel message to be thoroughly apolitical and oriented to the infinite worth of the personality. Jesus was
expecting the world to end very shortly, and so was indifferent to worldly
structures. When the expected end of the world failed to materialize,
Christians gradually began to adapt to worldly realities, primarily
through borrowing the ethics of the Greek Stoics. Therefore, Jesus's
teaching about social, ethical goals and ends ("eschatology") is viewed
as a major mistake for Troeltsch and his generation of religious scholars.

Troeltsch also does not see any continuity between Jewish social
and prophetic teachings and Jesus' message. On the contrary, he is critical of past Christian dependency on Old Testament social and political
teaching, which he feels reflects a lack of such in the New Testament:

> The New Testament was tortured and strained, but nothing was found [of a politi-
> cal ethic]. Church and theology accordingly had to rely on the Old Testament and
> to the much lower and less developed cultural level of the Jewish state that it
> represents. (PE, 32)

Thus the Jewish social, prophetic, and eschatological traditions not only
carry no positive meaning in Troeltsch's gospel reconstruction, they
are dismissed as "much lower and less developed." This devaluation of
Jesus' Jewish context explains how Troeltsch can arrive at a purely
apolitical Jesus (PE, 32–33).

The conception of the Kingdom of God, originally a Jewish Messianic concept, does appear in the background but is divested of its original political meaning. Troeltsch accentuates the contrast between the
"other-worldliness of the Kingdom of God" and the "this-worldliness
of the natural course of life, its laws, its conflicts and its worldly morality" (PE, 36). The soul is lifted up above the world into this mystical
Kingdom of God which never finds embodiment in the world.

Troeltsch also emphasizes the "profound difference" between the
Christian ethic of personality and the natural law ethic of late antiquity
with its idea of social equality. In fact there exists a "deep, material

opposition" between these two notions (PE, 33). Troeltsch emphasizes Christianity's acceptance of social inequality, whether on the traditional basis of original sin, or on the modernist basis of Darwinian nature. In both forms, Christian "ethics will accommodate itself" to social inequality and recognize "only equality before God" (PE, 34, 28).

Finally, Troeltsch deals with the Christian teaching on loving thy neighbor by subordinating it to the development of the personality before God:

> the Christian ethic is in the first place an essentially religious ethic, the fundamental conception of which is the completion and purification of the personality in love to God and the evidence of an attitude of brotherly love that is rooted in God. (PE, 34)

Again, it is an ethic oriented to the development of the inner person rather than to external social reality. Therefore, although Christian love is the highest ethical ideal, as a matter of the heart it has only the most indirect bearing on a political ethic: "wanting to derive state and society out of Christian love is like trying to square a circle," insists Troeltsch.[8] He concludes his discussion on neighbor love by reemphasizing the primacy of the personality on the one hand and "natural" inequalities on the other. Troeltsch explains that the state, nationalism, and "love of Fatherland" gain their legitimacy from independent sources; indeed, from the very being of the state itself:

> So it is a totally impossible undertaking to determine the political ethic from the central idea of Christianity. It will not be the central idea of love, but rather it will be both the *accompanying conceptions of the personality and the surrender to natural orders* that qualify Christianity to be a positive political ethic. On the other hand we must never expect that the influence of Christian ideas on the state will encompass the whole political ethic. The state has an independent ethical idea, the idea of nationalism, the ideas of love of Fatherland and political honor which are given in and of themselves and arise out of its essence.[9]

In fact, Troeltsch goes even further by arguing that the state not only enjoys its own independent source of legitimacy, but also stands in a prior relation to Christian ethics. Using the analogy of a tree, Troeltsch takes the state as a fundamental given upon which Christian ethics is grafted to lend strength (PE, 41). In another place he uses an analogy comparable to the base-superstructure formula of the economistic Marxism of his time. "Christian ethics stands above the state," that is, like the frosting on a cake (PE, 35). The state itself is legitimated by values that are more fundamental than Christian values. These include "love of the

Fatherland," "political sense of honor," great "personalities" and "aristocratic orders" (PE, 35). As mentioned, Troeltsch has earlier described aristocracy as rooted in patriarchy (*Patriarchalismus*) and possession of the immobile land, for example, "Mother Earth" (*die Unbeweglichkeit der Mutter Erde*) (PE, 18–19). The primacy of the state found here echoes Hegel's political theory which, as described in chapter 5, was adopted by both orthodox and modernist theologians of Imperial Germany.

In other words, Christian ethics is in no position to determine fundamental political values and structures, but is to humanize what is already established. Since its sphere is purely inward and attitudinal, it has only an indirect bearing upon political ethics (PE, 37).

Troeltsch summarizes his interpretation of the Christian ethic and its relation to politics as follows:

> No development of the personality without submission to the aristocratic orders; no aristocratic order without contributing to the value of the personality. That is the formula for the political outlook which is inspired by Christianity. Translated into political formulas it is: Christianity is at the same time democratic and conservative. It is democratic in that it demands to an ever further extent morality, independence and intellectual content of the personality and that it lets this personality come to fruition in the formation of state power. It is conservative in that it recognizes authority based on moral superiority and political balances of power, and that it understands the submission to authority as a submission to a source of moral power.[10]

Thus, Christian ethics primarily involves the complementary roles of "personality" and "aristocracy." Hierarchical authority provides the social structure within which personality or character is developed. The traits include on the "democratic" side, independence and intellectual maturity. At the same time, the developed personality finds its full expression in a strong nation state. Submission to established authority is virtuous.

This description captures the ideal of the German "bearer of culture"—Troeltsch's social stratum—as we have described in chapter 4. This ideal is critical of traditional conservatism in that authority must not rest merely on pedigree, but rather on "personality" or the superior "character." It produces two moral standards for two kinds of people. For those who rule there is the ethic of noblesse oblige, a paternal concern for ones inferiors. For the many who serve, there is the ethic of pious, humble submission to those of proven character.

Given this understanding of the Christian ethic, Troeltsch then proceeds to address the question of the relation of the churches to politics.

Here he evokes the traditional Lutheran position of the two separate spheres: the churches are not to meddle in politics, but are to attend to their first order of business, namely religion. On this point Troeltsch quotes with approval the emperor's dictum, "'Political pastors are nonsense.'"[11] He also paraphrases the classic saying of Jesus, "One can render to Caesar [Kaiser] what is Caesar's according to the natural course of things, if only one does the chief thing: if one renders to God what is God's."[12]

In the context of the Kaiser's attack on socialist pastors, the original political thrust of this saying was transformed. Jesus's point had been that Jewish dealings with Rome should be limited to paying taxes and performing required public service. Since further deference to Caesar had alien religious overtones for Jews, "Render to God what is God's" implicitly criticized the Jerusalem Temple elite for their active collaboration with Rome at the people's expense.

Troeltsch does not refer to this original context, which does not support his conservative and otherworldly interpretation of Christianity. Instead, he invokes St. Paul and the Bishop of Mileto: "In this way Paul understood his relation to the heathen empire and a hundred years later the Bishop of Melito celebrated the Augustan empire and the Christian church as twins with the same birthday" (PE, 29). In this spirit the early Catholic church maintained the corporate structures of the Roman Empire, even including slavery and the military profession (PE, 29). When church and state came together, there was a close alignment based on a common deference to "the aristocracy of the natural position of power" (PE, 30). Fashioned on the Roman model, the German churches and Imperial Germany ought also to be working together hand in hand: catechism and scepter.

Continuing his historical survey, Troeltsch acknowledges that the values of the French Revolution posed a serious challenge to this Christian aristocratic ethic. However, he reminds his readers of the rightward reaction of his own time evident in such authors as De Bonald, De Maistre and Stahl. While he would not wish to risk losing the centrality of the role of "personality" that they risk, Troeltsch finds their conservatism to contain an important truth:

> Yet all that must not deflect from the fact that in itself the Christian ethic contains an aristocratic, conservative tendency which accepts the results of the natural power formation process as natural fate and makes the ruling powers responsible only for the most feasible administration of their power as a moral office and divine vocation. And therein lies for countless people even now the ethical idealism of the conservative principle.[13]

Again this "aristocratic, conservative tendency" in Christianity, this acceptance of the political and social status quo as divinely ordained arises from the presupposition that it is a "natural...process" that comes about as the result of "natural fate." And so, the churches are not to meddle in the divinely ordained sphere of the emperor. They are to remain independent of politics.

This apolitical ideal, of course, involves a special definition of politics. As the term is generally used, one might think that being apolitical means neither supporting nor opposing political leaders or policies. Like many conservatives, however, Troeltsch labels support for the political status quo as "independence" from politics, and reserves the term "political" for those clergy who oppose established leaders and policies. The unspoken presupposition of this semantic usage is that the state itself is somehow outside and above the realm of politics.

Indeed, the emperor's original order for pastors to stay out of politics was not directed to all alike, but in particular to progressive pastors who were leaning toward support of the Social Democrats. Troeltsch's quotation of the emperor picks up this polemical thread and there are attacks on the left embroidered throughout his essay.

The double standard involved in Troeltsch's use of "politics" becomes glaring in the partisan logical conclusion he draws from his political ethic. Echoing Ritschl, he exhorts pastors to reject the legitimacy of class conflict, and even of French Enlightenment notions of natural law and equal rights. In his concluding remarks, however, he does not stop with these general principles, but actually endorses the specific political parties most supportive of the existing power structure of Imperial Germany.

Of the six major parties existing in his time he mentions only the three most conservative as serious options: the National Liberal and the two Conservative parties. Of these he writes:

> Here it can very well be a duty in the present situation to vote Liberal, even if one is not a Liberal. In practical politics a decision between the Liberal and Conservative parties may be necessary. (PE, 43)

As soon as Troeltsch gives his advice to vote the Liberal ticket, he comes back to his theme that "the political ethical ideal itself demands the unification of liberal-democratic and conservative thought" (PE, 43). In other words, this is supported by the Christian ethic.

For Troeltsch the choice between the conservative and liberal parties was clearly not an easy one. Troeltsch was a conservative in his emphasis upon divinely ordained hierarchical authority based upon "natural" inequality within a fallen world. He was a liberal in resting this authority upon the developed "personality," the mark of cultivation, rather than on pedigree and land ownership.

Troeltsch reconciled these impulses by recommending the National Liberal Party to voters, while endorsing the Conservative Party as possible coalition partners. In fact, just such a coalition was in the making when Troeltsch first made this address, as mentioned in chapter three. It was formed to promote colonialism and a revival of the *Kulturkampf.*

Beginning with his discussion of democracy, Troeltsch takes up the challenge of class conflict. To say that democracy is associated with class conflict is an illusion, he argues (PE, 13). There is really no difference between the principle of democracy held by the bourgeoisie and by the proletariat. When the Social Democrats argue otherwise they are indulging in rabble-rousing (PE, 15).

We have also mentioned that Troeltsch argues against those who interpret democracy in a way that diminishes the "Fatherland." This defense of nationalism is clearly aimed at the only groups in Germany that subordinated it to an internationalist orientation: the Catholic Center Party and the Social Democrats (PE, 13–15).

On the question of the life and teaching of Jesus, Troeltsch makes a particularly interesting reference to the Social Democrats who, he writes, claim for themselves the pure, historical Jesus. It is interesting that he does not describe them as rejecting Christianity and religion out of hand. Troeltsch's description of the Social Democrats reflects a knowledge of the contemporary writings of Karl Kautsky on the history of Christianity. It was Kautsky who, with one eye on the influx of Christian peasants into the proletariat, was arguing for a prophetic understanding of Jesus (PE, 17). Troeltsch also acknowledges that there were Protestant groups who believed that the gospel ethic, with its emphasis upon the poor, supports fully democratic structures (PE, 17).

Therefore, it is in the polemical context of refuting the Social Democrats and certain activist pastors that Troeltsch emphasizes a privatized Christian ethic. Their teaching is incorrect, he writes, since Christianity has to do with

> purely the sphere of private morality. Also if with its acts of love it heals social troubles, these acts of love themselves arise from the purely religious or from motives of private morality. Love of God and of the brethren is never at any time a political principle.[14]

Troeltsch continues to argue that the principle of democracy does not require "love and sacrifice, but rather law and reliable order" (PE, 24). Returning to his theme of Christian love being a private attitude of the heart, he then argues that it therefore does not provide a basis for the principle of democracy, "the enthusiasm of well-meaning idealists" notwithstanding (PE, 24).

Thus, Troeltsch does not formulate his theory of a politically indifferent and privatized Christian ethics from a standpoint that is itself politically indifferent, from a standpoint of "pure religion." Rather, his theory arises out of a politically charged context involving the Social Democrats and Christian activist pastors.

This is why, instead of leaving the sphere of the emperor to the emperor as he exhorts pastors to do, Troeltsch himself offers a concrete, political alternative to the teachings of the social activists: "We can demand reforms without being revolutionary and we can recognize the moral values of aristocratic orders of life" (PE, 34). Not that Troeltsch sanctifies the traditional forms of aristocracy: "We can see old aristocrats go under and new ones come into being and both are equally legitimate, since by grace they both are of the natural order" (PE, 34). As we have seen above, an aristocracy of "character" or "personality"—the German mandarin ideal—is actually his preferred form of aristocracy.

At the conclusion of his essay, Troeltsch makes very clear the concrete politics that the church is to adopt. It "will resist all deceptions of natural law and the idea of equality.... It will never sanction the identification of...[Christian] ideals with class conflict, with the spirit of the proletariat, or with the antithesis against the dominant classes" (PE, 40). Instead, Troeltsch continues, the church "will always demand that moderation and patience..., piety, obedience and helpfulness remain moral ideals" (PE, 40).

Note that these political values all have partisan correlates in Troeltsch's historical context. Equality and natural law were French Revolutionary values promoted by the Social Democratic and Progressive Parties. The Center Party, following Catholic social teaching, promoted a more conservative concept of natural law, but one that still threatened the status quo in the German context. And class conflict, of course, was the hallmark of the Social Democrats.

To be sure, Troeltsch accuses both the Social Democrats and the Conservatives alike of egotism, that is, of a lack of inward maturity of personality or of character. In such lack of character lies the basis of whatever class conflicts might arise (PE, 42). But his criticism of the Conservatives remains the friendly criticism of a coalition partner, while his criticism of the Social Democrats is not limited to their alleged "egotism." As the vehicle of both French Revolutionary and socialist values, the Social Democratic Party threatened everything Troeltsch stood for.

In summary, despite his emphasis upon inwardness and the indifference to politics purportedly found in the gospel, Troeltsch concludes with a very specific, concrete, political agenda. The underlying polemic against the Social Democrats primarily and the Center Party secondarily, becomes explicit in Troeltsch's clear directive: vote the National Liberal party.

Troeltsch also gives his final blessing to the Imperial German state of his time: "Conservatism may hold to the historical German state and its monarchical militaristic foundation; however, it will be allowed to do it only with willing recognition of the personality, of its self-assertion and its participation" (PE, 43). Thus, if the traditional aristocratic German state rooted in the feudal institutions of monarchy and the military makes way for leadership by men of personality, by those who have excelled in character development in the Christian virtues as taught through the gymnasium system, then its continuation is ethically justified. An aristocracy based on great personality should appease the growing alienation of various social groups (PE, 43).

Troeltsch's analysis of Christian ethics and his polemic against the Social Democrats that first surfaced in his essay of 1904 was soon elaborated in *The Social Teaching*.[15] Before turning there, however, it is appropriate to look more closely at the writings on the social history of Christianity by the Social Democrats' leading theorist, who was Troeltsch's principal antagonist.

Notes

1. In chapters 10, 11, and 12 the focus of the book shifts to the interpretation of primary texts. Unless explicitly noted to the contrary, the viewpoints being presented are those of Troeltsch and Kautsky, not the viewpoint of this author.
2. Ernst Troeltsch, *Politische Ethik und Christentum* (Göttingen: Vandenhök & Ruprecht, 1904). This is the final revised edition of an address originally given to the Evangelical Social Congress on May 25, 1904 under the title, "Christian Ethics and Today's Society." "Die christliche Ethik und die heutige Gesellschaft," *Die Verhandlungen des fünfzehnten Evangelisch-sozialen Kongresses* (Göttingen: Vandenhöck & Ruprecht, May 1904), 11–40.

   In conversation, Prof. Hartmut Ruddies of the Ernst Troeltsch Gesellschaft strongly recommended this essay as Troeltsch's most programmatic state-

ment on political ethics and as foundational to an understanding of *The Social Teaching*.

My translation of this text in the quotations may often err on the side of a
literal rendering for heuristic purposes. Because of their frequent occurrence,
subsequent references to this essay will be embedded in the text using parentheses with the identifying acronym, "PE."

Politische Ethik und Christentum, and Troeltsch's work generally, continue
to shape German political discourse today. Prof. Trutz Rendtorff of the University of Munich, past president and founding member of the *Ernst Troeltsch
Gesellschaft*, modeled his own 1978 programmatic essay on Troeltsch's, and
even borrowed Troeltsch's title. T. Rendtorff, *Politische Ethik und Christentum*,
(Munich: Christian Kaiser Verlag, 1978). The debate between proponents of an
"inward" Christianity and Christian socialists has continued as illustrated, for
example, in a 1980s debate between Rendtorff and D. Sölle on the implications
for Christians of contemporary military policy issues.

3.   "The actual political consequences of the Christian ethic which grasp the inner
structure itself are distributed between democracy and conservatism" ("Die
eigentlich politischen, das innere Gefüge selbst ergreifenden Konsequenzen der
christlichen Ethik verteilen sich auf Demokratie und Konservatismus"). PE, 25–
26.

4.   "Er [der nationale Character des Konservatismus] wird daher den Krieg für eine
unvermeidliche Folge der in der Natur der Dinge liegenden Machtkämpfe halten
und wird in her für die Kriegsführung notwendigen Disziplin und Autorität eine
Erweisung der höchsten sittlichen Kräfte sehen. Weiterhin wird er überhaupt
auch auf die Verhältnisse der Völker seinen aristokratischen Begriff übertragen.
Er wird die Leitung der kleinen Staaten durch die Grossen, die Unterwerfung
niederer Rassen durch die herrschaftsfähigeren und kulturreicheren billigen und
den Gedanken der Herrschaft der *weissen Rasse* halten." Emphasis mine, PE,
20–1.

5.   "Gedanken der Erlösung…als Erhebung zu der in Gott gegründeten
Persönlichkeit und als Überwindung der Welt durch eine höhere, sittlich
vollkommenere Welt." PE, 28.

6.   *"Die natürliche Ungleichheit der Lage* schafft tausend Unterschiede der
Herrschaft, des Eigentums, der Stände, der Geschlechter, der Gesellschafts-
zustände. So sind die Mächte und Zustände, wie sie in diesem *natürlichen Prozess*
sich bilden, von den Gläubigen als göttliche Zulassung und Ordnung
hinzunehmen und zu ertragen als der äussere Spielraum, innerhalb dessen die
innere religiöse und sittliche Kraft von jedem an seinem Ort betätigt werden
soll." Emphasis mine. PE, 29.

7.   The original German conveys Troeltsch's emphatic tone: "Die christliche Idee
ist eine *streng einheitliche nur*, solange sie in ihrer reinen Innerlichkeit bei sich
selber bleibt." Translation: "The Christian idea is a *strictly unified one only* as
long as it remains self-contained in its pure inwardness." Troeltsch's emphasis.
(Note: The idealist discourse is very difficult to translate into English.) PE, 36.

8.   "Staat und Gesellschaft aus der christlichen Liebe ableiten wollen, heisst die
Quadratur des Zirkels suchen." PE, 35.

9.   "So ist es ein völlig unmögliches Unternehmen, die politische Ethik aus der
Zentralidee des Christentums zu bestimmen. Es wird nicht die Zentralidee der
Liebe, sondern es werden die beiden *Begleitgedanken der Persönlichkeit und
der Ergebung in natürliche* Ordnungen sein, die das Christentum zu einer positiv
politischen Ethik befähigen. Andererseits werden wir auch nie erwarten dürfen,
dass die Beeinflussung des Staates durch die christlichen Ideen die ganze

politische Ethik erschöpft. Der Staat hat eine selbständige sittliche Idee, die Idee des Nationalismus, die Ideen der Vaterlandsliebe und der politischen Ehre, die mit ihm selbst gegeben sind und aus seinem Wesen erwachsen." Troeltsch's emphasis. PE, 35.

10. "Kein Werden der Persönlichkeit ohne Fügung in die aristokratischen Ordnungen, keine aristokratische Ordnung ohne Dienst am Werte der Persönlichkeit: das ist the Formel für die vom Christentum inspirierte politische Gesinnung. In politische Formeln übersetzt heisst das: Das Christentum ist demokratisch und konservativ zugleich. Est ist demokratisch, indem es in immer weiterem Umfang Versittlichung, Verselbständigung und geistigen Gehalt der Persönlichkeit fordert und diese Persönlichkeit in der Bildung der Staatsgewalt zur Wirkung kommen lässt. Es ist konservativ, indem es die Autorität in ihrer Begründung durch sittliche Überlegenheit und durch politische Machtverhältnisse anerkennt und die Beugung unter die Autorität als Quelle sittlicher Kräfte versteht." PE, 37–8.

11. "Das Wort des Kaisers 'Politische Pastoren sind Unsinn' is so, wie es vermutlich gemeint ist, daher nicht unberechtigt." PE, 39.

12. "Es kann dem Kaiser gegeben werden, was nach natürlichem Weltlauf des Kaisers ist, wenn man nur die Hauptsache tut, wenn man Gott gibt, was Gottes ist." PE, 29.

13. "Aber all das darf den Blick dafür nicht verdunkeln, dass an sich in der christlichen Ethik eine aristokratisch-konservative Tendenz enthalten ist, die die Ergebnisse des natürlichen Machtbildungsprozesses sich als natürliche Fügung gefallen lässt und den Machtinhabern nur die möglichste Handhabung ihrer Macht als sittliches Amt und göttlichen Beruf zur Pflicht macht. Und darin liegt heute noch für Unzählige der ethische Idealismus des konservativen Prinzips." PE, 31.

14. The entire German original is worth quoting here: "Das Christentum kann seinem ganzen Sinn und Wesen nach keine direkte politische Ethik haben. Es hat von Hause aus überhaupt keine politischen Gedanken. Es bezieht sich mit seinen sittlichen Geboten zunächst rein auf die Sphäre der Privatmoral. Auch wenn es mit seiner Liebstätigkeit soziale Schäden heilt, geht doch diese Liebestätigkeit selbst von rein religiösen oder von Motiven der Privatmoral aus. Die Liebe zu Gott und zu den Brüdern ist nie und nimmer ein politisches Prinzip." PE, 23.

15. Liebersohn contrasts the conservative pessimism toward the possibilities for social reform in Troeltsch's *Social Teaching* with the more politically interventionist tone of his 1904 essay. What Liebersohn doesn't take into account, however, is the specifically conservative political direction that Troeltsch assumes in his earlier work. Harry Liebersohn, *Religion and Industrial Society: the Protestant Social Congress in Wilhelmine Germany* (Philadelphia, PA: American Philosophical Society, 1986), 57.

11

Karl Kautsky's Social History of Christianity: The Communitarian Church

Introduction

After Friedrich Engels's death in 1895, the mantle of leading intellectual in the Socialist International passed to Karl Kautsky. From 1883 until 1917 Kautsky served as editor of *Neue Zeit* and wrote the theoretical section of the Erfurt Program of the Social Democratic Party.[1]

Partly because of the massive influx of rural Catholic peasants into the cities and into the ranks of the proletariat in the latter part of the nineteenth century, Kautsky wrote extensively on the question of the relationship of Christianity to Marxism, emphasizing the compatibility of the ethics of the early church with modern socialism. In fact, he remains the leading Marxist thinker on this issue.[2] It is therefore not surprising that Troeltsch would single him out for refutation even though as a socialist he was excluded from occupying a chair at any university.

Born in Prague in 1854, son of a Czech artist and an Austrian actress and writer, Kautsky is often mistakenly thought to have been Jewish by many otherwise informed people.[3] In fact, he grew up in a Catholic household, but he later left the Church. He attended the University of Vienna where he was influenced by the works of J. S. Mill and Charles Darwin, the latter reflected in his search for a theory of history along natural science lines. Hegel had fallen out of favor with his generation. Ironically, he became a Marxist through the influence of Eduard Bernstein, whose revisionism Kautsky later opposed. In 1883, the year of Marx's death, Kautsky collaborated with Friedrich Engels in editing *Neue Zeit*. As an organ of the Social Democratic party, it grew into the most influential socialist journal of the day. During the period of the Second International, Kautsky developed a non-Hegelian form of Marxist thought that utilized a base-superstructure model.[4]

Within the politics of the Social Democratic Party, Kautsky advocated a democratic path to power through a "revolutionary" or oppositional approach to politics.[5] As a committed democrat, he rejected all idealist reinterpretations of democracy. For Kautsky, democracy involved the active participation of all persons in public affairs. When there is no popular participation in decision making, it is due to certain economic and social relations, not to natural inequalities or forces.[6]

In fact, Kautsky observed an increase in autocracy with the rise of capitalism. The shift to a money economy created salaried public officials who could easily be dismissed. Under the agricultural economy of feudalism officials had been vassals who held property. Their relative self-sufficiency had made resistance to the liege lord more possible and likely. Army officers and clergy also became more economically dependent under capitalism, losing titles to land and becoming salaried civil servants who had to obey their superiors without question or risk losing their sole means of livelihood.

The clergy in the monastic orders of the Roman Catholic church were an exception to this trend. They remained economically independent of the dictates of the rising nation states and were internationalists with allegiance to Rome. This explains why they were so hated and persecuted by the National Liberals and other nationalists who considered the state to be the final political authority.[7]

In summary, Kautsky sees political freedom diminished with the rise of capitalism. His analysis stands in sharp contrast to that of Troeltsch, who considered the inequalities of his time to be purely natural and the German state to be ordained of God, as explained in the preceding chapter.

As mentioned, Kautsky engaged in scholarly investigations into the social origins and history of Christianity. In 1888 he published *Thomas More and his Utopia*.[8] In 1908 during the time Troeltsch was working on *The Social Teaching*, his *Foundations of Christianity* appeared, which was to become a classic work within Marxist studies.[9] Troeltsch does not explicitly refer to this work, but he does refer to its predecessor, a two-volume work entitled *Forerunners of Modern Socialism*, which Kautsky published in 1895.[10] In the Introduction to the *Foundations of Christianity*, Kautsky explains that he has not altered, but rather elaborated his earlier analysis in *Forerunners*.

Troeltsch is clearly familiar with Kautsky's overall analysis of Christianity, whether from the earlier or later work. As mentioned in chapter 6, Troeltsch also makes special reference to Kautsky's pamphlet entitled "Social Democracy and the Catholic Church."[11] This pamphlet appeared about the time when the Catholic Center and Social Democratic parties both opposed the Conservative-Liberal coalition under Chancellor Bülow, which favored a revival of Bismarck's persecution of Catholics and continuation of brutal colonial policies.

In his historical work Kautsky reconstructs the social history of the Christian churches, using the methods of social historiography that were frowned upon by Meinecke and most other German intellectuals.[12] For Kautsky the starting point and cornerstone of this history is the communal sharing of goods by the first Christians, the principle that the individual Christian's possessions belonged ultimately to God and were to be administered by the Christian community on behalf of all its members. This principle is not only central to the first Christian communities, but goes through several transformations over the centuries and is decisive in shaping the churches' social ethics. Therefore, Kautsky uses a method much like that of *Traditionsgeschichte* to reconstruct the origin and development of the Christian tradition of the communism of goods. What follows is a summary of his reconstruction:

Early Christian Communism

According to Kautsky, the social origins of the Christian community were almost exclusively proletarian, in the broad sense that its constituency was without property or a high level of education. It included both manual workers and the "lumpenproletariat," or masses of beggars and unemployed.[13] He begins with a sociohistorical sketch of the conditions of the Roman Empire at the time Christianity came into being. He describes the rise of an urban proletariat, who were attracted to the sects of the Essenes, to the nationalistic Zealots or to Christianity.

At the time the Christian community was born, the Roman Empire had witnessed the rise of the large landed estate based on cheap slave labor resulting from expansionist wars. This forced small farmers off the land and into the cities where they sought employment. Finding none, they swelled the ranks of the urban underclass, a lumpenproletariat of beggars subsisting on public feedings and other handouts. It was from the ranks of such as these that the first Christian communities originated. They were an urban phenomenon. In fact, the word "pagan," which became the common term for non-Christians, is Latin for "village inhabitant."

Widespread poverty was therefore the major social problem of this period in Roman history. At the time Christianity came into being, widespread cynicism had arisen about the capacity of the Roman state to bring about significant reforms. If people could not hope for a miracle, they lapsed into despair or escapist pleasures.

But there were some who became increasingly convinced that supernatural power could effect real social liberation. These were attracted to Christianity, which taught that Jesus would return as the Messiah to establish a paradisal Kingdom of God on earth.

The first Christians did not limit their vision of the Kingdom to a transformed society. They went so far as to believe in a transformed earth. As the Apocalypse describes, after ushering in a millennial rule of 1,000 years, God would bring into being a new heaven and earth and new Jerusalem. Kautsky also cites Ireneaus (second century) and Lactantius (fourth century) as other examples of early Christian apocalyptic thinkers (VNS, 21–3).

According to Kautsky, numerous statements by Jerome, Eusebius, and Origen attest to the proletarian origins of such utopian visionaries. There are also biblical references, such as St. Paul's statement in I Corinthians 1:26–28:

> Consider your own call, brothers and sisters: not many of you were wise by human standards, not many were powerful, not many were of noble birth. But God chose what is foolish in the world to shame the wise; God chose what is weak in the world to shame the strong; God chose what is low and despised in the world, things that are not, to reduce to nothing things that are. (NRSV trans.; FC, 328–29)

Given their social location, the first Christians did not espouse a work ethic nor were they concerned with methods of production. Their lack of a work ethic is indicated by biblical references to the lilies of the field that neither sow nor spin and yet come under the care of God[14] (VNS, 24). They practiced a form of communism, but in keeping with the large number of unemployed in their midst, it was a communism of goods rather than of production.

The idea of a communism of consumption was hardly unique to the early Christian communities. During the last years of the Roman Republic and early years of the Empire, public feedings and mass distributions of the basic necessities occasionally occurred. Certain communal sub-cultures also developed around this time, most notably the Essene community among the Jews. According to Josephus, this sect held all its goods in common, and therefore no member was either too rich or too poor (VNS, 25). The Essenes were spread throughout a number of cities in which they kept hospitality houses. A member could travel from city to city and be given room, board and whatever else he might need at the local Essene abode.

The first Christian communities were also communal, although Kautsky did not know if they consciously modeled themselves on the Essenes. However, this sect, with its Jewish nationalism, eventually disappeared. By contrast, Christianity adopted the international outlook of the Roman Empire and eventually took it over.

In response to the problem of poverty both the Essene and Christian communities tried to adopt a fully communistic lifestyle. Jesus is represented as saying to the rich young ruler that in order to be welcome, he should sell what he had and give it to the poor.[15] Quoting Acts 4:32,34–35, Kautsky described the communism of the first Jerusalem community as follows:

> no one claimed private ownership of any possessions, but everything they owned was held in common.... There was not a needy person among them, for as many as owned lands or houses sold them and brought the proceeds of what was sold. They laid it at the apostles' feet, and it was distributed to each as any had need. (NRSV, VNS, 25)

The story of Ananias and Sapphira, that follows in the Book of Acts, is about the judgment of God towards those who withheld a portion of the proceeds from the liquidation of private property.

In summary, Kautsky argues that it was the radical commitment to a community of equals sharing equally of their possessions that provided the dynamic spark to early Christianity. The apocalyptic expectations of the Kingdom of God coming to earth inspired the early Christians to believe that these radically altered social arrangements were the harbinger of the future[16] (VNS, 23).

While the egalitarian values of the early church may have anticipated modern socialism, Kautsky is careful not to superimpose the historical possibilities of his own industrial age back onto the Roman world. Inequality was inherent in the relations of production of preindustrial societies, in which most people had to devote most of their activity to producing the society's wealth through labor intensive methods. At this stage of technology, even if the church fathers could have conceived of revolutionizing the relations of production and had the will and political power to make the attempt, they could not have succeeded. The amount of surplus produced by such a society was only sufficient to support the good life for a minority; general equality would have meant the socialization of toil. Thus, the churches' egalitarian experiment could only be realized in the sphere of consumption and on a small scale; it was necessarily relegated to the margins of the Roman economy.[17]

As Christianity and its communism of consumption spread in the Roman world, the churches therefore necessarily came up against the inherent contradiction of socializing a preindustrial economy characterized by a small surplus and general scarcity. Before too long the early Christians tried to find ways to reconcile the communism of goods with the maintenance of private property. They began to allow the membership to keep title to their property and to require only the communal sharing of income. The distinction between private ownership of productive assets and collective ownership of consumable income was not explicitly conceptualized, however. This explains the contradiction regarding property in early church teaching, which advocated communism while simultaneously defending the rights of private ownership (VNS, 26).

In summary, Christians could eventually own and manage productive assets such as fields and even slaves. However, their surplus assets were still to be turned over to the jurisdiction of the Christian community to be redistributed. Each Christian, as a "brother" or "sister" within the community, had a right to use the possessions of the other members as the need arose. For example, one Christian who needed a place to live could ask another Christian who owned two houses to let him occupy the second house. The owner would have to comply; however, he would continue to own the second dwelling.[18] This accommodation to private property eventually weakened early Christian communism. However, it was inevitable given the limitations of a communism of consumption.

According to Kautsky, the communal arrangements of the early church were also undermined by a second factor: persistence of the family and of marriage. A communism of consumption requires a weakening of these private institutions. Plato's style of communism adopted the libertine alternative to marriage, that of holding wives and children in common. The Essenes adopted the ascetic alternative, that of celibacy. The early Christians also sought to weaken the preeminence of the family and marriage, primarily by adopting ascetic alternatives. However a few Christian Gnostic sects, the Adamites for example, taught and practiced the libertine alternative.

Accordingly, the Gospel of Matthew records Jesus as saying, "And everyone who has left houses or brothers or sisters or father or mother or children or fields, for my name's sake, will receive a hundredfold, and will inherit eternal life" (19:29). In the Gospel of Luke he says, "Whoever comes to me and does not hate father and mother, wife and children, brothers and sisters, yes, and even life itself, cannot be my disciple."[19]

In the *Foundations of Christianity* (1908) Kautsky added a feminist analysis. With the loosening of the traditional family ties, the social position of women improved. "Once [a woman] ceased to be bound to the narrow family activities, once she cast them off, she was enabled to devote her mind and her interests to other thoughts, outside the family sphere...to the much wider circle of the Christian congregation." Therefore, in early Christianity, there were not only prophets, but also prophetesses[20] (FC, 353–54).

The *agape* meals or daily love feasts of the early Christian communities were like the common meals of the Spartans and other Platonic states (Acts 2:46). They took the place of the family meal and went hand-in-hand with practicing a communion of goods (VNS, 27).

However, allowing private property in productive assets meant accepting the continuation of the family and the continued transference of property from father to son. The mode of production determined the character of the society in the final instance. As Christianity spread throughout the Roman world, it necessarily accommodated itself to the dominant institutions of family and private property. The communism of goods became relegated to the monasteries and certain individual sects. It did not and could not achieve general acceptance (VNS, 28).

The Decline of Early Christian Communism

Given the contradiction between the private family and the communism of consumption in early Christianity, an unusual degree of dedication was necessary to hold them together. As Christian membership increased, the zeal of each member decreased. Also, in a decadent Empire, dedication was increasingly hard to come by (VNS, 28). As the affluent moved into the churches, radical dreams of overthrowing the status quo faded (VNS, 22).

Along with the loss of revolutionary vision, the communism of consumption retreated, while the patriarchal family system regained its primacy. Only the family's surplus was handed over to the churches. The common use of goods was cut back to a sharing of what remained after the family's comfort was fully provided for.

In the *Foundations*, Kautsky also adds that with the renewed emphasis on the traditional family there was a conservative backlash against women's relative emancipation in the first Christian communities. This becomes evident in certain biblical passages such as in the Pastoral Epistles, generally considered to be of a later origin (FC, 353–54).

Nevertheless, the communist tradition of the first Christians did not die out. Again and again new communist sects arose. The ascendant Catholic church continued to be communist in theory (VNS, 28).

Prophetic voices harkening back to the original teaching arose throughout the history of the churches. Preaching against wealth and economic inequality, these prophets provide further evidence of the authenticity and power of the Christian communal tradition. Kautsky cites three of these prophets as examples: St. Basilius of the fourth century, Gregory the Great of the sixth century and St. John Chrysostom of the fourth century.

He quotes St. Basilius's condemnation of the rich: "'You miserable ones! How will you answer to the Eternal Judge?'" Basilius anticipates the rationalization of the rich who are accustomed to replying: "'How have I been unjust, since I only hold for myself what belongs to me?'" Basilius responds: "'Yet I question you, what do you call your property? From whom have you obtained it? You act like a man in a theater who hurries to secure all the seats and now wants to hinder others from entering'" (VNS, 28). Basilius then questions the validity of private property: "'Through what means do the rich become rich other than through the taking of possession of things that belong to all?'" (VNS, 29). Thus, all property justly belongs, not to private individuals, but to the community. Inequality of wealth indicates illegitimate greed on the part of some at the expense of the many: "'If each did not take for himself more than he needed for his maintenance, and left the rest to others, then there would be neither rich nor poor'" (VNS, 28–29).

Gregory the Great underscores this principle of the common ownership of property. Not only is the rich person a thief, stealing from the common wealth, but worse, he is a murderer. The rich person is responsible for the death of every poor person who dies from want, who would have lived had there been a more equitable distribution of wealth. Therefore, since property is owned by all, sharing ones goods with the poor is not an option but a requirement: "'If we share with those who are in need, then we do not give them something that belongs to us, but rather what belongs to them. It is not a work of mercy, but rather the settlement of a debt.'"[21]

It is hard to imagine a stronger statement in favor of common ownership of property than those of Basilius or Gregory. However Chrysostom not only endorses their position, he goes even further in making an elaborate concrete application to the situation in Constantinople where he served as patriarch. His radical stance proved to be too much for the emperor, who eventually sent Chrysostom into exile in Armenia where he died in 407 A.D. In his eleventh sermon on the Book of Acts, Chrysostom, whose name means "golden mouth," preached a bold and eloquent sermon on the subject of the communism of the first Christians.

The early Christians were blessed by God because they held all goods in common and renounced private property. Kautsky quotes extensively from Chrysostom's sermon:

> "Grace was among them because no one suffered scarcity, that is to say, because they gave so zealously, that no one remained poor. For they did not give a part and hold back another for themselves; rather they gave all, so to speak, as their property. They abolished inequality [*Ungleichheit*] and lived in great abundance; and they did this in the most praiseworthy way." (VNS, 29)

Chrysostom then describes how the apostles acted as property brokers, collecting the property from the wealthy and redistributing it to the poor (VNS, 29). He then makes the application: "'If today we did the same, we would live much more fortunately, the rich as well as the poor,'" for the rich would not impoverish themselves, yet they would raise the fortunes of the poor (VNS, 30).

Chrysostom elaborates his economic blueprint for the city:

> "Let us advance the idea. Everyone hands over what they have to the common property. No one need be troubled about it, neither the rich nor the poor. How much money do you think will be collected? I conclude—for one cannot declare with certainty—if every individual put in all his money, his fields, his possessions, his houses (I will not speak about the slaves because the first Christians possessed none since they probably released them), then very likely a million pounds of gold would be collected, indeed probably two or three times as much. Then I said to myself, how many Christians? Are there not 100,000? And how many heathen and Jews? How many thousands of pounds of gold must thereby be collected! And how many poor persons have we? I do not believe that there are more than 50,000. How much is necessary to feed them every day? If they ate at a common table, the cost would not be very great. What would we therefore begin to do with our enormous treasury? Do you believe that it would ever be exhausted? And would not the blessing of God pour out upon us a thousand times more richly? Would we not create a heaven on earth? If this was so spectacularly seen in the case of three or five thousand (the first Christians) and none of them suffered want, how much more must it stand the test with such a large crowd? Would not each of those newly coming in dispose of something?" (VNS, 30)

Using actual population estimates and projected figures for wealth that would be accumulated, Chrysostom argues that scarcity would be permanently eradicated.[22] He goes on to note how much more economical it is to feed people at a large common meal than within the individual family structure. In fact, he attributes the rise of scarcity to the emphasis away from common meals toward the family unit:

"The fragmentation of goods gave rise to greater expenditure and through this to poverty. Let us take a house with a husband, wife and ten children. They operate a weaving mill; he looks to the market for his support. Would they use more if they lived together in one house or if they lived separately? Obviously if they lived separately. If the ten sons leave home they then use ten houses, ten tables, ten servants and everything else is similarly multiplied. And how would it be in the case of the multitude of slaves? Will they not eat together at a table in order to spare the cost? The fragmentation leads again and again to extravagance; integration, to the saving of goods. So one now lives in the monasteries and so the believers once lived. Who starves then from hunger? Who is not richly satisfied? Yet, the people are more afraid of these conditions than of a leak in an endless ocean. May we make an attempt and boldly attack the issue!" (VNS, 30–31)

Despite his awareness that many people greatly feared it, Chrysostom returns to his original claim that all would be blessed by collectivizing the wealth:

"How great would be the blessing thereof! Then at the time when the number of the believers was so small, only three or five thousand, if at that time, when the whole world was hostile in opposition, when no one made a move toward consolation, our predecessors so resolved to move with this, how much more confidence should we now have where by God's grace believers are everywhere! Who then would still want to remain heathen? No one, I believe. We would draw and befriend all to us." (VNS, 31)

Chrysostom therefore believes that with the spread of Christianity, the possibilities for communal life are multiplied. The ethical example it would set would attract those who still remained outside the church fold.[23] He ends his sermon with a call to implement his proposal.

Kautsky highly praises Chrysostom's "sober, purely economic sermon" that is "free of every religious enthusiasm" (VNS, 31). His sermon underscores the authenticity of the communist principle within the Christian tradition. But it also underscores the fact that this tradition was one of consumption rather than of production. Chrysostom's entire argument turns on the economics of consumption, the fact that an extended household disposes of goods in a more efficient manner than many small family units, for example. Nothing in the sermon addresses the question of who is to produce the wealth or how (VNS, 31).

Kautsky also notes that Chrysostom's proposed economic policy was never put into effect. That the church father felt the need to speak against a widespread fear of communism was an indication of how far the churches had already shifted from their original economic arrangements.

The failure of St. Basilius, Gregory the Great, and St. Chrysostom to restore the early communism of Christianity illustrates for Kautsky the primacy of material relations over the power of ideas (VNS, 31). At the same time, however, Kautsky views their passionate declamations against economic inequality as clearly drawing their power and legitimacy from Christianity's original spirit of equality and solidarity. This had been a spirit that succeeded in eliminating slavery from the early Christian community and that strove after egalitarian, communal relationships (VNS, 31).

To summarize Kautsky's analysis, the impossibility of socializing the means of production under preindustrial conditions, without also generalizing scarcity, relegated all communal experiments to the margins of society (VNS, 31).

The fact that communist teaching and practice was central to the earliest Christian traditions meant that it could not simply be thrust aside by later church theologians, and that it continued to play an important prophetic role. Many felt the need to get around it through a series of sophistries. They no longer tried to solve the problem of poverty and of economic inequality. Instead, what the early Christians addressed as a problem of material relations in history began to be "spiritualized," according to Kautsky. Originally Christians had declared that no rich person could enter the Kingdom of God, that is to say, be accepted into the community, unless he or she gave all of his riches to the poor and became poor. This doctrine that only the poor could be blessed was eventually reinterpreted to refer only to an inner "poverty" of spirit.

As an example of this new nonmaterial interpretation, Kautsky quotes Ratzinger's *History of Ecclesiastical Poor Relief*:

> "the rich man had to separate his heart from all earthly property; he had only to so possess, as a householder of God, as if he did not possess; he should use only that which is most necessary to his maintenance. As a trustee of God, he should employ all the rest for the poor."[24]

Kautsky comments:

> However, the poor must strive after earthly property just as little as the rich; he must be satisfied with his lot and thankful to accept the crumbs which the rich throw to him. What a tap dance! [*Welch' niedlicher Eiertanz!*] The rich man needs to do nothing more than separate his heart from earthly property; he should own

as if he owns not! So is Christianity with its communist origins bought off. (VNS, 31–32)

Even in this compromised form, Christianity continued to play the single most important role in addressing poverty, which partly accounted for its continuing popularity, declares Kautsky. However, as the church became increasingly powerful and established, it eventually gave birth to a new ruling class: the clergy (VNS, 32).

To substantiate his point, Kautsky briefly reviews the history of early church organization, how it began with relative decentralization and a large degree of self-government on the part of individual congregations. This situation progressively gave way to increased centralization and the rise of a professional managerial class. Kautsky observes that the lumpenproletariat comprising the ranks of the first congregations were unable to continue sharing power within the church any more than within the Empire as a whole. They bartered away their freedom to the bishops in exchange for handouts just as they did to the Roman Caesars (VNS, 32). By the third century participation of the laity had been reduced to the right to confirm the appointment of church officials.

After Constantine the church no longer depended on free will offerings, but began to enjoy the fruits of taxation and state patronage. The tithe became a mandatory tax required from everyone including serfs. The church now became enormously wealthy and also fully independent of the laity. With enormous wealth and power came also corruption and greed. Here Kautsky declares that the institution that began as a communal movement now emerged as "the most colossal machine for exploitation that the world had seen."[25]

By the fifth century the church's tremendous wealth was divided into four equal parts and dispensed to (1) the bishop; (2) the other clergy; (3) administrative costs; and (4) the poor. In other words, the bishop himself received the same amount of money as all those in need (VNS, 34). In fact, this four-part budget was probably established to guarantee that the poor received even this much!

Until the Roman Empire collapsed under the Germanic invasions, the basic principle of *patrimonium pauperum*—the church property as property of the poor—remained in effect. Even though corruption abounded and the funds designated for the poor sometimes got used for administrative purposes, no clergy would have dared to actually lay claim to it. This would only happen after the fall of the Roman Empire, and a total restructuring of the churches within a new socio-political context (VNS, 34).

Church Property in the Middle Ages

Kautsky describes how the Germanic tribes were organized according to a simple form of agrarian communism at the time they conquered Rome. While house and court were already the private property of individual families, the surrounding land was apportioned among them for their usage with ultimate title belonging to the tribe. Also pasture, forest, and water remained the property of all, both in usage and title.

With the Germanic invasions came a dramatic decrease in the level of poverty. If people were poor, it was only a temporary condition caused by war or epidemic. Whenever individuals suffered a lack of necessities, the community stepped in to remedy the situation (VNS, 35).

The charity function of the church therefore became less important during the early Middle Ages. Gradually the church moved from being an institution concerned with charity to becoming an institution concerned with power, Kautsky explains. As the Germanic states embraced Christianity, the church evolved into the largest property-owning institution holding title to a third of the land or more. This is in contrast to the collective ownership of other major parcels of land. Furthermore, with the disappearance of the lumpenproletariat, the church finally dispensed with the ancient principle of *patrimonium pauperum*—property of the poor.

Kautsky describes how Emperor Charlemagne of the Holy Roman Empire wanted to maintain the tradition of setting aside a quarter of the church property for charity. However, while the policy remained on the books, it was not enforced. Some years after his death the Isidorian Decretals appeared, which provided the basis for establishment of the papacy. These fraudulent documents made the argument that the "poor" of the gospel actually refer to the *clergy* who have taken a vow of poverty. This then justified the clergy's possession of church property. By the twelfth century this teaching was further modified to justify all church property belonging to the head of the clergy, namely, the Pope, who could dispose of it as he wished.

Kautsky sees a connection between the development of the clergy as church property holders and the vow of celibacy. The papacy wanted to ensure that clergy would not divide church property among their children, but rather would keep it permanently within the church. For example, Kautsky cites Pope Benedict VIII's complaint about, "great parcels of land, large pieces of property which the vile fathers [the married clergy] could always acquire for their vile sons from the church treasury—because they didn't own anything else." The rise of clerical celibacy had an economic motive which actually carried more weight than the ascetic rationale that is commonly given, according to Kautsky.[26] In summary, the clergy with their vows of poverty and chastity came to displace the truly poor as rightful owners of the church property.

Although the church's wealth no longer belonged to the poor, the medieval church did take some steps to alleviate temporary poverty caused by war, plague, and famine. Every wealthy institution and person was expected to give to the poor, not to mention the richest of them all: the church. Now, however, the church fulfilled its obligation, not because of a special Christian ethic, but rather a pagan ethic: the Germanic custom of "*hospitality*" (emphasis Kautsky's. VNS, 37).

Kautsky saw this German ethic reflecting the "natural economy" of the period: production for family and community, rather than for markets and customers. The wealthy property holders—royalty, high nobility, top clergy—accumulated huge surpluses of perishable items that they could not sell. In Kautsky's words, "they could only—feed." Accordingly, the surplus provided for large retinues of soldiers, artists, servants—and also went to the poor.

Therefore, when the church gave to the poor during the Middle Ages, it was only doing what the rich were supposed to do under an ancient Germanic code of ethics. It gave more, only because it owned more (VNS, 38).

When the natural economy gave way to a money economy, and surplus produce began to be sold in markets that developed in Italy and southern France and spread northward, the wealthy grew less generous. They were now able to sell perishable goods for money which they could save. In Kautsky's words, "In place of the joy of sharing surplus steps the joy of storing up treasures. Generosity is dead because of greed" (VNS, 38). As liberality diminished, poverty increased. The development of production for exchange produced a new, permanent underclass that quickly spread into many regions.

Because the monasteries adapted to the newer capitalist economy more slowly than wealthy individuals, they continued the older tradition of charity. Yet even the monasteries increasingly restricted their hospitality to provide only "soup for beggars." Furthermore, what they could do was limited in relation to the increasing demands of the growing masses of poor (VNS, 38).

With the permanent impoverishment of masses of people comparable to the earlier conditions under the Roman Empire, communist experiments were attempted. Some of them were influenced by Plato and some by the early Christians. For example, the radical Waldensians were a socialist lay group that was organized by reform-minded weavers in the woolen industry (VNS, 103). The entire Reformation movement gave impetus to such class movements. Kautsky viewed Martin Luther as an ambivalent figure who both provided religious legitimation for communist oppositional groups, and curried favor with a new nationally based ruling elite. He saw Thomas Münzer as the more consistent reformer, who took a firm stand against autocratic social structures (VNS, 239–51).

These social movements marked the emergence of a new mode of production unknown to both Plato and the first Christians—capitalism with its foundation in wage labor. In turn, capitalism gave rise to a new development in the age-old theory and practice of communism: modern social democracy (VNS, 39).

Christianity and Socialism in Modern Germany

Even though early Christian communism failed, it was so central to Christian identity that it could not simply be cast aside. Throughout the centuries it remained a thorn in the side of an increasingly corrupt and hierarchical church. Prophetic voices repeatedly rose up to recall it. These voices were repressed, but the tradition still remained to be explained in one way or another, whether by confining it to the monasteries, or by giving it an ahistorical, spiritualized interpretation. According to Kautsky, the most creative sophistry prevailed throughout the Middle Ages, equating the clergy with the poor based on their vow of poverty, thereby legitimating their entitlement to church property. The very need for such rationalizations, however, only underscores the centrality of communism to the original Christian social ethic. To Kautsky this tradition of the communism of consumption was a harbinger of modern socialism.

Therefore, Kautsky went on to argue, individual Christians would find their faith more compatible with modern socialism than with capitalism, even though the modern institutional churches opposed the social democratic parties of the Socialist International. Nor was he surprised that individual priests and pastors had actually joined the Social Democrats. He exhorts the parties' leadership not to hesitate in welcoming such Christians into the ranks of socialism. He also counsels Christians not to feel they must give up their religious beliefs to be good socialists. They should not be surprised, however, if they meet with resistance from church establishments (SDK, 8–9).

Kautsky's understanding of the nature and history of Christianity informed his political responses to the organized Christianity of his own day. First, his reconstruction of Christian communism and assertion that it lies at the heart of Christian social ethics guaranteed a hearing for socialists with the Catholic and Protestant peasants moving into the cities and swelling the proletariat. Here Kautsky ideologically positioned modern socialism as a more legitimate heir of authentic Christianity than the corrupt churches of Imperial Germany.

Second, he agreed with August Bebel that organized Christianity would wither away once the state began to take over the welfare function that the churches had traditionally assumed. It was therefore not necessary to use state power to suppress organized Christianity, as the Bolsheviks were later to undertake, but simply to stop funding the clergy and religious instruction with state revenues. Kautsky therefore advocated the elimination of religious instruction from the public schools and the separation of church and state. Considering religion to be a private matter, he defended the freedom of individuals and groups to practice whatever religion they chose and fund their own religious schools.[27]

August Bebel first developed this socialist policy towards religion in 1873 in the context of opposing Bismarck's anti-Catholic *Kulturkampf*. At that time a coalition comprised of the two Conservative parties, and the right wing of the National Liberal party supported "exceptional" legislation against the Roman Catholic church particularly against the religious orders. Kautsky quoted Bebel's position with approval:

> "to fight clericalism…there is only one means open to the bourgeoisie and to the government, but neither is willing to use the only means of stopping clerical forces of reaction, and that is the separation of the school from the church, of the church from the state, and the major improvement of elementary education; instead of this the government uses violence against increasingly troublesome clerical opposition. This is why the Liberals and the government support coercion. In so doing they speak of liberty, order and the public welfare as governments always do. Legal coercion against the clergy, expulsion of Jesuits, etc., have all been adopted by the Reichstag to the great joy of the Liberals, except for a few who hold to certain ideals."[28]

In arguing for separation of church and state, Kautsky was applying a single, consistent standard against both Catholic regional power in

Southern Germany and Protestant state power in the Prussian dominated Empire. By contrast, the Empire depended on the legitimation
it received from the Protestant clergy, and so preferred to use force
against the Catholics rather than cut its own ties to the Protestant
churches. Thus, Kautsky's position simultaneously subverted the
power of Catholic clergy, Protestant clergy, *and* the German political
and military elites.

Kautsky explicitly addressed the question as to whether the German
Social Democratic party should bow to pressure from the right-wing
coalition of parties which favored staging another *Kulturkampf* against
the Catholic Center party. First, he argued that clerical forces of reaction would be more effectively weakened by removing state privileges.
Second, he argued against such persecution on grounds that it would
violate basic principles of civil liberties. In what would prove to be a
most prophetic statement, he declared that if today Catholics were persecuted by the state, tomorrow it would be socialists and Jews (SDK, 3,
9, 10, 18–23):

> If a law is passed against them [Roman Catholics], then it may be argued that it is
> alright to legislate against unpopular political opponents. These may be anarchists
> today and Social Democrats tomorrow. The laws against the Catholic clergy [un-
> der Bismarck's *Kulturkampf*] preceded the laws aimed at the socialists.... [Such a
> law that] confiscates the property of the religious orders today [would mean] that
> of the Jews tomorrow. (SDK, 22–3; SDC, 359–60)

Although Kautsky believed institutional religion would eventually
wither and die without state support, he did not believe this would mark
the end of religion as such. On this point he is often misunderstood.
While he is often criticized for reducing religion to an external social
phenomenon, in fact, his view was more complex. Ironically, in the
very essay Troeltsch cites as an example of reductionism, Kautsky carefully distinguishes two definitions of religion:

> But we cannot speak of the church without first defining religion, and this is no
> easy matter. The idea of religion is very confused and varied, and there is a mul-
> titude of definitions.... However, all definitions of religion can be considered
> under two headings. They have often been confused, and yet they are mutually
> exclusive. Schiller has already referred to them in his famous couplet, 'What is
> my religion? None of those you name. And why? Because I am religious.' On the
> one hand, religion may be defined as a certain individual outlook—as personality
> rising above self-interest; it is a form of moral idealism or exaltation. On the other
> hand, religion is a general historical phenomenon, a universal system which is not
> formulated by reason, but by an act of faith which is accepted by the masses on
> trust, and which becomes the guide for their thoughts and actions....

> Religion, looked at as a matter of the heart, as a private affair, and religions of the masses, are not only different but are often hostile. For the first only recognizes personal conscience as a guide; the second demands that conscience should submit to a social power which claims a supernatural authority. The constitution of this authority is the social condition inherent in all collective religion, and that alone concerns us. (SDK, 3–4; SDC, 163)

Here Kautsky makes a radical distinction between (1) the religion of a Schiller, namely a private matter in which the conscience functions as an autonomous moral authority and in which the personality transcends mundane interests, and (2) mass institutionalized religion in which authority is necessarily heteronomous. He makes it clear that in his social treatment of religion he is addressing only the latter phenomenon. Yet his recognition of the validity of the former is one reason he defended freedom of religion as a matter of public policy.

Further, as his social history of Christianity demonstrates, Kautsky believed that even organized religion can contain liberating elements under certain historical circumstances. The communism of consumption practiced by the early churches was certainly one such important case.

In summary, Kautsky by no means held the one-dimensional view of religion his critics often attribute to him. Although Troeltsch frequently presented his own ideas as a defense of religious individualism from Marxist reductionism, it was Kautsky and the Marxists who actually championed religious freedom in Imperial Germany. Ironically, most National Liberals including Troeltsch supported a renewal of the *Kulturkampf.*

These differences regarding the politics of religion had implications for a range of other political phenomena, including nationalism, colonialism, and militarism. As the state religion, German Protestantism played an important role in legitimizing Imperial Germany and its military and colonial ambitions. For German Catholics, by contrast, the highest earthly authority rested not with the state but with the international papacy. Thus removed from the mainstream of German nationalism, the Catholic Center party criticized both Germany's military buildup and its brutal Africa policies, as mentioned in chapter 6.

From his very different starting point as a leader of the Socialist International, Kautsky came to similar political conclusions. He viewed the nation state as serving the interests of big capital, and saw colonialism and militarism as expressions of the capitalist drive for expanded markets. Just ten years before the outbreak of World War I, Kautsky argued that the German military buildup should be sharply curtailed.

Further, he made connections between such geopolitical questions and domestic questions regarding religion and culture. There simply was not enough public revenue to support both an arms race and good public education, he argued. Public education would only be able to compete effectively against church-sponsored parochial education if it received much of the revenue currently going into military spending:

> The bourgeois state has no intention of destroying clerical influence over the people by making the public schools better.... That is because this educational policy costs money, and a bourgeois state cannot find the necessary means if it will continue to pursue *militarism* and is opposed to taxation that would seriously affect the rich. (Emphasis mine. SDK, 24; SDC, 361)

This is a rare word of dissent at a time when the Emperor, with his war lords and compliant government, was embarked on an unprecedented arms build-up. In this situation only the socialists dared to call for demilitarization and increased taxation of the rich.

At another point Kautsky addressed the relation of the military to the working class:

> The proletariat must attempt to put curbs on the army. Unfortunately however they cannot do without it entirely. Although it truly is a means of keeping the people in subjection, it is also a means of defence against outside enemies, especially against the Eastern enemies (SDK, 20; SDC, 289)

Thus, Kautsky did not reduce all questions of national security to class politics, nor did he embrace pacifism as an absolute ethical principle. However, he recognized the role of the military as an instrument of class domination within the politics of the nation state. On this basis, he adopted a far more critical stance on the military than Troeltsch's National Liberals, who actively supported the arms race leading to World War I.

Kautsky's social history of Christianity, first published in *Forerunners of Modern Socialism* (1895) preceded *The Social Teaching* (1912) by seventeen years. Most commentators consider the work by Troeltsch to be the first "social history of Christianity."[29] However, it was neither the first, nor was it really social historiography.

Intending to provide a German idealist alternative to Kautsky's social history, Troeltsch followed the Dilthey school in writing intellectual history, as explained in chapter four. Whereas Kautsky wrote a history of Christianity as a social system, Troeltsch wrote a history of the social *teachings* of Christianity. A closer look at *The Social Teaching of the Christian Churches* will illuminate this difference.

Notes

1. John H. Kautsky, *Karl Kautsky: Marxism, Revolution & Democracy* (New Brunswick: Transaction Publishers, 1994), 1–2; idem, *The Political Thought of Karl Kautsky*, (Ph.D. diss., Harvard University, 1951), 3f; Ingrid Gilcher-Holtey, *Das Mandat des Intellektuellen: Karl Kautsky und die Sozialdemokratie* (Berlin: Siedler Verlag, 1986), 13f.
2. Kautsky's strengths as a Marxist thinker lay in his combining, almost paradoxically, a strict Marxist orthodoxy with an openness to new and developing social phenomena. He had a keen eye for discerning new problems that Marx and Engels did not anticipate, and breaking new ground in addressing them. Not only did Kautsky first see the need to address the relationship of democracy and socialism, he was also the first Marxist theorist to explore fully the relationship of religion and socialism. He still provides the best analysis of the latter, according to Professor Bertell Ollman in conversation with this writer. Massimo Salvadori, *Karl Kautsky: Karl Kautsky and the Socialist Revolution 1880–1938*, trans. Jon Rothschild (London: NLB, 1979), 18.
3. The Nazis accused him of being Jewish, perhaps because his grandfather owned property in the Jewish section of Prague. The popular association of Jews with socialism may have also contributed to the error. Kautsky's second wife, Luise Ronsperger, was a Jew who died in Auschwitz. Steenson, *Karl Kautsky*, 11.
4. Although compared with Antonio Gramsci, Kautsky used a relatively nondialectical approach to Marxism, he shared with Gramsci a concern for the relations between society, state and parties. Despite different approaches, Gramsci and Kautsky arrived at the common conclusion that democracy was necessary to socialism. Massimo Salvadori, *Karl Kautsky and the Socialist Revolution 1880–1938*, 13.
5. For example, Kautsky concluded his programmatic essay on socialist policy regarding religion by arguing that it must be specifically socialist and "can have nothing in common with liberalism." Karl Kautsky, "Die Sozialdemokratie und die katholische Kirche," 2nd ed. (Berlin: Buchhandlung Vorwärts, 1906), 31.
6. Lenin and Trotsky claimed that Kautsky rejected Marx's concept of the dictatorship of the proletariat. They failed to realize that Kautsky had always defined this notion in democratic terms, even in the earlier years when Lenin hailed Kautsky as a master of Marxism. Kautsky envisioned the dictatorship of the proletariat to be a constitutionally based parliamentary system with free elections and respect for civil liberties. In fact, Kautsky believed that political democracy was necessary to true socialism. Salvadori, *Karl Kautsky*, 12–13.
7. Karl Kautsky, "Die Sozialdemokratie und die katholische Kirche," 16–17.
8. Karl Kautsky, *Thomas More and his Utopia*, trans. (New York: International Publishers, 1927), first published as *Thomas und seine Utopie* (Stuttgart: J. H. M. Dietz, 1888).
9. Karl Kautsky, *Foundations of Christianity*, trans. (New York: International Publishers, 1925; reprint ed., New York: Monthly Review Press, 1980), first published as *Der Ursprung des Christentums. Eine Historische Untersuchung* (Stuttgart: J. H. M. Dietz, 1908), 7. Following references will be referred to by the acronym "FC" and cited parenthetically in the text of this chapter.
10. Karl Kautsky, *Die Vorläufer des Neueren Sozialismus*, 2 vols. (Stuttgart: J. H. M. Dietz, 1895). Subsequent references will appear parenthetically in this chapter with the acronym, "VNS."
11. Karl Kautsky, "Die Sozialdemokratie und die katholische Kirche," hereafter referred to as SDK; idem, "Social Democracy and the Catholic Church," *The So-*

cial Democrat, vol. VII (London, 1903), 162–69, 234–43, 288–91, 359–62, 430–36, hereafter referred to as SDC.

12. See chapter 4.

13. Karl Kautsky emphasized divisions within classes and stressed the complexity of social conflicts, thereby lending nuance to the Marxist concept of class struggle. He arrived at an understanding of social conflict similar in some respects to the interest group approach of modern political science. John Kautsky, *Karl Kautsky: Marxism, Revolution & Democracy*, 25–26; SDK, 5; FC, 323–27.

14. Mt. 6:28–30; Lk. 12:17.

15. Mt. 19:21; Mk. 10:21; Lk. 12:33, 18:21.

16. In the apocalyptic discourse of the New Testament, neither "world" nor *die Welt* adequately convey the sense of the original Greek. "Cosmos" did not mean in the first instance the physical earth or universe; it meant the socio-political or human order (Stephen Charles Mott, *Biblical Ethics and Social Change* [New York: Oxford University Press, 1982], 4–6). Thus, in Jesus's day the imminent "end of the world" meant the imminent collapse of the existing social and political arrangements, rather than the physical destruction of the earth, although the latter is an apt metaphor for the former. Jesus believed he was instituting a new social order that would take the place of the old.

17. Kautsky's concept of equality as a value that can only be fully realized at a certain stage of history under highly developed material conditions, a concept that originated with Marx, contrasts with Troeltsch's concept that inequality is rooted in nature, and is thus eternal and unchangeable. For further discussion, see the description of Kautsky's appropriation of Chrysostom below.

18. Kautsky is drawing upon the work of J. L. Vogel, *Antiquities of the Early Christians* (Hamburg: 1780). VNS, 26.

19. NRSV, Lk. 14:26; see also Mt. 10:37, 12:46f.; Mk. 3:31f., 10:29; Lk. 8:20, 18:29.

20. No doubt the growing suffragette movement of his own day prompted Kautsky to be sensitive to feminism. As mentioned in chapter six, the Social Democrats chose a feminist leader to join their executive council during the pre-World War I period, long before any of the other parties became responsive.

21. Kautsky's source for these references to the church fathers was F. Villegardelle, *Histoire des idees socialistes avant la revolution francaise* (Paris: Guarin, 1846), 71ff. VNS, 29.

22. Chrysostom is arguing that scarcity of basic necessities, that is, poverty in an absolute sense, would be eradicated. As discussed above, Kautsky apparently believed that economic scarcity *as such* could not be eradicated under pre-industrial conditions. While the two propositions are compatible, they are ultimately empirical questions in economic history; testing them is beyond the scope of this book.

It should be mentioned, however, that Kautsky's proposition could be tested by a close examination of the economics of medieval monasteries, which tried to maintain the ideal of apostolic communism in its original purity. Even these communities apparently developed a class system, where one group of monks maintained a high level of culture while another group toiled to produce the necessary surplus. This would appear to indicate that under preindustrial conditions, equality could only be achieved at the expense of imposing *some* scarcity (i.e., scarcity of leisure time, if not scarcity of basic necessities) on everyone. While Chrysostom mentioned "the cloisters" as an illustration of the abundance available through communism, he did not deal with the compromises these communities made with class stratification. Given his historical situation, of course, neither could he have conceptualized what for Kautsky was the material origin

of this compromise: a scarcity of leisure time resulting from the economic inadequacy of preindustrial production methods.
23. His reference to the "heathen" is, unfortunately, a reflection of his historical period.
24. Ratzinger, *History of Ecclesiastical Poor Relief* (Freiburg, 1860), 9, 10; VNS, 31–2.
25. "Aus einer kommunistischen Anstalt wurde sie die riesenhafteste Ausbeutungsmaschine, welche die Welt gesehen." VNS, 34.
26. Kautsky was not the first to see the connection between clerical control of church property and the rise of celibacy. He cited the church historian Johann Karl Ludwig Gieseler who argued this connection in his *Lehrbuch der Kirchengeschichte* (Bonn, 1831). VNS, 36n.
27. Kautsky viewed the separation of church and state in the United States as a model of good public policy regarding religion. However, his prediction that organized religion would wither away under such conditions proved incorrect, at least in the case of the U.S. This suggests the inadequacy of Kautsky's economistic understanding of organized religion.
28. As we know, the "few" with ideals to which Bebel referred were eventually to split from the National Liberal party and form the Progressive party. SDK, 25.
29. Claude Welch, *Protestant Thought in the Nineteenth Century*, vol. 2: 1870–1914 (New Haven, Conn.: Yale University Press, 1985), 291.

12

Troeltsch's *Social Teaching*:
The Legitimation of Social Inequality

Introduction

The growing popularity of the German Social Democrats among Christian believers and the socialist appropriation of the earliest Christian traditions helps to explain why Troeltsch begins *The Social Teaching* with a polemic against the principle of class conflict.[1] I have mentioned that during the years he was writing *The Social Teaching*, Troeltsch was also sitting in the Badenese upper house as a member of the National Liberal Party. As in the case of Kautsky, Troeltsch's own values and political agenda in this partisan context informed his reconstruction of the social history of Christianity. It was an agenda that first surfaced in his essay, "Political Ethics and Christianity" (1904), and that continued in *The Social Teaching*.

In chapter 1 I discussed how Troeltsch's polemic against the socialists of his day focuses upon Karl Kautsky in particular. The crux of Troeltsch's reply to Kautsky in *The Social Teaching* is to substitute the doctrine of "religious individualism" for the doctrine of communism as the heart of the gospel social ethic. Rather than communism, "religious individualism [*religiöse Individualismus*] is and remains the root idea."[2] Therefore, the communism practiced by the Early Church, which for Kautsky was central, for Troeltsch "was a by-product of Christianity and not a fundamental idea. The fundamental idea was solely that of the salvation of souls" (ST, 63; GS1, 50).

In other words, the central problematic of Christianity is one of "pure religion"; that is, involving the soul, afterlife and worship: "in the whole range of the Early Christian literature…there is no hint of any formulation of the 'Social Question'; the central problem is always purely religious" (ST, 39; GS1, 16). Questions of ethics are secondary and when they do arise, they deal primarily with personal ethics. Personal ethics begins with "severe self-discipline" in seeking after "personal holiness" (ST, 39; GS1, 16). "Christ requires men to be indifferent to material happiness and to money, to practice sexual self-restraint, to have a mind that values the unseen and eternal more than the seen and temporal" (ST, 54; GS1, 37).

In formulating the problematic in this way Troeltsch places himself in the neo-Kantian tradition of Ritschl and Harnack, with echoes of Lagarde. In fact, he makes explicit reference to Harnack's *History of Dogma* and *The Mission and Expansion of Christianity in the First Three Centuries.* "The latter," writes Troeltsch, "contains the best material known to me for the social history of Christianity"[3] (ST, 165n; GS1, 17n). He also refers to Harnack's programmatic address presented to the Evangelical Social Congress in 1894.[4] Harnack represented the conservative wing of the Evangelical Social Congress and was its president while Troeltsch was writing *The Social Teaching*, as mentioned in chapter 7. By this time the moderate and progressive leadership had been forced out. The interventions of the emperor played no small role in this change, as discussed in chapter 7. Harnack, on the other hand, pleased the monarch so much he eventually received ennoblement the year World War I broke out.

Like his friend Harnack, Troeltsch chose to side with the emperor against the activist wing of the Evangelical Social Congress, which sympathized with the Social Democrats. In his address of 1904 given to this Congress Troeltsch supported his own arguments by quoting the emperor's edict: "Political pastors are nonsense!" Troeltsch's reference to "pure religion" reflects Harnack's emphasis on "essence" as discussed in chapter 5.[5] It should be noted that it was Harnack who used his influence to get Troeltsch a university chair in Berlin in 1915, and who delivered the final oration at his funeral in 1923. Wilhelm Pauck concludes his survey of Troeltsch: "Few creative men who have become famous have been praised by their peers as Troeltsch was by Harnack."[6]

Following Harnack, Troeltsch distinguishes between the eternal and the temporal realms, giving primacy to the former. The spirituality that he describes is disembodied, focusing on the salvation of "souls."[7] This emphasis on the union of souls with God makes concern for material and social redemption seem trivial by comparison (ST, 1005; GS1, 978). Thus, class differences "were lost sight of" in favor of the "supreme question of eternal salvation and the appropriation of a spiritual inheritance" (ST, 40; GS1, 16).

Troeltsch builds upon and extends this theological paradigm in his discussions of the "independence" of religion:

> In reality, however, all impartial religious research reveals the fact that, to some extent at least, religious thought is independent; it has its own inner dialectic and its own power of development; it is therefore precisely during these periods of a total bankruptcy of human hope and effort that it is able to step in and fill the vacant space [*den frei gewordenen Raum*] with its own ideas and its own sentiment. (ST, 48; GS1, 31)

In contrast to the Marxist view of an *interdependence* between religion and political economy, with the latter having primacy, Troeltsch argues for a neo-Kantian interpretation of religion as an *independent* force. To be sure, he weakens this formulation by the phrase "to some extent at least," but he then strengthens it by asserting that religion actually has primacy in certain historical situations. The origin of Christianity was presumably one of these situations of "a total bankruptcy of human hope and effort."

That political economy is eclipsed in Troeltsch's neo-Kantian formulation is apparent in his understanding of the ascendancy of religion as coinciding with a historical "vacant space." In the case of early Christianity, this would mean that the period from the birth of the Roman Empire to the peak of its power in the second century was a "vacant space." The cult of the emperor, which was the ideological apex of this great power structure, was during this time the bearer of "human hope and effort" for much of the Mediterranean world. Whereas Kautsky and other Marxists viewed early Christianity as an opposition movement rooted in the oppressed and marginalized classes of this Roman world, for Troeltsch it was a phenomenon with "its own inner dialectic and its own power of development...step[ping] in and fill[ing] the vacant space with its own ideas and its own sentiment."

Thus, Troeltsch interprets Jesus as involved in purely religious pursuits that had little bearing on questions of political economy. While he agrees that Jesus began his ministry by proclaiming the Kingdom of God as the hope of redemption, he quickly adds that this had nothing to do with correcting social injustice, but rather with ushering in "values of pure spirituality" (ST, 40; GS1, 16). Paul was to transform Jesus' original proclamation to mean a redemption already achieved through the life and death of Christ. Here, too, "the values of redemption were still purely inward, ethical and spiritual, leading inevitably and naturally to a sphere of painless bliss" (ST, 40; GS1, 16–17). One may recall that in "Political Ethics and Christianity," Troeltsch explicitly linked redemption with conservative political values. The triumph of the spiritually elect individual over the things of the world goes hand in hand with "authority, not majority."

Lest his readers be tempted to think that his reference to the Kingdom as a realm of bliss suggests social betterment, Troeltsch, in true Ritschlian form, argues against any connection to socialism and eudaemonism:[8]

> The whole conception of Eudaemonism, or the fundamental ethical principle of happiness, which implies that moral excellence and political and economic well-being coincide, has been altered [with the Christian message].... Bliss itself is conceived increasingly as the state of the future life, and thus it becomes increasingly possible to do without earthly happiness. (ST, 49; GS1, 32)

Forswearing earthly happiness and waiting for the reward in heaven became possible for the first Christians in light of human depravity and bondage to things material, earthly or bodily:

> The value of the present life was further depreciated by the idea that man is by nature totally corrupt, and also that this life is inextricably bound by the chains of material things. (ST, 49; GS1, 32–33)

While Kautsky viewed history as the evolution of social relations, Troeltsch viewed it more statically as an expression of nature. Thus, history itself becomes the problem for the God-seeker. Troeltsch summarizes:

> [T]he new hope offered by Christianity...does not offer simply a transformed social ideal, expressed in transcendental terms, the promise of a world in which equality, freedom, painlessness, and satisfaction shall reign, effected by a Divine and miraculous intervention when human effort has proved unable to achieve this end; *the Christian ideal means rather the entire renunciation of the material social ideal of all political and economic values*, and the turning towards the religious treasures of peace of heart, love of humanity, fellowship with God, which are open to all because they are not subject to any difficulties of leadership or organization. (Emphasis mine. ST, 48–49; GS1, 32)

In other words, Troeltsch understood the Christian ideal to involve the complete renunciation of *the questions themselves* having to do with social justice, not merely the renunciation of socialist solutions. These questions have only relative or historical value. The "Christian ideal" is that which remains foundational and normative, that which distinguishes Christianity at its core, not merely for a particular time frame, not merely within history. For Troeltsch the uppermost questions of reality stand outside of history.

Troeltsch is not concerned to reconstruct merely the first century worldview in the foregoing statements. In the beginning chapters of *The Social Teaching* he is replying above all to interpretations of "the Christian ideal" being offered in his own time by Kautsky and certain Christian socialists, as mentioned. Troeltsch's alternative reconstruction given here "is and remains the root idea" of Christianity.[9]

Troeltsch's dichotomy between the things of the spirit and things of the world provides a context for understanding his argument that Kautsky allegedly reduces religion to social causes.[10] In the very pamphlet Troeltsch cites as exemplary of this error, however, Kautsky was careful to distinguish between two types of religion: organized religion on the one hand and the private mysticism of a Schiller on the other.[11] His critique of Kautsky's analysis of organized religion in terms of material conditions echoes the German professors' disapproval of any focus on the material or the concrete as "soulless" pedestrianism. Apart from his devaluation of the material realm, however, Troeltsch ignores Kautsky's recognition of private mysticism as authentic religion, even though it is entirely consistent with Troeltsch's own preference for the mystical over the church types discussed below.

According to Troeltsch, Jesus came to announce the coming of the Kingdom of God, which he expected would bring about the end of history within his own generation. Because the end was thought to be at hand, Jesus was indifferent to social concerns. His ethic concerned only the spiritual preparation of the individual for a Kingdom that was either beyond history (ST, 52; GS1, 36) or within the soul: "'The Kingdom of God is within you'" (ST, 1013; GS1, 986). The Kingdom was certainly *not* the ushering in *within history* of a utopian communal society as the socialists were claiming. Furthermore, Troeltsch follows Harnack in interpreting the doctrine of the Incarnation—Jesus Christ uniting in himself the divine with the human and the heavenly with the earthly—as a much later development in church dogmatics that does not belong to the original gospel. For Troeltsch the Absolute is never found within history, which contributed to the problem of relating faith to history. For him God is never made flesh; the material realm is never sacralized.

According to Troeltsch, preparation for the coming Kingdom involves two things: (1) awareness of God as All-Knowing, All-Holy, and the Judge of all; and, (2) preparation of the soul through nurturance of the virtues of utter surrender, self-sacrifice, sincerity, integrity, humility, conscientious behavior in daily life, self-denial, the sacrifice of love of self, sacrifice of love of pleasure, indifference to material happiness and willingness to serve.

Like Ritschl, Troeltsch found a harshness in the moral claims of Jesus. "It is not ascetic, but it is very severe" and it is a "severity [*eine strenge*] which makes almost superhuman demands" (ST, 54; GS1, 38). Jesus embodied "an idealism which is certain that it can break down the dull resistance of the masses and of utilitarian reason."[12] Whether or not this is an accurate description of Jesus' ethic, it is an accurate description of an ethic likely to be prescribed for "the masses" by a German professor of Troeltsch's own time. We saw in chapter 4 that his academic peers spoke contemptuously of "the masses" and had no love for Anglo-French philosophies such as utilitarianism.

Indeed, Troeltsch adds that the kind of person who can best embody Jesus' ethic is one who is "bowed down with a sense of sin and guilt" (ST, 52–53; GS1, 36). In fact, this is the reason he gives for the emphasis on poverty in the Gospels. It is the poor and humble who can accept this gospel, who can flee from their problems to religion for spiritual deliverance (ST, 52–53; GS1, 36). In this regard, Troeltsch agrees with Kautsky's view that the *Lumpenproletariat* of the Roman Imperial period played a significant role in the formation of the Early Church and notes that Max Weber's *Hunger-proletariat* referred to much the same social group (ST, 169n; GS1, 22n):

> To put it quite plainly: Christianity was not the product of a class struggle of any kind; it was not shaped, when it did arise, in order to fit into any such situation; indeed, at no point was it directly concerned with the social upheavals of the ancient world. The fact, however, remains that Jesus addressed himself primarily to the oppressed, and to the 'little ones' of the human family, that he considered wealth a danger to the soul, and that he opposed the Jewish priestly aristocracy which represented the dominant ecclesiastical forces of his day.[13] It is also clear that the Early Church sought and won her new adherents chiefly among the lower classes in the cities, and that members of the well-to-do, educated upper classes only began to enter the Church in the second century, and then only very gradually. (ST, 39; GS1, 16)

But rather than coming to provide palpable deliverance for those who were oppressed, Jesus apparently came to save souls through flight from material reality. Furthermore, he provided an ethic that reinforced the low self-esteem that often accompanies the experience of oppression. But Troeltsch does not make use of a historically based analysis of why the poor often feel "humble." They simply *are* that way by nature. The early Christians were not encouraged to fight to overcome social oppression; quite the contrary, they were encouraged to resign themselves to it. According to Troeltsch:

> [S]ubmission to the world domination of the Empire drove the individual into his own inner life, and forced him to concentrate his energies on the effort to elevate private and personal morality...[to find] comfort in religious exaltation as a compensation for the hopelessness of the temporal outlook. (ST, 47; GS1, 30)

It was not the historical quest for social justice, but rather the submission to power and withdrawal from history that distinguished the first Christians, declared Troeltsch. They recognized the futility of entering into the historical process to try to deal with social injustice, which was due to corrupt human nature:

> The failure of so many great plans owing to the pettiness and selfishness of the masses, and the criminal, unbridled license of their leaders, aroused a sense of sin and weakness, and...the desire for eternal values in a higher sphere. (ST, 47; GS1, 30)

Thus, Troeltsch blames "the masses" as much as "their leaders," the victims of oppression as much as the perpetrators of their woes. Rather than analyze history and social structure, which would expose the oppressors, he assigns ultimate blame to the "sin and weakness" of human nature in general, which obscures the differences in guilt between the victims of power and the power holders.

It is clear from his description of "the Christian ideal" that Troeltsch either misunderstood or chose to misrepresent the Marxist critique of religion. While Marx and his followers did deny that religion could be independent of the social totality, they held the same view of science, art, politics, and indeed all forms of human consciousness. Their specific critique of religion was not to question its independence, but to question its *authenticity* or its *truth-claims*. Their critique was not that religion arose out of society, which was true of all forms of consciousness, but that religion is a form of *false* consciousness.[14]

Troeltsch does not address this fundamental question. In fact, his portrayal of the original Gospel message as a flight of consciousness from the struggles of existence only serves to lend credence to the Marxist view of religion as false consciousness. Kautsky, in the very pamphlet Troeltsch cited above, argued that organized religion has traditionally provided a doctrinal system accepted, not by reason, but by an act of faith by the masses. It demanded that the people submit to a social power which claims a supernatural authority.

By the time of the Roman Imperial period, the customary social structures that once protected the average person had disappeared and new religions stepped in to fill the vacuum. Kautsky's description of the inducements of new religions to the people living at that time in many ways parallels Troeltsch's portrayal. However, Troeltsch views these escapist and authoritarian/submissive elements as the essence of Christianity. Kautsky, on the other hand, views them as features Christianity had in common with all the other religions of the day, including the cult of Caesar:

> He is now placed in a dreadful society, in a society full of misery and toil which is hastening to destruction. Terrified, he searches for a solution, for a savior. Frightened and timid, he humbles himself before any new power and tends to look on it as superhuman and as divine. In the midst of general ruin, an ordinary human power cannot save him. Without hesitation he accords divine honors to the Caesars, he believes in the divine origin of a new community which, confident and undefeated, gains ascendancy in the midst of general decay. Man believes the new doctrines and submits to those who teach them.[15]

Christianity offered opportunities for "escape" and "submission" that were formally similar to, but substantively different from most of the other religions of Roman antiquity. According to Kautsky, this substantive difference was Christianity's communism of consumption, which addressed the material sources of alienation in the Roman world more authentically and profoundly than its religious rivals.

Thus, Troeltsch's description of the nature and origins of Christianity as an escape of the "soul" while the body submits to social oppression actually lends weight to the Marxist contention that religion is an opiate, a form of false consciousness. Troeltsch's emphasis on the values of self-denial and willingness to serve actually adds credibility to the charge that Christianity is another form of self-alienation. In sum, Troeltsch's focus on the question of the "independence" of religion fails to address the fundamental Marxist challenge.

Early Christian Communism

How did Troeltsch view the tradition of early Christian communism that Kautsky reconstructed? Troeltsch conceded that it existed, but gave it a neo-Kantian interpretation and relegated it to the periphery of the gospel message. He argued that the ethic of Jesus "develops an idealistic anarchism and the communism of love, which combines radical indifference or hostility towards the rest of the social order with the effort to actualize this idea of love in a small group."[16]

Troeltsch viewed the historical reality of communal living arrangements that addressed the Social Problem of the Roman period as an epiphenomenon of a purely religious reality: the expression of an ahistorical "idea of love" on the part of the individual Christian. Troeltsch did not believe that the embodiment of this "idea" in history and society was central to Christianity and constitutive of it. Rather, "love" was one of many teachings oriented to the spiritual development of individual souls, and as such subordinate to "religious individualism."

From a religious standpoint "all that matters is that all the members shall sacrifice something and that they all have to live; how this is carried out in practice does not matter." The fact that this communism was apparently later relinquished "without even a struggle for the principle, is only a further sign that this communism was a by-product of Christianity and not a fundamental idea" (ST, 62–63; GS1, 49–50).

Troeltsch agreed with Kautsky's view that the early Church only practiced communism on a small scale and only with respect to consumption, relying on "private enterprise" to maintain production. For Kautsky, however, the scale of this communist experiment simply reflected the small scale of early Christianity itself; communism was coterminus with these early churches and central to their identity. Further, Kautsky viewed their dependence on private ownership of the means of production as a contradiction that helped explain the experiment's eventual failure, a contradiction that modern socialism was attempting to overcome. Troeltsch, by contrast, interpreted the same evidence as a vindication of capitalism and confirmation of an inherent human selfishness that makes socialism on a large scale impossible.

Like Kautsky, Lujo Brentano in his *The Economic Teaching of Christian Antiquity* had also "[insisted] upon the communistic character of the Christian doctrine of property" (ST, 183–84n; GS1, 113n). Troeltsch summarily rejected this view, arguing that "[Both Kautsky's and] Brentano's treatment of the subject betrays an absence of all understanding of the ideas of the spirit of the early Church; indeed, [their] one desire seems to be to prove that the ideas of Early Christianity are of no use for a liberal capitalist economic policy" (ST, 175n; GS1, 51n).

In Troeltsch's eyes, Jesus with his communism of love was a terribly attractive and inspiring figure—Ritschl's hero. He was too lofty a figure to be addressing workaday concerns of social reform. His Sermon on the Mount reached Olympian heights to which few could aspire in the real world. Above all, he was concerned to help the individual prepare the soul for an imminent Kingdom that was not of this world. Thus, he saw the main elements of the Gospel ethic to be primarily the fostering of purity of heart and submission to God the Father as an obedient child; even loving the neighbor was a secondary element. Religious individualism provided the foundational idea (ST, 70; GS1, 59).

In his treatment of Jesus, Troeltsch does not address the question of why Jesus was executed, if his mission was so thoroughly concerned with a "higher sphere." According to Kautsky, virtually no other Jewish sectarians except for the Zealots were being executed at that time.[17]

Later, in *The Materialist Conception of History* (1927), Kautsky specifically critiqued Troeltsch's portrayal of Jesus as a religious innovator cut off from his Jewish roots by citing Jesus' own words:

> "Do not think that I have come to abolish the law or the prophets; I have come not to abolish but to fulfill. For truly I tell you, until heaven and earth pass away, not one letter, not one stroke of a letter, will pass from the law until all is accomplished." (Matt. 5: 17,18 NRSV)[18]

Troeltsch also disputed Kautsky's view that early Christian communism incorporated a principle of social equality (*Gleichheit*) and loosened traditional patriarchal family ties. On the contrary, Troeltsch found an ethic of "Christian patriarchalism" (*Typus des christlichen Patriarchalismus*) in the early churches that strengthened the institution of the family. Wives are ethically required to submit to their husbands, because this is part of the natural order (ST, 78, 81, 176n; GS1, 67, 71, 19n). The operative principle is that equality "in Christ" is not to be confused with social equality. In Troeltsch's words:

> As stewards of God the great must care for the small, and as servants of God the little ones must submit to those who bear authority; and, since in so doing both meet in the service of God, inner religious equality [*die innere religiöse Gleichheit*] is affirmed. (ST, 78; GS1, 68)

He therefore invokes the conservative ethic first described in "Political Ethics and Christianity"—"authority, not majority"—a far cry from Mommsen's call for active citizenship.

Indeed, Troeltsch uses a similar logic to argue for a transcendental "socialism." By locating socialism somewhere other than here on earth, Troeltsch is able to appropriate this popular word while continuing to espouse individualism. In the conclusion to *The Social Teaching*, he summarizes this theme:

> The Christian Ethos alone, through its conception of a Divine Love which embraces all souls and unites them all, possesses a Socialism which cannot be shaken.

It is only within the medium of the Divine that the separation and reserve, the strife and exclusiveness which belong to man as a natural product, and which shape his natural existence, disappear. Only here do the associations formed by compulsion, sympathy and need of help, sex instinct and attraction, work and organization attain a connection which transcends them all, a connection which is indestructible because it is metaphysical. (ST, 1005; GS1, 978)

Troeltsch argued that the concept of human equality derived not from Christian but from Stoic principles which inferred the principle of abstract equality for all based on reason. "Christianity will always instinctively fight shy of all ideas of equality [*alle Gleichheitsideen*]" (ST, 76; GS1, 65).

To underscore this principle of Christian inequality Troeltsch again invoked predestination, as he did in his 1904 essay. Following Ritschl and Harnack in their break with Baur, he did not place the Jesus movement within its Jewish context by referring to, for example, the Hebrew creation tradition of humankind being created in the image of God, the Exodus tradition of release of slaves from Egypt, the legal tradition of Jubilee involving radical redistribution of property, nor the radical prophetic tradition. Rather Troeltsch dismissed as unimportant this Jewish context of the Kingdom of God or Jesus' Messiahship: "We need not here discuss the question of the connection of these ideas with the Jewish law" (ST, 52; GS1, 36).

Furthermore, the "Jewish Decalogue" was "adopted as a summary of Christian ethics quite late in the history of the Church" as part of a Judaizing trend. This trend brought with it a "casuistry which weaves a complicated web of commandments...but which...is triumphantly broken through by all interior souls" (ST, 172n; GS1, 39n). This echoes the association of Judaism with materialism so prevalent during the Second Reich, as mentioned in chapter 2. It was certainly compatible with, if not directly linked to, the pervasive anti-Semitism of Troeltsch's own time and place, heightened during the 1880s when he was a university student, as we have seen above.

Breaking with the mainstream scholarship of the time, Kautsky, particularly in his 1908 study, interpreted early Christianity in light of its Jewish heritage.[19] According to Troeltsch himself, whenever the Jewish context of Christianity was taken into account, usually by sectarian groups, these groups would take on a revolutionary character:

Where, however, the idea [of Natural Law] is also directed against the unnatural and ungodly conditions within the State and Society, it develops into a democratic socialistic revolution, which does not shrink from violence, but justifies it by appealing to the Old Testament and to the Apocalypse. (ST, 345; GS1, 379–80)

It was not until after the Holocaust that Christian biblical scholars and theologians again took Jesus's Jewish heritage into serious consideration.[20] In this respect Kautsky anticipated contemporary Christian scholarship and theology.[21]

In his statement, "Christianity will always instinctively fight shy of all ideas of equality," Troeltsch was not merely describing one phase in the history of Christian teaching, but was prescribing the normative Christian social ideal (ST, 76; GS1, 65). As we saw earlier, this rejection of equality, which he also made explicit in "Political Ethics and Christianity," was in keeping with mainstream German academic values of his own time. After 1848, the German mandarins maintained a distance from the ideals of the French Revolution: freedom, equality and solidarity. Instead Germanic, feudal values of noblesse oblige and obedience to one's superiors were proudly upheld. Thus, in gazing at early Christianity Troeltsch saw mirrored there the values of his own class.

Troeltsch was able to find conservative social values of obedient servility and kindly lordship in the original Gospel message only by subordinating some parts of the New Testament to other parts. The books of Luke, James, and the Apocalypse of John which place stress on social justice were assigned an inferior status. Troeltsch also subordinated the ethics of Jesus to the ethics of Paul.

Troeltsch reinterpreted certain parts of these troublesome portions of the New Testament. For example, the preoccupation with the poor that plays a prominent role in the Gospel of Luke is not a concern for social justice. Rather, it has to do with "the ethico-religious effect of poverty in producing a better religious disposition" (ST, 170n; GS1, 28n). Troeltsch does not address the fact that the refrain running throughout the Gospel of Luke, that the last shall be first and the first, last—the theme of revolution—is also found in the other Gospels.

Examples of Troeltsch's canon within the canon could be multiplied. For example, his argument for a principle of Christian inequality overlooked sayings of Jesus found in both Mark and Matthew, such as the following:

> "You know that among the Gentiles those whom they recognize as their rulers lord it over them, and their great ones are tyrants over them. But it is not so among you; but whoever wishes to become great among you must be your servant, and whoever wishes to be first among you must be slave of all."[22]

According to Troeltsch, "the Apocalypse of John simply preaches hatred against the Roman Empire and against the worship of the Caesars, and pays no attention to social inequalities" (ST, 170–71n; GS1, 28n). It would appear that Troeltsch is here reading his own lack of attention to social inequalities back into the biblical text, since the Apocalypse equates the Roman Empire with the evils of ancient Babylon and insists on her judgment because "in you was found the blood of prophets" (NRSV; Rev. 18:24). Later her judgment is meted out by one whose "judgments are true and just...; he has avenged on her the blood of his servants" (NRSV; Rev. 19:2).

How did Troeltsch handle the Epistle of James with its passionate declamations against the rich who drag the poor into court? With an abrupt dismissal: "This [book] is the spirit of people with a narrow outlook." Troeltsch did not give serious alternative interpretations to such texts; instead, he resorted to ad hominem argumentation.

Waving aside the Synoptic Gospels, James and the Apocalypse, Troeltsch came back to the Gospel of John which, he insisted, knew nothing of social justice issues. "On this question the essentially religious idea stands in direct opposition to the 'spirit of small minds'" (ST, 171n; GS1, 28n). In dismissing the Synoptic Gospels, James and the Apocalypse of John as the "spirit of people with a narrow outlook" and the "spirit of small minds," the professorial disdain for things material again comes to the surface.

It was Paul, however, who provided the "canon within the canon" for Troeltsch. With Paul the apocalyptic expectations receded and the church was established along socially conservative lines. Troeltsch understood the Pauline social ethic to be the classical formulation of the Christian social ethic "right down to the beginning of the modern era." Troeltsch also did not view the ethic of love to be at the center of the Gospel ethic. With Paul,

> love of one's neighbor becomes...the principle of love in general, in praise of which Paul sang his famous hymn...; this love rests upon a religious individualistic foundation, and religious individualism is and remains the root idea. (ST, 70; GS1, 59)

As with the ethic of Jesus, Paul's ethic of love is subsumed under the overarching rubric of individualism.

Further, it was Paul who came to recognize the need to accommodate to the world as it is. He was the first "realist." He understood the necessity for compromise. Following Weber's typology of leadership, Troeltsch viewed Jesus as the charismatic leader who launched his movement through force of character. Jesus had a utopian vision of the

Kingdom. It was the realist, Paul, who routinized or institutionalized the charisma within the world. Paul was less idealistic, less inspiring, but he understood what giving permanence to the movement required. This distinction is compatible with the distinction that Weber later made between an ethic of ultimate ends versus an ethic of responsibility, the latter requiring compromise with the world as it is.[23]

Thus, Troeltsch disputes Kautsky's view that beginning with Paul the Christian movement began to undergo a process of internal corruption. Troeltsch writes:

> Further, however, we must admit (what Kautsky himself, owing to his conception of Christianity as a socialistic movement, cannot see) that the conservative religious attitude, which accepts the world-order as natural, and also the possession of private property as an integral part of it, and therefore the refusal of all revolution, is forced to give up communism. (ST, 176n; GS1, 71n)

Here Troeltsch himself explicitly identifies the fundamental presupposition at the basis of his debate with Kautsky: the belief that the "world-order" is simply a part of God-ordained nature rather than a product of social relations operating within history.[24] It follows from this presupposition that the status quo, including private property, is mandated by God, and that any revolutionary movement, particularly one that wishes to introduce socialism, is not. The "conservative" viewpoint to which Troeltsch refers is his own, as was seen in the discussion of Troeltsch's 1904 essay, "Political Ethics and Christianity" in chapter 10.

If it is true that the Gospel message did not address social living arrangements, Troeltsch is left without a motive for the early Christians' decision to live communally. Nor does he explain just how the institution of the family was strengthened under communal arrangements. These problems do not arise for Kautsky, who viewed communism as a constitutive part of early Christianity, and who welcomed the evidence that communism undermined the patriarchal family structure and promoted greater social equality.

While Troeltsch rejected Kautsky's explanation for the rise of early Christian communism, he did accept his explanation for its demise— its failure to address the problem of private ownership of the means of production. Troeltsch took what he wished from Kautsky to build his own argument for the natural primacy of private property and the individual within the original gospel message. Whereas Kautsky's interpretation of Christianity delegitimized the power structure of Imperial Germany, Troeltsch's religious individualism served the ideological needs of that power structure.[25]

Kautsky's extensive quotation of Chrysostom as further evidence of the authenticity of the communal tradition in Christianity likewise sparked a reply from Troeltsch. While admitting that Chrysostom's Homily XI on the Acts of the Apostles was "very remarkable," Troeltsch viewed its socialist character as more a reflection of the Ananias and Sapphira story on which it is partly based than of Chrysostom's own politics. He felt constrained to say that it was "a striking phenomenon" but hastened to add that "the Church gave no practical expression to these ideas at all."[26]

The Ideal Types of Church, Sect, and Mysticism

In *The Social Teaching*, Troeltsch accepts the concept of class as a social factor. However his typology of church, sect, and mysticism militates against the concept of class struggle as a political response to injustice. This typology views class inequality as a reflection of nature, rather than history. Troeltsch adopted the typology of church and sect from Max Weber; to this he added mysticism,[27] reflecting the influence of Paul de Lagarde.

Embedded in Troeltsch's typology are political presuppositions about the wisdom of accommodating to existing power relations and the futility of struggling to transform them. The church type is associated with "realistic" accommodation to the world as it is and as it must be. The sect type is characterized by a refusal to compromise and a commitment to "utopian" values. The mystical type is associated with the pursuit of pure inward experience (ST, 378–82; GS1, 422–26), which in theory should be equally compatible with church and sect. As will be explained below, however, Troeltsch gives his concept of mysticism a conservative twist by tending to conflate it with the church type.

Given this rubric, it is not surprising that Troeltsch strongly denounced Kautsky's interpretation of the rise of the medieval clergy as the rise of a new ruling class. Kautsky's analysis, he wrote, is "amazingly meagre and a travesty of the real facts; all that is right is his statement that the ethic of the Church is certainly connected with a natural economy" (ST, 399n; GS1, 248n). Although Troeltsch gave recognition to the economic context, even to the fact that a new class did come into being after the time of Constantine, he did not attempt to show how these factors shaped social relations. (ST, 138–42; GS1, 139–43). Also in contrast to Kautsky, he gave no recognition to class division occurring *within* the churches. Nor did he address Kautsky's observation of how the natural economy, which limited the possibilities for accumulation of wealth, led to extensive works of charity. I will return to the issue of private charity below.

Troeltsch also took strong exception to Kautsky's interpretation of the Reformers, in particular to Luther:

> To [Kautsky] Luther is an agitator who provides a religious sanction for the communistic-democratic opposition, and an unprincipled courtier who supplies a religious sanction for the rising absolutism; his great influence is supposed to be due to this dual position. The real hero of the Reformation is Thomas Münzer, who did not possess Luther's second detestable characteristic. Reasons for these statements are not given in this superficial sketch, which is entirely lacking in understanding. (ST, 821n; GS1, 433n)

Kautsky is said to entirely lack understanding because his fundamental presuppositions are different, as we have seen. Once social justice issues are viewed as essential to the Christian ethic, Luther's stature might well be diminished and Münzer's increased. But as we have seen, Troeltsch does not include these issues in the core of Christian ethics.

In the conclusion to his work Troeltsch emphasized that he interpreted the great personalities of church history as having specifically religious rather than social or economic motivations. It is supposed that they transcended their historical context of class and economic pressures. On the other hand, however (and for Troeltsch there is often an "other hand"), the economic factors are "co-operating elements" that lend "causal connections." In other words, social and economic factors can be added secondarily, but not in such a way as to disturb Troeltsch's idealist framework (ST, 1002; GS1, 975).

Thus, Troeltsch by his own admission is concerned to portray Luther and the other major figures of Christianity as shaped primarily by their inner religious life. They are shaped by history to the extent that they must accommodate to social reality, but this influence is not constitutive of who they are.

Kautsky later specifically criticized Troeltsch's portrayal of Luther as governed, like Jesus, primarily by inner "illumination." Kautsky argued that:

> Luther is anything but unique.... The number of his precursors is great, and no less great is the number of his contemporaries who were active to the same end as he was. The agreement among them becomes explicable if it is traced back to the new impulses and conditions of the environment they all lived in.[28]

In other words, as discussed in chapter 4, Kautsky preferred to emphasize the importance of social conditions and earlier cultural traditions in the shaping of leaders such as Jesus and Luther.

Despite his insistence that Kautsky's class-based analysis is "entirely lacking in understanding," Troeltsch not only referred to class as a social factor, but was actually much indebted to it. Kautsky used class struggle to explain what occurred between the dissenting and dominant groups in church history, linking the dissenters with the ethic of communal love found in the early church. Similarly, Troeltsch found class to be a decisive factor distinguishing the church and sect types. He admitted that the church type was dominated by the ruling classes and controlled from the top down. The sect type was comprised of disempowered elements of society, the working classes, and controlled from the bottom up:

> The fully developed church, however, utilizes the State and the ruling classes and...from this standpoint the Church both stabilizes and determines the social order; in so doing, however, she becomes dependent upon the upper classes, and upon their development. The sects, on the other hand, are connected with the lower classes, or at least with those elements in Society which are opposed to the State and the Society; they work upwards from below, and not downwards from above. (ST, 331; GS1, 362)

Thus, Troeltsch proposed a class analysis substantially similar to Kautsky's.

While agreeing on the importance of class, however, the two thinkers interpreted it very differently and had very different attitudes towards economic inequality. For Troeltsch, class differences derived not from history but from nature and were therefore to be accepted, as we have seen. This presupposition leads to his double morality, one for those ordained to positions of authority and one for those called to serve. For Kautsky the class structure represents the domination and exploitation of one group by another, such that the exploited group drives forward a historical process oriented to abolishing domination, and hence of the class system itself.

This fundamental difference surfaced in the way both thinkers described the sectarians, for example, who often claimed to be recovering the original gospel ethic. Troeltsch interpreted such claims in light of his view that Jesus had no social ethic because he was indifferent to the problems of a world he believed was about to pass away. Arguing that the classical ethic of Christianity derived from Paul, Troeltsch viewed any attempt to recover a social ethic from Jesus as primitive, unhistorical and impractical:

> Finally, like all dreamers and primitive folk (who lack the practical and the historical sense), they [the sectarians] believed in the possibility of reforming Christian Society from within outwards, shaping it according to their own ideal, and according to that which had been laid down in Scripture. (ST, 353; GS1, 388)

Thus, *The Social Teaching* stressed the continuity of development between Rome, Wittenburg, and Geneva. Jerusalem was left out of the equation, since it represented for Troeltsch an immature "sect" stage of Christianity that was quickly outgrown. While sects reappeared throughout the history of Christianity, the "church" type remained the realistic option. We turn now to Troeltsch's examination of this church type in its Roman Catholic and Protestant variants.

The Roman Catholic Church

Only with the rise of medieval Catholicism did Christians begin to think of their faith as addressing social structures in terms of a uniform social philosophy, according to Troeltsch. We have seen how he interpreted the early church as disconnected from larger social structures. Christian social ethics began when the church fathers, drawing upon Paul and Stoicism, invoked natural law to interpret secular structures as a divinely ordained part of a fallen yet natural order. Patriarchy, violence, law, capital punishment, war, private property and trade defaced the ideal society. Yet these features had to be endured as penalty and discipline for sin (ST, 280–81; GS1, 286). Such a view led to both condemnation of, and resignation to, the status quo.

This somewhat ambivalent posture is captured in Augustine's philosophy, Troeltsch continued. On the one hand he described an ascending series of goals with earthly acts performed for heavenly objectives. Yet with his emphasis on sin and predestination, Augustine radically rejected and condemned earthly social structures. Nor did he put anything else in their place (ST, 282; GS1, 289–90).

Only with Thomas Aquinas was a comprehensive Christian social philosophy formulated, argued Troeltsch. It began with affirming the possibility of a Christian society that could be universal. A new interpretation of natural law minimized the difference between the absolute Primitive State and the relative state of fallen human nature. More emphasis is placed on the prospect for healing and for progress towards a higher ideal than on devolution and punishment. Natural law is no longer equated with a state of original sinless perfection, but rather with a process leading gradually to the mystical community of grace.

Here Thomas invokes Aristotle's idea of evolution as the working out of natural reason (ST, 282–83; GS1, 290–94).

This new medieval synthesis was consistent with earlier Christian attitudes towards society. Whereas the status quo had been passively accepted as part of the "fallen order," now it was accepted as merely "lower" rather than "fallen." As with all church-types, Thomas built upon Paul's ideas of the church as an organism and as patriarchal (ST, 285; GS1, 296–97).

In contrast to Kautsky, Troeltsch could not emphasize enough the centrality of patriarchy, from the inception of Christianity to the medieval church:

> From the very beginning, in the ethic of the Primitive Church, the original model of all social relationships was that of the domination of the husband within the family over wife and children, and the willing subordination of the members of the family, as well as of the servants, to the authority of the housefather. (ST, 286)

> The ideal of the family in the Middle Ages remained the same(ST, 287).... In this respect all that Christianity did was to modify from within this idea of male domination by its teaching about love and good will...; externally, however, it permitted the conditions of authority and subordination to continue as they were before, although with important and increasing security for the individual personality of women, children and servants. (ST, 286–87; GS1, 299–300)

Thus, as he went on to elaborate, "the patriarchalism of natural authority gives place to the patriarchalism of love [*der Liebespatriarchalismus*]" (ST, 287; GS1, 300). In other words, early Christianity did not at all challenge the patriarchal family model through its communal relationships, as Kautsky claimed. Rather Christianity accepted the patriarchal order and simply tried to make it more benevolent. The idea of the patriarchal family is then generalized to all of society:

> This sociological ideal of the Family as the original ideal of human relationships is applied to all the conditions of rule and subordination in general. Repeatedly we are reminded that Christendom is a great family. (ST, 287; GS1, 300)

Troeltsch's view of patriarchy as universal and part of the core Christian teaching had the effect of delegitimizing the women's suffrage movement of his own day.[29]

Similarly, Troeltsch views the communal traditions within Catholicism to be essentially innovations, rather than expressions of core Christian teaching. The religious orders placed a new emphasis upon communal arrangements, eclipsing the fundamental Christian values of individualism and private property, he claimed (ST, 290; GS1, 306–7).

Even within Catholicism the communist tendencies are not decisive. The centrality of patriarchy provided a "conservative, stabilizing aspect." People were encouraged to remain in their place within a "cosmos of callings" and serve others cheerfully and selflessly (ST 293f.; GS1, 311). Although Catholicism permitted revolution in the case of a tyrannical king, the Pope held absolute power (ST, 289; GS1, 305). Therefore, in general, Catholic social teaching was conservative. It led to quietism, not social reform (ST, 296; GS1, 313). It represented the pure church type (ST, 461; GS1, 427).

Troeltsch could not end his section on medieval Christianity, however, without commenting on Roman Catholicism's economic doctrines and hopes for social reform in his own day. This included putting restraints on financial speculation and restructuring the property relations of capital, so as to give workers a share in ownership. In this context, Troeltsch tried to minimize Thomas' condemnation of lending with interest by arguing that it referred in the first instance to usury, and that interest, with certain restrictions, would be tolerated. (ST, 320; 428–29; GS1, 346–48).

The Protestant Churches

Troeltsch defined Protestantism as embodying only the groups that fit the church type. "[Protestantism] rejects the sect-type as the tendency towards legalism and loveless division" (ST, 512; GS1, 507). Therefore, the Baptists, Mennonites, Pietists and Quakers, for example, are not truly Protestant. He then concluded: "This rejection of the sect-type led Protestantism to an ever-increasing recognition of the life of the world and of the morality of the world" (ST, 512; GS1, 507). By defining Protestantism in this way, Troeltsch virtually equates it with the state churches of northwestern Europe. While he refers to dissent from these as "loveless division," he does not apply this description to the dissent by Protestantism as a whole from Roman Catholicism.

Having so defined Protestantism, Troeltsch then gives a general description of how its social teachings evolved from medieval Catholicism. It's emphasis on patriarchy, classes and callings, for example, is indebted to Aquinas' social philosophy. Reflecting a pessimism about the individual's capacity for absolute holiness, however, Protestantism applied a single moral standard to all social and occupational groups.

Protestantism also stressed interiority over law.[30] (ST, 512; GS1, 508). Here Troeltsch's understanding of the Biblical legacy including the message of Jesus is informed by neo-Kantian concepts such as "pure spiritual freedom" (ST, 513; GS1, 508). But he admitted that the link between this gospel of the inner life and the conception of the church as the objective instrument of redemption for a Christian society remained elusive. "The Protestant solution of the difficulty in the dualistic ethic of a 'personal' and an 'official' kind is no solution; it is simply a new formulation of the problem" (ST, 513; GS1, 509).

Protestantism's equal moral demand on all alike brought a renewed emphasis on individualism. Nevertheless, because this individualism is maintained within the context of the church as the objective instrument of grace, "the social teaching of Protestantism is much nearer to Catholic social doctrine than to that of the sect-type" (ST, 513; GS1, 511). In other words, according to Troeltsch, the great divide within western Christendom lay not between Protestant and Catholic but between church and sect.

While there was much continuity between medieval Catholicism and the Lutheran church for Troeltsch, an important development occurred: the newly emerging nation state gained ascendancy over the nationalized churches. In principle, the Lutheran church was no longer ruled by the Papacy but rather "was ruled by Christ and by the Word; in practice, it was governed by the ruling princes and the pastors" (ST, 520; GS1, 518). The separation of church and state, of sacred and secular did not yet exist. Civil authority and religious authority were two different aspects of a single Christian society (ST, 522; GS1, 523).

The Catholic notion of an orderly succession of ascending steps from nature to grace is replaced by the immanence of God's love in the world; therefore, there occurred a sanctification of the existing order (ST, 528; GS1, 531). The State became truly divine.[31] (ST, 548; GS1, 561). In effect, the authority that the one universal church irrevocably lost with its division into national Protestant movements is reinvested in the nation state.

In Luther's Catechism, the centrality of patriarchy and the Catholic view of society as an organism are united in absolute patriarchy (ST, 541; GS1, 551). As in Catholicism, patriarchy and the family remain central as a model for all society. The Prince simply took over the duties of Pope as the ultimate earthly Father (ST, 542; GS1, 552).

Informing the Prussian-German Restoration of the nineteenth century, these teachings legitimized Prussian conservatism, Troeltsch declared. "[Lutheran social theory] became a weapon in the hands of a ruling class and produced that blend of masculine hardness and class-conscious ruthlessness which distinguishes modern Lutheranism from the older kind" (ST, 544; GS1, 555).

A split between private and public morality also occurred in Lutheranism. This legitimized the use of force by the state, even though violence was opposed to the Christian spirit of love (ST, 548; GS1, 561). However, Luther's teaching limited war to defensive purposes and excluded all ideas of holy war or crusades. Religious causes merit only spiritual weapons (ST, 550; GS1, 563). At this point, Troeltsch pauses from his description to criticize Luther from the right:

> It is easy to see what a disastrous effect this kind of outlook [defensive war only] would have upon Lutheranism in the political sphere, and although the Lutheran princes, diplomats and jurists, and later on even Luther himself, did not bind themselves to follow this policy, it was still everywhere a dangerous drag on Lutheran politics; it determined the expansion and fate of Lutheranism, which was unable to extend beyond the land of its birth. What a contrast was presented by Calvinist politics, with their treaties and alliances and their Wars of Religion. (ST, 551; GS1, 563–64)

Thus, Troeltsch criticized the Lutheran rejection of imperial uses of force as "a dangerous drag on Lutheran politics." The "disastrous effect" of this policy was the inhibition of the Lutheran countries' colonial expansion. He specifically cited the Calvinist churches as wise enough to strengthen and build their movements through such colonial expansion.[32]

Troeltsch's colonialism largely reflected the era of European and American colonialism in which he lived. Such policies became even more attractive for Imperial Germany with the discovery of diamond and copper mines in the German African colonies.

It should be noted, however, that colonialism was controversial in German politics when Troeltsch was writing *The Social Teaching*. At that time, Catholic Center Party leader Matthias Erzberger was attacking the Second Reich's colonial policy for its brutality toward indigenous peoples. As discussed earlier, the Social Democratic and Center Parties both opposed the coalition of conservative and liberal parties that supported Chancellor Bülow's expansionist agenda.

In his essay "Social Democracy and the Catholic Church," Kautsky was deeply critical of colonialism, viewing it as capitalist greed in search of new markets and raw materials. Troeltsch's approval of colonial imperialism, articulated as a critique of Luther's defensive war position, served to support his procolonial position in the foreign policy debate of his own time.

Troeltsch also critiqued the Lutheran teaching on economics as "thoroughly reactionary," because it accepted the Catholic doctrine against usury and accumulation of capital. It did not involve a work ethic to nearly the same degree as Calvinism nor did it foster competition between individuals (ST, 554–57; GS1, 571–80). "Luther waged war not only on the forms of early capitalism" but also "against the new principle itself." Luther entirely opposed the "egotism and worldly self-confidence which are implied in all desire to possess property at all" (ST, 558; GS1, 576–77). Although socialists of his own day could agree with this critique of possessive individualism,[33] Troeltsch found it "reactionary," because it undermined the legitimacy of emergent capitalism.

To what extent did Lutheranism attempt to reform society? After the time of Luther, Troeltsch argued, the church became increasingly passive with respect to questions of reform (ST, 563–64; GS1, 585–86). Particularly during and after the Peasants' War, Luther himself took a conservative turn and carved out his "two kingdom" theory to justify two exclusive spheres of responsibility. Social issues were the legitimate concern of the state alone; the church was to be concerned only with spiritual issues (ST, 565; GS1, 587–88).

Church charity continued for the Lutherans as it had for the Catholics, but with greatly diminished means of implementation (ST, 566; GS1, 588). Social welfare now belonged to the province of the state (ST, 567; GS1, 589). We shall see below that Troeltsch himself favored a strict policy of private charity as opposed to state welfare. Yet Lutheranism legitimated public welfare policies precisely because of the church—state distinction that it emphasized. As we have seen, certain Lutheran pastors in Troeltsch's own day had joined the Social Democratic Party, much to Troeltsch's chagrin.

Lutheranism was therefore capable of being Janus-faced with respect to political alliances, making common cause with feudal elements on the one hand, and social democratic elements on the other. Rejecting both, Troeltsch in his 1904 essay attributed "egotism" to feudal aristocrats and social democrats alike. In that same essay, however, he advocated coalition with the feudal elements in German politics, while rejecting coalition with the socialists. In this context, and in view of his criticism from the right of the Lutheran doctrine of defensive war, it would appear that Troeltsch found the socialist potentialities of Lutheranism more problematic than its conservatism.

At the conclusion of his treatment of Lutheranism Troeltsch leaped ahead through the centuries to sketch the rise of several nineteenth-century Lutheran social movements including Wichern's Inner Mission, the Christian socialists of the Naumann persuasion and the Evangelical Social Congress (ST, 567–68; GS1, 589–94). The dominant form of Lutheranism of his own time, however, was still that of the feudal Conservative party which took Stahl's position: "that the social order should be entrusted to a Christian government, whose duty it should be to ensure the maintenance of the class organization of callings" (ST, 568; GS1, 590).

In summary, Troeltsch viewed Protestantism as collapsing the moral double standard of Catholicism with respect to clergy and laity. But he agreed with Stahl's view that it actively maintained separate ethical standards for the ruling and subservient classes. Troeltsch's critique of Lutheranism centered on its resistance to the bourgeois revolution sweeping Western Europe and its failure to accommodate to European colonial expansion.

In his discussion of Lutheranism, Troeltsch touches upon Kautsky's analysis of corruption of the church by a ruling class. He raises Kautsky's question: "to what extent are these social doctrines the reflection of existing political and social conditions?" But unlike Kautsky, he emphatically rejects such an analysis: "So far as the actual ideal is concerned which floated before the minds of Lutheran thinkers, we must give a directly negative reply to this question" (ST, 569; GS1, 594).

In other words, the ideal underlying Lutheran social theory was not shaped by contemporary social forces such as the rise of the modern nation state. Rather, Troeltsch argued, this ideal marked the renewal of the original teaching of the early Church with its purported indifference to "the world with its law, property, might, and force" (ST, 569; GS1, 594). This use of the word "world" presupposes that social relations of domination are simply part of the natural order, rather than an object of historical struggle.

Troeltsch grants that the social environment did play a role, insofar as Protestantism accommodated to social realities:

> To a far greater extent than Catholicism, certainly, Protestantism has accepted the life of the world, and it is therefore similarly determined by the spirit of general social development, which forced itself upon the attention of the Church. (ST, 569; GS1, 594)

On one level then, acceptance of the status quo by the Protestant churches is inevitable. Having said that, however, Troeltsch returns to his theme of the social independence of the Christian ideal:

In so doing, however, Protestantism has carefully preserved the dualism of the Christian ideal which arises out of this conception, and which, in contrast with Catholicism, it has both deepened and intensified. (ST, 569; GS1, 594–95)

He then reinforces his argument for the social independence of the Christian ideal with reference to the social continuity between the Catholic and Protestant worlds:

Since Protestantism supported the mediaeval ideal of a social hierarchy and the anti-capitalistic spirit, expressed in agrarian and middle-class ways of living, along with a patriarchalism based on authority and reverence, as the right way of reconciling both sides, it drew its conclusions from the ethical and religious ideal, and not from the circumstances which happened to prevail at the time. (ST, 569; GS1, 595)

By emphasizing the continuity of the social context of Catholicism and Protestantism, Troeltsch argues that the ethical and religious differences between them stemmed from Protestantism's return to the classical Christian ideal, rather than its adaptation to new social circumstances. In his desire to emphasize continuity, he fails to develop and draw out the implications of his earlier reference to the relationship between Protestantism and the emerging nation state.

In summary, Protestantism generally reconciles "the life of the world" with "the ethical and religious ideal" on the basis of the ideal's own conservatism. To be sure, Protestant reconciliation with the world sometimes takes a more corrupt form:

Whenever the social doctrines of Lutheranism are treated solely as the religious sanction of the existing situation, as often happens in orthodox Lutheranism, this always means that Lutheran thought has been weakened and *despiritualized*; the main impulse of the real Lutheran ethic in its *mystics* and *spiritual thinkers*, in its ethical reformers, and finally in the *Pietists*, has always reacted against this tendency with great vigour. (Emphasis mine; ST, 570; GS1, 595)

In other words, Christianity's legitimation of state power is sometimes problematic, but in such instances the churches have abdicated their authentic spiritual mission. In most instances, however, this legitimizing role is not problematic, because it is authentically motivated by Christianity's own conservative values.

For Kautsky, the churches' function in legitimizing unequal relations of power fundamentally calls into question the authenticity of the Christian message. Troeltsch responds by invoking the "dualism of the Christian ideal" reflected in Luther's two-kingdom theory. If the primary objective of Christianity is the mystical development of souls, then its legitimation of existing power structures becomes peripheral. Moreover, Troeltsch implicitly endorses this ethical position by viewing it as an accommodation to "reality" itself.

Seeing this "realism" in the original Christian ideal, and viewing Protestantism as a return to that ideal, Troeltsch felt methodologically justified in leaping through centuries with little or no transition in thought when describing Lutheranism or any of the other major denominations. Despite his claim to being historical, he repeatedly argued that the religious and ethical ideal transcends the flux of time.

As I have discussed throughout this book, the reader of Troeltsch cannot make sense of this contradiction except in the context of his debate with Marxism. "The religious and ethical ideas of Lutheranism," he argues, "are not a glorification and intensification of definite class and power interests by means of a world outlook based upon those interests" (ST, 570; GS1, 596). Furthermore, Luther made his peace with the German princes

> not in any kind of class interest, but in the authoritative conservative temperament of Luther himself, and in his peculiarly penetrating conception of the nature of authority and power, as well as the essential inequality [*der wesenhaften Ungleichheit*] of the fundamental elements in all human social groups. (ST, 570; GS1, 596).

Reference here to "the essential inequality" of all human society recalls Troeltsch's invocation of conservative ideology in his 1904 essay, as discussed in chapter ten. In that essay and in *The Social Teaching*, the inequality allegedly inherent in society is cited to justify the conservative call for "authority, not majority." This would appear to be a polemical reply to Kautsky's critique of social inequality.

Troeltsch's account of Lutheranism can therefore be summarized as follows: through embracing the patriarchal model of the family, Lutheranism stood in continuity with Catholicism. Both churches were socially conservative, but in its acceptance of the state, Lutheranism was more worldly than Catholicism. To be sure, Lutheranism was unduly passive with respect to waging religious warfare, and it did not accommodate well to capitalism. More importantly, however, it recovered the dualism of the classical Christian ideal. In its two-kingdom theory, Lutheranism returned to the original Gospel emphasis on the spiritual development of souls, Jesus's indifference to the affairs of this world, and Paul's realistic accommodationism.

In Calvinism, Troeltsch found a church ideology that was expansionist and that did not shy away from using force if necessary to achieving its ends. It attempted to exert more control over the state and was much more affirming of capitalism and private property. Again, Troeltsch insisted that the characteristic features of this religion came about independently of social factors such as the rise of capitalism. On the contrary, Calvinism had the capacity "to penetrate the political and economic movements of Western nations with its religious ideal," a quality Lutheranism did not have (ST, 577; GS1, 605). Calvinism produced a political and social way of life called 'Americanism' which today has lost its religious origins, (ST, 577; GS1, 607) as Max Weber observed.[34]

In keeping with Troeltsch's emphasis on the independence of religion, Calvinist ideology is described as self-shaping. An offshoot of Lutheranism, its distinctiveness centers on a different image of God. Luther's loving and merciful Father became for Calvin the absolute, sovereign, majestic Lord who in arbitrary freedom stood above conceptions of justice and law. The human being became "the creature, in its misery" (*die elende Kreatur*) who had no ontological claim to justice because "it" deserved none (ST, 582; GS1, 615).

This sovereign Lord created the "creature" and "law" to glorify himself. Indeed, all else was created by "the inscrutable Will of God" merely as instruments to reflect the glory of God. With emphasis on predestination, "God ordained the sin of Adam." This would imply that God is also the author of evil as we conceive of it, again, for his own glory (ST, 582; GS1, 616).

The problem of theodicy is thus solved by subordinating it to the awesome glory of God. "To Calvin the chief point is not the self-centred personal salvation of the creature, and the universality of the Divine Will of Love, but it is the Glory of God" (ST, 583; GS1, 616). In other words, God and God alone is the subject of history.

Human beings and the earth are bereft of subjecthood and reduced to the status of instruments, pawns of an inscrutable Will. "As an elect person the individual has no value of his own, but as an instrument, to be used for the tasks of the Kingdom of God, his value is immense" (ST, 589; GS1, 623). "Immense" perhaps, but purely derivative, not inherent in being human. By no stretch of the imagination could Calvin be compared to the Christian humanists like Thomas More or Erasmus. Human beings and the planet are objectified and instrumentalized.

Troeltsch considered Calvin's theological sources to derive only indirectly from Paul and to include also the ideology and policies of Israelite kings, the Decalogue, King David, and the Psalms. Reflecting his own canon-within-the-canon, however, Troeltsch interpreted Calvin as neglecting the prophetic books and the radical part of the Mosaic legacy (ST, 583, 600; GS1, 317, 637).

Calvin's inscrutable Lord "elected" some persons to "become Christ's warriors and champions, subjects in his Kingdom" (ST, 584; GS1, 618). Proof of their conferred status did not consist in contemplation of the *Unio mystica* as in Lutheranism, but rather in energetic action. The goal was to "mold" the world for Christ (ST, 589; GS1, 623).

Does Troeltsch find "individualism" surfacing in Calvinism? In a way, yes:

> This individualism differs not only from Catholic and Lutheran individualism, but also from the optimistic, rationalistic individualism of the Enlightenment. Founded upon a crushing sense of sin, and a pessimistic condemnation of the world, without colour or emotional satisfaction, it is an individualism based upon the certainty of election, the sense of responsibility and of the obligation to render personal service under the Lordship of Christ (590). It finds its expression in the thoughtful and self-conscious type of Calvinistic piety, in the systematic spirit of self-control, and in its independence of all that is "creaturely." *The value of the individual depends wholly upon the merciful grace of election*, and it may give honour to none save God alone. This leads to the result that against a background of the severest self-condemnation there stands out in clear relief in Calvinism the sense of being a *spiritual aristocracy*; this produces a detached and aloof manner of handling all that is secular and creaturely, solely with reference to their secular purposes, which extends into all merely secular and natural personal relationships. (Emphasis mine. ST, 589–90; GS1, 623–24)

While he is critical of Lutheranism, Troeltsch is relatively comfortable with Calvinism, with its "active" element that caused people to build colonial empires. Indeed, the Calvinist doctrines of predestination and redemption are easily reconciled with his conservative political ethic, as discussed in chapter 10.

Troeltsch emphasized that Calvinism did not rest upon the ethic found in the Sermon on the Mount. Unlike Catholicism or Lutheranism, Calvin saw no need to balance the claims of Jesus with the claims of the world. For him the glory of God outweighed the claims of neighbor love (ST, 599; GS1, 636). There is no relationality in this ethic or in the image of God that accompanied it. God is the subject and end of history—a despot above law; humans are the pawns.

Although his description supports this authoritarian picture, Troeltsch himself gives it a more positive spin:

> Wholly instinctively, and with piercing insight, Calvin singles out of the Christian morality of love the religious element of activity for the glory of God, and of

sanctification for God and for His Purpose, which has always distinguished Calvinism from any mere sentimentality and humanitarianism. (ST, 599; GS1, 636)

Troeltsch's rejection of "sentimentality and humanitarianism," it should
be noted, is consistent with his support for the Second Reich's policies
of colonial expansion abroad and suppression of civil liberties at home,
as we shall see below.

Finally, Troeltsch took up the issue that Calvinism led "to a kind of
'Christian socialism.'" (ST, 602; GS1, 642). Accepting Weber's view
that Calvinism was particularly compatible with capitalism (ST, 645f.;
GS1, 715f.), and given his own description of Calvinism's low anthropology, his term "socialism" in this context took on a special meaning.

Troeltsch was apparently referring to efforts of the Calvinist theoc-
racies to promote social justice within the framework of emerging capitalist institutions. This "ecclesiastical Socialism gave way certainly to
the pressure of modern political and social developments. When, however, the technical and social effects of these developments revealed
their dubious tendency, once again it was Calvinism which came forward with a new 'Christian Socialism,' adjusted to modern conditions,
yet still bearing traces of the Puritan spirit" (ST, 623; GS1, 677–78).
This modern version of Calvinist "socialism" apparently refers to the
social outreach efforts of the Reformed churches of his own time, including the work of the Evangelical Social Congress.

By "socialism" in this context, Troeltsch meant the view that "the
Church ought to be interested in all sides of life" (ST, 602; GS1, 642).
This definition is so elastic as to be virtually meaningless, particularly
when Calvinism involved active support of capitalist structures. While
intellectually dubious, however, Troeltsch's definition enabled him to
co-opt the popular term "socialist" on behalf of organized religion. In
effect, Troeltsch was saying that Social Democracy is not necessary; socialism is already being implemented in the form of Christian socialism.

In conclusion, the three major manifestations of the church type were
Catholicism, Lutheranism, and Calvinism. All three were governed from
the top down by the ruling classes and came to terms with the world as
they found it. Although, Troeltsch emphatically rejected a Marxist analysis, he nevertheless viewed the greatest division within Western
Christendom to fall not among these three church bodies, but between
them and the sect movements of disempowered peoples who kept rising in rebellion.

Indeed, the one issue that the established churches of Troeltsch's
own time agreed upon was the need to address the Social Problem, that

is, to combat socialism. While he appropriates the word "socialism" in an imprecise way to designate a certain tendency within Calvinism, he classified Christian socialists like Leonhard Ragaz as "aggressive sectarians," as will be discussed below.

The Sects

Did not the presence of the sects lend evidence to Kautsky's analysis of class struggle within Christendom? No, Troeltsch insisted, because the sects were not legitimate expressions of the true gospel message.[35] While he did acknowledge a correlation between class and the church/sect dimension, he views this dimension as more fundamentally reflecting the difference between realists and dreamers—those who were capable of adapting to the world and those who were not.

At one point Troeltsch admitted that the word "sect" was originally "used in a polemical and apologetic sense, and it was used to describe groups which separated themselves from the official Church, while they retained certain fundamental elements of Christian thought" (ST, 333; GS1, 367). Nevertheless, he appropriated this loaded term in his own typology and did not address the question of whether such terminology would compromise his ostensibly scientific purposes. No less an authority than Weber had set the precedent for using "sect" as an ideal type.

Consequently, the most varied groups fell under the rubric of "sectarian," groups that had little more in common than the fact that they were of the lower classes and marginalized from the mainstream of society. Some like the Moravian Brethren were inclined to withdraw from secular life and assume an otherworldly orientation. Others like the Christian socialists wanted to realize the Kingdom of God on earth. Groups like the Mennonites were pacifist, while the Taborites espoused armed revolution (ST, 371; GS1, 412). Troeltsch believed that the teaching of Jesus anticipated that of the Moravian Brethren more than that of the Taborites or other "aggressive sectarians" such as the modern Christian socialists (ST, 371, 802–3; GS1, 412–13, 942–43). But the social ethic he felt they all had in common was the following:

> [It] is expressed in the refusal to use the law, to swear in a court of justice, to own property, to exercise dominion over others, or to take part in war. The sects take the Sermon on the Mount as their ideal; they lay stress on the simple but radical opposition of the Kingdom of God to all secular interests and institutions. They practise renunciation only as a means of charity, as the basis of a thorough-going communism of love. (ST, 332; GS1, 363)

The Waldensians and many other sects believed that the fundamental idea of the gospel was the equality of believers, including women (ST, 354–55; GS1, 389). Troeltsch accepted Kautsky's observation that the social base of the Waldensians was the subculture of weavers in the woolen industry where ideas for social reform flourished. Nevertheless, they too numbered among the "dreamers and primitive folk" of Troeltsch's world of sects.

In his description of the sect type, Troeltsch regarded the recessive tendency to be the socialist transformation of the world, and the dominant tendency, the anarchistic withdrawal from the world. This is compatible with Kautsky's analysis. In today's concepts, one could think of the socialist/anarchist alternative as the social equivalent of the psychological fight-or-flight response. One understandable though somewhat alienated way for oppressed peoples to react to their condition is social withdrawal. It is this apolitical response to oppression that Troeltsch prefers to dignify with the weight of historical precedent within Christendom traceable to Jesus himself.

The socialist option involves oppressed peoples forming alternative social structures that would have the potential to challenge the established structures. This alternative approach was preferred among certain sectarian movements which Troeltsch labels "aggressive sectarians." It is this activist tradition that Kautsky claimed could be traced to the original Jesus movement. This, of course, Troeltsch vigorously denied, as we have seen; to admit that this form of sectarianism had its precursor in the Jesus movement would be to give far too much legitimacy to activist pastors, with their ties to the Social Democratic party.

However, Troeltsch did acknowledge that the activist form of sectarianism had deep roots in the history of Christendom. In *The Social Teaching* he surveys the teachings of a wide variety of sectarian groups, in particular, those spawned by the Reformation. We will look briefly at a representative sect from the socialist as well as the anarchist alternatives before moving to his treatment of modern Christian socialism.

The Anabaptist movement broke out in Zurich in 1525 mostly among members of the lower classes:

> [Its] principles were in close agreement with the democratic tendencies of the masses; primarily it was recruited from the ranks of the manual labourers, miners, and similar groups. (ST, 703; GS1, 812)

Their principles included living apart from the world which was considered to be the dominion of the devil and the domain of suffering.

There was also the refusal to hold public office, to swear an oath in a court of law, to engage in warfare, violence or use capital punishment (ST, 696; GS1, 803). Membership was comprised of truly converted believers and symbolized by adult baptism. The sacramental system was replaced by a simple worship service centered around the reading and interpretation of Scripture.

Clergy were ordained through the laying on of hands by local synods that arose "from the bottom up." The clergy were generally "tent-makers" in the manner of the apostle Paul; that is, volunteers who earned their living at a secular occupation. Generally, they were educated and from a more privileged strata of society than the people they served, although they tried to be sensitive to the democratic tendencies of their people. The Anabaptists advocated strict separation of church and state. In sum, they tried to abide by the precepts of the Sermon on the Mount (ST, 695–707; GS1, 797–809). In Troeltsch's mind they embodied an "extreme idealism" (ST, 697; GS1, 806).

This movement spread like wildfire and soon all of Central Europe was covered with a network of Anabaptist communities. Chief centers were located in Troeltsch's hometown of Augsburg, Moravia, Strassburg and later, Friesland and the Netherlands (ST, 704; GS1, 813).

Harsh, violent persecution followed from the official churches which viewed the movement as a fundamental threat to the structures of society. They could see in it "nothing less than the destruction of the very basis of society itself" (ST, 704; GS1, 813). One might well imagine the reaction of the great banking families of Augsburg, for example. Anabaptist leaders were tortured and burned at the stake. Their people were persecuted "with savage cruelty." This persecution fed apocalyptic tendencies leading finally to the revolt in Münster where it was believed that the New Jerusalem could be established. In Troeltsch's words:

> This terrible pressure of persecution then drove the Baptist communities into an excited Revivalism and Chiliasm, and thus some fanatics in the Netherlands…came to the conclusion that the Last Days were at hand, and that they were justified in attempting to set up the Heavenly Jerusalem by force. They based their argument upon the example of the Old Testament and the Apocalypse. This led to the horrors of Münster, which was a disaster for the whole movement, and only made their persecutors feel still more sure that their oppressive attitude was justifiable and right. (ST, 705; GS1, 814)

Apparently the "horrors of Münster" were not the fact that Anabaptists were tortured and killed there; after all, that was happening all over Europe. Rather what was unique to Münster was the fact that they succeeded in wresting control of the city, the seat of a bishopric, from the established authorities and establishing their own government—that is, until the ousted bishop came back with reinforcements, lay siege and savagely regained it.

The real fear was that the Anabaptist movement was providing impetus to the peasant rebellions. Thus, the "horrors of Münster" reflect Troeltsch's own fear of revolution, no doubt heightened by the threat of social democracy in his day. As another center of the Anabaptists during the sixteenth century, his own hometown of Augsburg probably experienced unprecedented grassroots rebellion, which was perhaps recounted in horrific tones to Troeltsch while studying at the exclusive Augsburg gymnasium of St. Anna, as discussed in chapter 8.

While Troeltsch admitted that the workers were oppressed, his fear of revolution was apparently stronger than his concern for their well-being. At any rate the threat of revolution is his primary concern.

A sect similar to the Anabaptists but which adopted the anarchist model was that of the Mennonites. They established peaceful communities and tried to abide by the precepts of the Sermon on the Mount, to take a pacifist position toward war and to foster egalitarian relations within their own communities. In the Netherlands, their land of origin, they had no civil rights and endured much persecution from the Calvinist authorities. Not surprisingly, they responded by maintaining a strict separation from the world (ST, 705–6; GS1, 814–15).

Eventually the Anabaptists and to a lesser degree the Mennonites became more accommodating to existing social structures and took on the features of what Troeltsch called "Free Churches"—a mixed type embodying a blend of features of church and sect. In Troeltsch's own time, however, the rise of industrial capitalism and the associated development of the Social Problem

> has reawakened in the modern world the old ideas of world-renewal which characterized the aggressive sects. These ideas have again come into prominence through the Bible, particularly in the Sermon on the Mount, and the idea of the Kingdom of God. (ST, 725; GS1, 843)

Here Troeltsch is referring to the rise of modern Christian socialism.

The Christian socialists were not "armies of saints" trying to overthrow the social order. However, they believed that Christian love required "the creation of just and suitable means for a sufficient material existence for all, as a basis for the development of spiritual values" (ST, 726; GS1, 844). In other words, they made an argument that could

be said to predate Maslow's "hierarchy of needs" by several generations: one cannot attend to things of the spirit on an empty stomach.
Therefore, to provide the material needs of persons is to foster their
spiritual well-being, also.

With Marxism, Christian socialism took on a more militant character, declared Troeltsch, explicitly referring to the influential role of Social
Democracy:

> [At present] Christian Socialism...claims to present the demand of the Gospel for
> brotherhood, and the coming of the Kingdom of God in its undimmed clarity and
> uncompromising character, after its eyes had been opened by Social Democracy
> to these inferences drawn from the Gospel. (ST, 726; GS1, 844)

Most readers of Troeltsch's period would have known that he is referring here to Kautsky's extensive historical work on early Christianity.
Clearly, this work was having a wide impact on many Christians who
were concerned about the Social Problem. Troeltsch's enumeration of
Christian socialism's characteristics reflects Kautsky's influence:

1. It rejected the "glorification of the prevailing bourgeois order."
This order was not divinely ordained nor could it be legitimated by
reference to natural law or sinful nature (ST, 726; GS1, 844).

2. Christianity must go beyond an exclusive focus on spiritual development to include material well-being, as mentioned above. Troeltsch
used the base-superstructure model to convey this idea: "the possibility of a spiritual and ethical development depends entirely upon the
substructure of a healthy collective social constitution, and...spiritual
factors are very closely connected with physical and economic factors"
(ST, 727; GS1, 844).

3. Christian socialism rejects the option of withdrawal into a sphere
of spiritual life, which would amount to despair towards the world (ST,
727; GS1, 845).

4. The Kingdom of God refers not to the church alone nor to the
hereafter, but rather to a realm on this earth. For contemporaries it means
moving beyond capitalist competition and social Darwinism (ST, 727;
GS1, 845).

Having enumerated the basic tenets of Christian socialism as influenced by Marxism (i.e., Kautsky), Troeltsch gave his commentary:

> In...[modern Christian socialism], we perceive once more the familiar character-
> istics of the primitive Christian tendency, the characteristics of the aggressive
> sect which believes in an actual transformation of conditions in this world. The
> Kingdom of God and reason, the Kingdom of God realized *on earth*, the invin-

cible faith in the victory of goodness and in the possibility of overcoming every human institution which is based upon the mere struggle for existence, the Christian Revolution: this is the primitive, splendid ideal of the sect. It is only the Chiliast ideal translated into human and intelligible terms. It is the ideal of a Christianity without compromise, formulated in harmony with modern social views. (Emphasis his. ST, 727; GS1, 845)

The term "Christian Revolution" captures the essence of his concern; the hope for social revolution on earth may be "splendid" but is also "primitive" and associated with aggressive sectarianism. It rests upon belief in the "victory of goodness" and belief that the social order can be replaced with something better. It believes that "every human institution which is based upon the mere struggle for existence" can be overcome. Whereas Kautsky and other Marxists view these institutions as the product of unequal social relations evolving in history, Troeltsch views them as adaptations to a natural order that undergoes only superficial change. Once the reader accepts Troeltsch's presuppositions, Christian socialism becomes unacceptable. After all, who could be in favor of something "primitive" and "aggressive" attempting to overthrow the natural order?

In a footnote Troeltsch briefly surveyed the contemporary Christian socialists by name, referring in particular to Walter Rauschenbusch and Leonhard Ragaz. Thus, he included the Social Gospel movement of America under Christian socialism and therefore under the rubric of aggressive sectarianism. He goes on to describe the Ragaz circle in Switzerland as the strong case. (The "*Kirchlich-Sozialen*" of the Catholic and Lutheran churches are not socialist at all [ST, 962n; GS1, 846n].)

The widespread concern with and variety of responses to the Social Problem of his time prompt Troeltsch to raise again his concern for individualism:

In any case, it is clear that everywhere individualism is being restricted, and that soon there will no longer be too much individualism, but too little. As political tendencies are becoming increasingly Democratic, religion may once again provide a refuge for individualism. (ST, 962n; GS1, 847n)

In this most telling statement, Troeltsch made explicit another fear concerning the Social Problem: the threat not only to social stability but to individualism as well. While it is possible to have "too much individualism," that is not the concern now; rather the Social Democrats, together with the Christian Socialists, threaten to introduce a situation that could bring about more democracy and "too little" individualism.

However religion, correctly conceived, has the potential to restore this endangered value. This statement clearly shows that, consistent with Steven Lukes' interpretation, German individualism is not to be associated with democracy.[36]

Thus, modern Christian Socialism was a sect that particularly concerned Troeltsch. Like some of the older sects it was working class and activist. We have seen in chapter 7 that Ragaz focused on the words of the Lord's Prayer: "Thy Kingdom come, Thy Will be done on earth."[37] Troeltsch knew of this emphasis and it caused much uneasiness for him and his peers. He worried about the possibility of social revolution and the loss of individualism.

For Troeltsch, therefore, the primary division within Christendom in his own time and place is indeed not between Catholic and Protestant, but between churches and sects. The churches were governed by elites and closely intertwined with the established social order. The working-class sects challenged the authority of the dominant church structures, whether actively and directly or simply through withdrawal. This division closely paralleled the class tensions within Christendom upon which Kautsky had focused. Troeltsch's analysis, however, subordinates the class dimension to a realist/utopian dimension predicated on a view of social inequality as natural and inevitable.

Mysticism

With his concept of mysticism, Troeltsch added a new dimension to Weber's bipolar typology of church and sect. Whereas Weber's typology had defined a sociological dimension, Troeltsch understood mysticism as a dimension of pure experience unrelated to the dimension of society: "In the widest sense of the word, mysticism is simply the insistence upon a direct inward and present religious experience" (ST, 730; GS1, 850). As such, it "has no impulse towards organization at all" (ST, 800; GS1, 940). "Thus mysticism becomes independent of concrete popular religion, timeless and nonhistorical, at most concealed under historical symbols" (ST, 735; GS1, 855). Troeltsch's two dimensional typology and his application of it to concrete historical examples can be represented as shown in Figure 12.1.

Perhaps the most anomalous application of Troeltsch's typology is his classification of Jesus as a nonmystic (ST, 733; GS1, 852–53). Troeltsch's own canon-within-the-canon elevated the Gospel of John over the Synoptics, since the latter contain abundant support for the politics of the "aggressive sectarians." But the protagonist of the Gospel of John is nothing if not a mystic.

This contradiction resulted from Troeltsch's tendency to conflate the mystical type with the church type: "many mystics remain within the Church, which they do not wish to replace by any other new organization." But they have a certain indifference towards the larger church (ST, 747; GS1, 868). Given this understanding of the mystical type, Troeltsch could not apply it to Jesus, whose "radical indifference or hostility to the rest of the social order" led to social withdrawal, rather than conformity.

FIGURE 12.1
Troeltsch's Two-Dimensional Typology of Christianity[38]

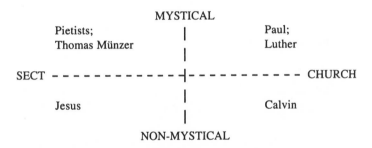

It also explains an ambivalence in *The Social Teaching* about applying the mystical type to sectarians generally.

Had Troeltsch consistently maintained the independence of mysticism from society, his concept of mysticism would have approximated Schiller's concept of inward religion, which Kautsky cited with approval (see chapter 11). By linking mysticism with outward conformity, however, Troeltsch was distorting this concept of pure inwardness in a conservative direction.

The key to understanding Troeltsch's tendency to conflate the mystical and church types is his appropriation of Harnack's essence of Christianity model as discussed in the introduction to this chapter. Since the essence of divine truth is above and outside of history and society, true mystics understand that outward conformity to existing social arrangements does not compromise their union with the divine.

For the mystic, the Kingdom of God is within (ST, 747; GS1, 868). While mystical sectarians may share this insight, for Troeltsch their efforts to withdraw from society or transform it indicate a less perfect religious consciousness than the "spiritual reformers," who conform to the institutional church outwardly while inwardly remaining indifferent to it (ST, 744; GS1, 863). From the vantage point of their universal religious consciousness, true mystics perceive all historical manifestations to be relative (ST, 750; GS1, 872). The highest good comes about through nurturance of the Inner Light, not through natural law. The goal is personal salvation; ethics is subordinated to "religion." Social problems fade into the background of relative values, as does history itself (ST, 753; GS1, 876).

Harnack's description of German Protestantism in 1900 illustrates what both Troeltsch and Harnack meant by mysticism:

> What do all our discoveries and inventions and our advances in outward civilisation signify in comparison with the fact that today there are thirty millions of Germans, and many more millions of Christians outside Germany, who possess a religion without priests, without sacrifices, without "fragments" of grace, without ceremonies—a spiritual religion![39]

Harnack's description, of course, is a far cry from the synergy of "catechism, bayonet and scepter" described in chapter 5. In his view, the cultural and social embodiment of these "souls" is rendered insignificant in favor of the essence of their religion. Symbols and myths are likewise considered foreign matter. The same presuppositions are at work in Troeltsch's *Social Teaching*. True religion progressively sloughs off the husks of history and culture.

Troeltsch's focus on mysticism and his positive characterization of it suggest that it describes his own faith position. Here he abruptly departed from Ritschl, who eschewed mysticism and the pan-German ideology associated with it. Troeltsch explicitly appeals to the authority of one of these reactionary mystics, Paul de Lagarde, who was one of his professors (see chapter 5):

> It is, of course, true to say that these [mystical] tendencies have a sociological fundamental theory, a union of the hearts of all in one common aim, and a complete toleration of all other souls on an equal basis, because as Lagarde says, 'upon the ascent towards God the various lines do not cut across each other but converge and meet'. People of this type, however, do not carry this fundamental theory systematically and actively into Society. (ST, 801; GS1, 940)

Thus, mystically based equality is not to be embodied in social equality.

As discussed above, Troeltsch recognized a class basis to the church/sect dimension: while the disaffected masses gravitated to the sect, the ruling classes gravitated to the church type so as to control the docile masses (ST, 798; GS1, 938). While he may have attempted to transcend this class conflict in his conceptualization of mysticism, he did not ultimately succeed. In order to do so, he would have had to consistently maintain a typology with two independent and unrelated dimensions: a dimension of inner experience, and a dimension of social adaptability (see Figure 12.1 above). Instead, what he intended to be a dimension of pure inwardness became skewed to coincide with his own class-based form of mysticism.

The class content of Troeltsch's concept of mysticism is evident in his comment that mysticism had become the "secret religion of the educated classes" (ST, 794; GS1, 931). Given this understanding of mysticism, it becomes apparent why he could not classify Jesus as a mystic. Whereas most German mandarins conformed outwardly to their society, Jesus did not conform to his.

In summary, Troeltsch's typology of church, sect and mysticism validates organized religion and the mysticism of the educated elite, while characterizing prophetic religion as "aggressive," or at best, "unrealistic."

"Socialist Churches are an Impossibility"

After his detailed treatment of church, sect, and mysticism, Troeltsch summarized his findings with respect to the relation of Christianity to the Social Problem.

He repeated his position that Jesus was "indifferent towards the world" and oriented to an imminent Kingdom of God that was beyond history (ST, 803; GS1, 944). If Jesus preached to the poor, which he did, it was because they were "in a more advantageous position than others, since they feel more warmly and humbly towards God" (ST, 803; GS1, 944). The poor had the proper attitude of heart to respond to the Gospel. This was the important thing; their material oppression in and of itself was a secondary issue.

The early church adapted to the world only as absolutely necessary, while maintaining an attitude of detachment. In his summary, Troeltsch dismisses the communism of the first Christians. Nowhere in *The Social Teaching* does he treat Kautsky's observations that one quarter of all church property was designated for the poor during the early Catholic period (ST, 803; GS1, 944).

The medieval period gave rise to increasing harmony between the

Christian ideal and the status quo as the church gained political ascendancy. Extensive charity was dispensed through the emerging monastic institutions (ST, 803; GS1, 944). No mention is made of Kautsky's observation that church property originally designated for the poor eventually ended up in the hands of the clergy by virtue of their vows of poverty.

Though continuing the practice of charity, Lutheranism primarily delegated matters of social concern to a government that was to be guided by Christian values within a Christian society. The Gospel of love was expected to inspire and shape the secular institutions in a Christian direction (ST, 803–4; GS1, 944).

Calvinism put forth the ideal of the Holy Community also found in the sects. However, it upheld the existing civil order, arguing that it could be the foundation of a Christian society if guided by relative natural law, good-will and Christian earnestness (ST, 804; GS1, 944).

It was only the sects that entertained the idea of radical social reform, because they did not believe that the existing social order and unequal distribution of property were compatible with Christian values. Even the sects ranged from passive endurance of the status quo in hopes of a reward in heaven to active striving for social revolution and the ushering in of the Kingdom of God on earth. Thus, it cannot be emphasized enough that "[the 'aggressive sectarians'] were the sole supporters of a Christian social ethic which was radical, allowed no compromise and did not accept the existing social order" (ST, 804; GS1, 945).

After describing the sects, Troeltsch reached the climax of his summary:

> Then Christian Socialism arose, with its penetrating criticism of the existing social order. It threw out a clear challenge, claiming that the urgency of the situation demanded either a radical change in the fundamental social outlook, or the destruction of the present economic system in order to make room for a new social order, which would be in harmony with the ideals which also dominate the Socialistic Reform parties, groups which have sprung into existence under the pressure of the economic situation. These demands show, however, that Christian Socialism again is fired with the old spirit of the aggressive sect...; it renews the hope of realizing the Kingdom of God upon earth, and revives the sense of the intimate connection between mind and body. (ST, 804; GS1, 945)

Thus, Christian socialism with its ties to Social Democracy demanded fundamental social change. It wished to realize the Kingdom of God on earth. It anticipated feminist theory by emphasizing the unity of mind and body, the spiritual and the material, religion and history. These characteristics qualified the movement to be classified once again as an "aggressive sect."

Having said this, Troeltsch rehearses once again the differences between church and sect: "the Church requires the masses to acquiesce in existing social conditions because they have been appointed by God...; its only idea of social reform is charitable activity" (ST, 805; GS1, 946). Thus, the church-type legitimates the status quo and works to keep the "masses" in a subordinate position. For Troeltsch this class-based arrangement is simply part of the natural, divinely ordained order.

From this observation Troeltsch draws a very strong, unequivocal conclusion: "Socialist churches are an impossibility [*Sozialistische Kirchen sind ein Unding*]" (GS1, 946). Indeed, his words vividly recall those of the emperor in 1896, whom he quoted in his address to the Evangelical Social Congress discussed in chapter 10: "Political pastors are nonsense!"[40] He then goes on to acknowledge, "But a Christian Socialism which is separate from the Church in spirit can appeal to the Gospel." This statement is merely an elaboration of his more general observation that the sect type, of which Christian Socialism is one manifestation, derives its legitimacy from the ethic of Jesus.[41]

Troeltsch then summarizes: "The heart of the problem...lies in the contrast between an ecclesiastical institution realistically focused towards mankind and a free voluntary community unconditionally striving after the ideal" (ST, 805; GS1, 946). If his pejorative characterization of socialist churches did not make it clear, his choice of words to describe the church type as "realistically focused towards mankind" as opposed to the sect chasing after an ideal leaves no doubt as to where Troeltsch's own sentiment lies.

Christianity and Socialism

Although Troeltsch concluded his exhaustive survey of Christian churches and sects with the eighteenth century, he ended *The Social Teaching* as he began it: on a polemical note regarding the Social Problem of his own day.

Troeltsch first expresses his indebtedness to "the 'Marxist' method... [which] is gradually transforming all our historical conceptions" (ST, 1002; GS1, 975). In an obvious reference to Kautsky and his followers, he refers to the wide impact of the "scholars of the 'class-war' school [who] have undertaken to represent the whole of Christianity as an ideological reflection of economic development" (ST, 1002; GS1, 975).

Because of this Marxist scholarship, church historiography will never be the same.

The Social Teaching has been written, he continues, "in opposition to the exclusive and doctrinaire application of this method" (ST, 1002). Troeltsch's specific concern, of course, is application of Marxist historiography to Christianity:

> the whole of this survey has shown that all that is specifically religious, and, above all, the great central points of religious development, are an independent expression of the religious life. Jesus, Paul, Origin, Augustine, Thomas Aquinas, Francis of Assisi, Bonaventura, Luther, Calvin; as we study their thought and their feeling we realize that it is impossible to regard them as the product of class struggles and of economic factors. (ST, 1002; GS1, 975)

Although Troeltsch verbally concedes that economic factors are "co-operating elements," in practice his analysis works to establish the *independence* of religion, rather than the *interdependence* of religion and political economy.

The doctrine of class struggle and the analysis of history as the product of social relations set the terms of Troeltsch's debate. For example, his typology of church and sect—building on Max Weber's sociology and developed largely in response to socialist interpretations of Christianity—is informed by class analysis and corresponds to class divisions. This appropriation of Marxism, however, is essentially tactical, since Troeltsch puts his typology in the service of a conservative ideological agenda.

Whereas Marxists viewed workers as the subjects of history and their social movements as the hope for larger structural transformation, Troeltsch viewed such movements as ultimately deluded, since his view of reality militated from the outset against the possibility of structural transformation. Troeltsch uses his typology precisely to invalidate revolutionary aspirations, and to reinterpret class-based religious phenomena in terms of "purely religious" factors. Similarly, his method of *Geistesgeschichte* (see chapter 4) is intended as a neo-Kantian alternative to historical materialism. Thus, Marxism's influence on Troeltsch is primarily negative.[42]

Having indicated the polemical context of *The Social Teaching*, Troeltsch returns to his original question: Is the core Christian message compatible with socialism? His reply: "The Christian ethos [*das christliche Ethos*] alone possesses, in virtue of its personalistic Theism, a conviction of personality and individuality" (ST, 1004; GS1, 978). This "personalistic Theism" involved "socialism," according to

Troeltsch, but a socialism that transcends the natural world, as mentioned earlier in this chapter. "The Christian ethos alone...possesses a Socialism which cannot be shaken. It is only within the medium of the Divine that...[natural] strife and exclusiveness...which shape [ones] natural existence, disappear"[43] (ST, 1005; GS1, 978).

Here Troeltsch again invokes the argument that nature is the source of social conflict, not historical social relations. This argument based on nature in effect attributes the pathologies of power to humanity as a whole, rather than to those who actually create and maintain systems of domination. The argument from nature blames the victim of power as much as the power holder. All share the guilt of having selfish and aggressive instincts, whether acted out or not.

Professing this equality in sin, and a corresponding equality "in Christ," is the extent of Troeltsch's egalitarianism. He writes: "Only the Christian ethos solves the problem of equality and inequality, since it neither glorifies force and accident in the sense of a Nietzchian cult of breed, nor outrages the patent facts of life by a doctrinaire equalitarianism" (ST, 1005; GS1, 978). After thus appealing again to nature— "the patent facts of life"—Troeltsch went on to argue for social and personal inequalities. These differences are established by God and shaped into structures of voluntary submission on the one hand and paternal care on the other.

> [The Christian ethos] recognizes differences in social position, power, and capacity, as a condition which has been established by the inscrutable Will of God...then transforms this condition...into an ethical cosmos. The ethical values of voluntary incorporation and subordination on the one hand, and of care and responsibility for others on the other hand, place each human being in circumstances where natural differences can and should be transmuted into the ethical values of mutual recognition, confidence, and care for others. (ST, 1005; GS1, 978)

In effect this is a new double standard, different from that of the medieval church, which prescribed one standard for monks and another for laity. Echoing the aristocratic ethic first invoked in "Political Ethics and Christianity," Troeltsch describes the central Christian ethic as upholding one standard for members of the elite, or those in authority, and another for the common people, or those in submission.

The Christian ethos is therefore characterized by the primacy of individualism, by a special ahistorical religious realm of the soul, by a transcendental socialism and equality "in Christ" that is not of this world, and by an ethical double standard between classes. In this context, Troeltsch provided his solution to the Social Problem:

Through its emphasis upon the Christian value of personality, and on love, the Christian ethos creates something which no social order—however just and rational—can dispense with entirely, because everywhere there will always remain suffering, distress, and sickness for which we cannot account—in a word, it produces charity. (ST, 1005; GS1, 978–79)

Troeltsch's answer to Social Democracy, in other words, is a process of private individuals helping other private individuals. The problem of evil is formulated in apolitical terms, since "suffering, distress, and sickness" are just "there," not embedded in an historical process in which some people secure a relatively comfortable existence at the expense of others. The ethical implication again is that power-holders are no more responsible for the evils of history than the victims of power; the political implication is that nothing decisive can be done to ameliorate human suffering. Troeltsch thus succumbs to a fatalism comparable his friend Meinecke's after the Great War had begun, and so typical of his colleagues, as discussed in chapter 9.

As for charity, Troeltsch admitted its inadequacy for meeting the extreme social needs of his day. "All Christian social work is in a problematic condition," he wrote (ST, 1012; GS1, 985). Ultimately what is needed are "thoughts…which have not yet been thought" (ST, 1012; GS1, 985). This is more of an empty wish than an actual orientation for he had just pessimistically declared that "everywhere there will always remain suffering, distress, and sickness for which we cannot account" (ST, 1005; GS1, 979).

Thus, following Harnack, Troeltsch views private charity as the practical expression of the Christian ethos. As mentioned, Troeltsch failed to address the long tradition of church property belonging to the poor which, according to Kautsky, led in its final decayed form to the practice of charity, that is, the giving of an economic surplus. Troeltsch also did not address Kautsky's observation that the charity system of the medieval church was weakened with the break-up of Western Christendom. The rise of capitalism also led to massive cutbacks in charitable contributions. Both the new possibilities for the accumulation of wealth and the desire to instill workplace discipline by making unemployment an unattractive alternative led to parsimony, according to Kautsky.

Socialists therefore regarded private charity as effective as rain falling on hot stones. Even Friedrich Naumann had conceded this point, as we saw in chapter 7. Despite these criticisms Troeltsch, following Harnack, persisted in hailing private charity as the best possible response to the Social Problem.

Civil Liberties and Individualism

Troeltsch also criticized Kautsky and Social Democracy for their proposed separation of church and state. Although in theory he saw the free church system as the wave of the future, in practice, he aligned with his party in protecting Protestant state patronage. He opposed socialist proposals to abolish religious instruction in the public schools, and supported exceptional legislation persecuting Catholic religious orders (ST, 1010; GS1, 983).

Kautsky had appealed to the leading role of the United States on the separation of church and state. Troeltsch replied:

> It [the Social Democratic Party] accepts the communistic tendency hidden under the veil of religion, and protects the ideas of religion by the statement that religion is a private matter, and it secures the sympathies of the Catholics by fighting against all exceptional legislation, as, for example, that against the Religious Orders. At the same time the power of the clergy is to be broken through the separation of Church and State, the abolition of religion from the schools, and the fight against the idea of religion by the stress laid on Socialistic science.... [This is a] contradictory church policy, which aims at protecting and annihilating religion at one and the same time. (ST, 36n; GS1, 7n)

To this, Kautsky might well have replied that the socialist position was to neither protect nor annihilate religion *as such*, but rather to consistently protect the rights of individuals and groups to freely practice religion if and as they choose. On the contrary, it was Troeltsch's own National Liberal Party that sought to protect the state privileges of Protestantism while annihilating the civil liberties of Catholics through exceptional legislation.

As mentioned in an earlier chapter, Kautsky did believe that without state privilege and with a welfare state supplanting the role of private church charity, organized Christianity would eventually wither away. One might have expected Troeltsch to argue against this prediction by attributing it to Kautsky's failure to understand religion as an independent impulse, which is one of Troeltsch's central themes.

Further, given his theory of the independence of religion, one might have expected Troeltsch to welcome the separation of church and state. Instead, he takes the opposite position, contradicting his own theory by accepting Kautsky's presupposition that with the end of state privilege, "religion" would wither away. As a National Liberal he finally supports his party's platform maintaining Protestant privileges and supporting a new *Kulturkampf* against the Catholic church.[44] While advocating the independence of religion in his theories, Troeltsch in practice endorsed state privilege as necessary to ensure the future of organized religion.

Troeltsch's policy positions on civil liberties also shed important light on his claims to be defending religious individualism from the Marxists. What he meant by "individualism" was clearly different from how the word was used in Anglo-French thought. Like Lagarde, Troeltsch understood individualism in a suprapersonal, mystical sense to refer to the manifestation of *Geist* in the most important and creative personalities of the community. It was these bearers of culture who wore the mantle of legitimate leadership. It so happened that in Germany the culture-bearers were Protestant and therefore their churches were entitled to certain privileges.

As discussed in chapter 6, it was the Social Democrats and not the National Liberals who chose to champion the Anglo-French liberal values of liberty, equality, and fraternity in the politics of the Second Reich.

Troeltsch concludes *The Social Teaching* with a parting reflection on the Kingdom of God. For him, the Kingdom will never come, on earth as it is in Heaven. There is no dialectic between the Kingdom within, and the Kingdom on earth. Rather Troeltsch adopts the view he had attributed to the mystics: "The truth is—and this is the conclusion of the whole matter—the Kingdom of God is within us."[45]

In his conclusion Troeltsch not only failed to find hope for social change that would signify the coming of the Kingdom on earth, he had ominous forebodings about the future: "For every threatening abyss which is closed, another yawning gulf appears" (ST, 1013; GS1, 986). The imagery of a "threatening abyss" and "yawning gulf" is drawn from nature, as if the German war machine that two years later cut a bloody swath through Belgium was beyond the control or responsibility of human agents.

In the face of such brutal realities, Christian ethics must accommodate—to exploitation, to militarization and to colonization. Those who resist on behalf of justice—Kautsky, Ragaz, and their ilk—are "doctrinaire idealists or religious fanatics":

> Thus the Christian ethic of the present day and of the future will also only be an adjustment to the world-situation, and it will only desire to achieve that which is practically possible.... Only doctrinaire idealists or religious fanatics can fail to recognize these facts. (ST, 1013; GS1, 986)

Notes

1. Troeltsch, *The Social Teaching*, 39. The German original is worth quoting: "die Predigt Jesu und die Bildung der neuen Religionsgemeinde *keine Schöpfung einer sozialen Bewegung ist*, das heisst nicht aus irgend einem Klassenkampf hervorgegangen oder auf ihn zugeschnitten ist und überhaupt nirgends direkt an die sozialen Umwälzungen der antiken Gesellschaft anknüpft" (Troeltsch's emphasis). Thus, a close reading of the German would be: the Jesus movement was emphatically "*not the creation of a social movement.*" It had nothing to do with "class conflict" (*Klassenkampf*) or creating "radical social changes" (*Umwälzungen*) in ancient society. Troeltsch, *Gesammelte Schriften*, vol. 1 (Tübingen: J. C. B. Mohr, 1923), 15–16.

   Because of the frequency of occurrence, subsequent references to *The Social Teaching* (Eng. trans.) will be indicated parenthetically in the text with the acronym "ST." References to the German original will be designated as "GS1" for *Gesammelte Schriften*, vol. 1.

2. ST, 70, 85. "*der religiöse Individualismus ist und bleibt die Kernidee.*" GS1, 59. Thus Troeltsch himself chooses to use "*religiöse Individualismus*" to describe the core teaching of Christianity. The immediate context of this statement is Troeltsch's description of the shift from the message of Jesus to that of Paul. One of the few things Jesus and Paul shared in common, he says, is this "kernel" of "religious individualism." In fact, he goes on, so central is this principle of "religious individualism" that even the Christian principle of love stands in a relatively subordinate position.

   The question of whether or not Troeltsch and Kautsky were being anachronistic in using "individualism" or "communism" respectively to describe early Christianity is beyond the scope of this dissertation.

3. Troeltsch made no pretense of knowing the primary sources. Instead, he selected the best ten or twelve secondary works to reconstruct the teachings of each period. Of these secondary works, Troeltsch claimed to be the most dependent on Harnack's. Bainton argued that greater depth of research cannot be expected, given the scope of the task undertaken; accordingly, the conclusions must be regarded as only tentative. Bainton, "Ernst Troeltsch—Thirty Years Later," 71–72.

4. Specifically in response to the socialist interpretations, Troeltsch wrote, "Cf. also the address of Adolf Harnack at the Protestant Social Congress in 1894: "Die Evangelisch-soziale Aufgabe im Lichte der Kirche," *Reden und Aufsätze*, vol. 2 (Gieszen: J. Ricker, 1904), 23–76. ST, 165; GS1, 17n.

5. In his 1903 essay, "What does 'Essence of Christianity' Mean," Troeltsch clarifies his own position in relation to Harnack's on Christianity's "essence." At the outset he clearly states that he does not dispute the application of the term, but rather it's content (127–28). He also states that he stands in continuity with "Schleiermacher, Baur, Ritschl and Harnack," each of whom attempted to define the essence of Christianity somewhat differently, but all of whom stood in the tradition of German idealism. The presupposition of German idealism, that "historical events are the development of an idea," created the concept of "essence" in the first place, according to Troeltsch. E. Troeltsch, "What does 'Essence of Christianity' Mean?" *Ernst Troeltsch: Writings on Theology and Religion*, ed. R. Morgan and M. Pye, trans. S. W. Sykes (Atlanta, GA: John Knox Press, 1903, 1977), 129–30.

   Having established his continuity with German idealism, Troeltsch then takes up the issue of the content of Christianity's essence. He agrees with Harnack that it should be centered in "the classical period" (147). But in contrast to Harnack he argues: "it cannot be an unchangeable idea given once for all in the teachings of Jesus…; [rather] it must be a developing spiritual principle, a 'germinative principle'" (151). There is the need to add "the preaching of Paul" to that of Jesus. (p. 149) Thus, in the classical moment, there are "two distinct accents" (149). "Thus the essence of Christianity contains a polarity within itself and a statement of it must be dualistic. To take over an image which Ritschl used in a rather different sense, it is like an ellipse which does not have one centre like a circle but which has two focal points" (154).

Thus, for Troeltsch, Harnack's "kernel" becomes an "ellipse" containing two foci, the preaching of Jesus *and* Paul, creating a tension that sets in motion a process of dialectical development. Troeltsch does not break with German idealism, but rather attempts to offer his own variant of it. According to S. W. Sykes, the translator of this essay, "the essay remains in conception an expansion of Schleiermacher's work" (181).

Benjamin Reist argues that Troeltsch's essay was "a scathing critique" of Harnack. But he also comments that while Troeltsch rejected Schleiermacher, Hegel and Harnack's attempts to define an essence of Christianity, he *de facto* makes his own attempt. Reist, *Toward a Theology of Involvement*, 182. His view complements Rubanowice's that Troeltsch did not quite agree with anyone and was eclectic almost as a matter of principle. Rubanowice, *Crisis in Consciousness*, 136. I would argue that calling the essay "a scathing critique" is an overstatement. As shown above Troeltsch clearly states that he retains the concept of essence and stands in continuity with the tradition of Harnack and Schleiermacher. Rubanowice's reference to Troeltsch's alleged eclecticism also tends to ignore the broader conceptual framework to which Troeltsch adhered.

Troeltsch's differences with Harnack are eclipsed as he turns his attention to the historical materialist paradigm of the socialists in *The Social Teaching*. Again, Rubanowice loses the forest for the trees when he argues that *The Social Teaching* is a "broad assault on all customary church history and all accepted history of doctrine that generated it." (See discussion of common misconceptions of Troeltsch's methodology in chapter 8.) Rubanowice, *Crisis in Consciousness*, 44.

Again, Troeltsch makes explicit in *The Social Teaching* that he is more indebted to Harnack's historical works than to any other secondary source for reconstructing the history of Christian social teaching (ST, 165n; GS1, 17n). Considering the fact that, as Bainton observed, he relied primarily on secondary sources, this is a telling statement indeed.

Claude Welch not only observes an "essence" in Troeltsch but argues that it takes the form of "the Christian ethos." Welch, *Protestant Thought in the Nineteenth Century*, 296.

6. Pauck, "Ernst Troeltsch," 135.
7. Troeltsch's focus on the "soul" occurs in conjunction with exhortations to self-renunciation, thus accentuating the disembodied nature of Christian spirituality. Note, for example, his description of the ethical ideal of the gospel: "the infinite and eternal value of the soul [*Seele*] [is] to be attained through self-renunciation for the sake of God. These ideas are more easily understood by the soul which is bowed down with a sense of sin and guilt than by a 'righteous' man" (ST, 52–3; GS1, 36). Troeltsch then elaborates by emphasizing the need for "self-sacrifice," "self-surrender," "self-denial" and "self-restraint" to achieve the soul's union with the "All-Knowing and All-Holy" (ST, 53–4; GS1, 37).

Thus, the image of God invoked here is that of a transcendent God, standing over the individual, whose will is to be obeyed without question. There is no suggestion of an immanent divine presence, a "divine spark" within the individual. Therefore, the soul must renounce and transcend the "self" in order to merge with this higher Being. A Marxist of his time would have considered this to be a formula for self-alienation and therefore, a description of "false consciousness." Troeltsch himself explicitly credits Paul de Lagarde for his views on mysticism, as discussed towards the end of this chapter.

8. The reader may recall that Ritschl argued against Enlightenment eudaemonism; see chapter 5.

9. "die Liebe ruht auf religiös-individualistischem Grunde, und der religiöse Individualismus ist und bleibt die Kernidee" GS1, 59; ST, 70. For Troeltsch religious individualism is more fundamental to Christianity than is love.

10. Kautsky's programmatic pamphlet, "Die Sozialdemokratie und die katholische Kirche," 2nd ed. (Berlin, 1906) is cited as a good example of this error. ST, 28; GS1, 7.

11. K. Kautsky, "Sozialdemokratie," 3–4; see chapter 11.

12. "den stumpfen Widerstand der Masse und des Nützlichkeitsverstandes." GS1, 38; ST, 54.

13. "dem jüdischen Priesteradel wie der herrschenden Theologenwelt feindlich gegenüberstand." GS1, 16.

14. This failure of Troeltsch to address the Marxist critique of religion was observed in general terms by Hans Bosse, *Marx, Weber, Troeltsch* (Munich: Christian Kaiser Verlag, 1971). In this chapter I will show that Bosse's thesis is borne out by a thorough analysis of Troeltsch's text.

15. K. Kautsky, "Sozialdemokratie," 4.

16. "der idealistische Anarchismus und der Liebeskommunismus." GS1, 72; ST, 82.

17. K. Kautsky, *Foundations of Christianity*, 398f.

18. Karl Kautsky, *The Materialist Conception of History*, ed., John Kautsky (New Haven, CT: Yale University Press, 1988), 172–73.

19. K. Kautsky, *Foundations of Christianity: A Study in Christian Origins* (New York: Monthly Review Press, 1925, reprinted 1980), 187–382.

20. For sharp criticism of scholars who refuse to take seriously Jesus's Jewishness, see E. P. Sanders, *Jesus and Judaism* (Philadelphia, PA: Fortress Press, 1985).

21. See, for example, a collection of essays by contemporary Christian and Jewish interpreters such as James H. Charlesworth, Daniel J. Harrington and Alan F. Segal on the meaning of the Jewishness of Jesus. *Jesus' Jewishness: Exploring the Place of Jesus within Early Judaism*, ed. James H. Charlesworth (New York: Crossroad, 1991).

22. NRSV; Mark 10:42–44; Mt. 20:25–28.

23. Max Weber, "Politics as a Vocation," *From Max Weber: Essays in Sociology*, trans. and ed., H. H. Gerth and C. Wright Mills (New York: Oxford University Press, 1918, 1964), 123–28.

24. Bosse also observed this difference between Troeltsch and the Marxists. Bosse, *Marx, Weber, Troeltsch*, 49–57.

25. In his selective and eclectic assimilation of Marxist ideas, Troeltsch even tried to appropriate concepts that were not compatible with his neo-Kantian assumptions, such as the base-superstructure concept:

> the Marxist idea of the dependence of the spiritual super-structure upon the social-economic substructure...if accepted with due precautions, seems to me to be a justifiable and illuminating idea. (ST, 407n; GS1, 281n)

Troeltsch apparently did not think through the contradiction between this fundamental Marxist idea and his own neo-Kantian preoccupation with establishing the independence of religion. As in the case of his attempt to appropriate the concept of class struggle (ST, 818), Troeltsch viewed certain elements of Marxism as "newly discovered causalities" to be somehow added to older findings of social science (ST, 1002–4; GS1, 975–77).

26. ST, 175n; GS1 51n. Kautsky himself was aware that the church of the fourth century was not receptive to the ideas of Christian communism and that Chrysostom himself later abandoned these ideas. However, Kautsky understood this lack of receptivity in terms of the changed historical situation of the church compared to the time of Jesus. His point is precisely that communism must have been central indeed to the original church if leaders such as Chrysostom continued to resurrect its memory under later inhospitable conditions. Troeltsch apparently either missed this point or chose not to address it.

27. Welch, *Protestant Thought in the Nineteenth Century*, 293–94.

28. Karl Kautsky, *The Materialist Conception of History*, 172–73.

29. In a comparative study of Troeltsch with his colleague, Gottfried Traub, Troeltsch and Traub are understood to take the same approach to "the social question," except for one issue: the role of women. Unlike Traub, Troeltsch takes the conservative, antisuffragette position, unconditionally supporting "the principle of the 'patriarchal state [*Männerstaat*].'" Shinichi Sato, "Ernst Troeltsch und die soziale Frage im Wilhelminischen Zeitalter unter besonderer Berücksichtigung des Zusammenhangs zwischen Troeltsch und Gottfried Traub," *Mitteilungen der Ernst Troeltsch Gesellschaft*, Vol. IV (Augsburg, 1989), 6.

30. In the German, "die gesetzesfreie Innerlichkeit des Christentums" GS1, 508.

31. "Insofern ist der Staat etwas wirklich Göttliches." GS1, 561.

32. Further on, Troeltsch observes that international Calvinism, after its period of worldwide colonial expansion, began to adopt a more pacifist position. Troeltsch comments that this was a positive trend, that now Calvinists "struggle hard against the Imperialistic tendencies, which are indeed closely connected with the process of economic development of the nations to which they belong" (ST, 652; GS1, 728). However, it is also clear that he views the strength of international Calvinism which resulted from its Wars of Religion, as a virtue to which "the very individualistic Lutheranism of the present day...cannot in any way compare" (ibid.). In summary, Troeltsch prized the fruits of colonial expansionism— a well organized, international church—which Lutheranism failed to achieve. After the harvest was in, however, he believed it was appropriate for Calvinists to adopt a more civilized posture.

33. For a critical reconstruction of this nascent capitalist ideology as it developed later in British political thought, see C. B. MacPherson, *The Political Theory of Possessive Individualism: Hobbes to Locke* (New York: Oxford University Press, 1962).

34. Max Weber, *The Protestant Ethic and the Spirit of Capitalism*, trans. Talcott Parsons (New York: Charles Scribners, 1904, 1976).

35. This *a priori* delegitimizing of the religious left using an ostensibly scientific typology is also characteristic of Peter L. Berger's typology of responses to the contemporary crisis of religion, as discussed in chapter 14.

36. See discussion in chapter 4.

37. Leonhard Ragaz, *Dein Reich Komme*, 3rd ed. (Zurich: Rotaphel, 1922).

38. Troeltsch does not explicitly formulate his typology in terms of two independent dimensions as illustrated graphically in figure 12.1. However, I would argue that such a conceptualization is implicit in Troeltsch's discussion, which posits a polarity between the church and sect types, while viewing the mystical type as compatible with both, at least in theory.

Thus, as discussed in the section on Protestantism, Troeltsch regards Lutheranism's role in legitimating the state to be compatible with the former's mystical essence, but only when such legitimation arises as an unintentional byproduct of authentic mysticism (ST, 569–70; GS1, 549–95). The same compatibility with mysticism and the same caveat should logically also apply to the sects' legitimation of revolution. But in practice Troeltsch avoids making such an argument, which would have attributed to his opponents a capacity for religious motivation as profound as that of his political allies. In summary, Troeltsch conceptualizes mysticism as theoretically independent of the church/sect dimension but in practice tends to conflate it with the church type, whose politics he prefers.

39. Adolf Harnack, *What is Christianity* (Gloucester, MA: Peter Smith, 1978), 268.

40. "Politische Pastoren sind Unsinn." Troeltsch, "Politische Ethik und Christentum," 39. In fact, Olive Wyon translates Troeltsch's statement in *The Social Teaching* as if *Unding* were *Unsinn*. Her rendering is, "Socialistic churches are nonsense."

41. That Christian Socialism is said to be separate from the church (type) in spirit reinforces Troeltsch's earlier claim that it belongs to the sect type. The fact that Christian Socialism is said to have its roots in the Gospel recalls Troeltsch's earlier observation that the sect type appeals to the ethic of Jesus. This does not necessarily legitimate Christian Socialism in Troeltsch's mind; he has already emphasized the impractical, apocalyptic nature of Jesus' ethic.

42. Michael Pye argues, in opposition to Bosse, that Troeltsch took a middle position between Max Weber and Karl Marx. He emphasizes Troeltsch's indebtedness to Marx by making a distinction between "practical" and "theoretical" socialism, then arguing that Troeltsch eschewed the former in favor of the latter. He goes on to say that Troeltsch also rejects Marxist materialism and the notion of class struggle, but accepts Marx's "economically defined social classes." Michael Pye, "Troeltsch and the Science of Religion," *Ernst Troeltsch: Writings on Theology and Religion*, eds. Robert Morgan and Michael Pye (Atlanta, GA: John Knox Press, 1977), 244.

Pye's argument overlooks the historical context of Troeltsch's ideas, which I have reconstructed in this book. When Troeltsch was writing *The Social Teaching*, Marxism in Germany was not an academic outlook that could be separated from politics. Before 1918, the Social Democratic Party was the only organized expression of Marxism in Germany and no socialist was known to hold an academic chair in a German university (see chapter 4). Troeltsch's relation to Marxism must therefore be understood in the context of his opposition to the SPD and to Kautsky's Marxist interpretation of Chrisitianity. This supports Bosse's thesis that a gulf exists between Troeltsch and Marxism. Hans Bosse, *Marx, Weber, Troeltsch* (Munich: Chr. Kaiser Verlag, 1971).

43. For the complete quotation see the introduction to this chapter.

44. Kautsky's, "Die Sozialdemokratie und die katholische Kirche," which Troeltsch specifically argued against on this issue, was written as a response to the "exceptionalist" policies, which Troeltsch's National Liberal party supported.

45. "Es bleibt dabei—und das ist das alles zusammenfassende Ergebnis—das Reich Gottes ist inwendig in uns." ST, 1013; GS1, 986.

13

God and Caesar

The purpose of this study has been to recover the historical context of Ernst Troeltsch's *Social Teaching*, which has largely been lost to interpreters. This context, which Troeltsch shared with his contemporaries, must be our frame of reference for understanding Troeltsch's intentions in undertaking this massive project.

A reconstruction of this context brings to light that *The Social Teaching* was largely a polemical response to Karl Kautsky's *Forerunners of Modern Socialism* published 17 years earlier. Both works take up a common problematic, namely, the relationship of Christianity to modern socialism. This is particularly evident in the way *The Social Teaching* opens, not with an introduction to early Christianity as one might expect in a disinterested historical work, but rather with a discussion of "the Social Problem" of Troeltsch's own time. It concludes on this same note, a note which recurs throughout the intervening pages as we have seen.

Therefore, to try to understand *The Social Teaching* without a knowledge of either Kautsky's work or "the Social Problem" is a bit like trying to understand one side of a long telephone conversation without hearing the other party, knowing who it is, or even knowing that what you are hearing is part of a dialogue. The fact is, although Kautsky and Troeltsch were political antagonists, they did share certain presuppositions and concerns common to the time and place. Their shared frame of reference is as important to our understanding of *The Social Teaching* as are the differences between them. For this reason I reconstructed their common historical context in chapters 2 through 9. Only then did I turn to survey Kautsky's work. With this contextual reconstruction in hand I then proceeded to a fresh reading of Troeltsch's *Social Teaching*. In this concluding chapter I shall briefly summarize my findings.

The Social Problem, with which Troeltsch began and ended his work, involved at least two dimensions. First, it was an ethical problem. Enormous suffering characterized the lives of masses of urban working poor who were forced to endure twelve-hour day, six-day work weeks only to come home to overcrowded slum dwellings. Not surprisingly, such conditions spawned the social base for the precipitous rise of the Social Democratic party in the latter half of the nineteenth century. Therefore, and secondly, the Social Problem was a political problem of the first magnitude for the German military-industrial state, otherwise known as the Second Reich.

Social Democracy constituted a frontal attack on the established political order. At the top of the social pyramid stood a constitutional (but very powerful) monarch, with a growing military sector, an industrialist class, the German academics and the Protestant churches closely associated with him. An Imperial parliament with very limited powers gave a taste of democracy to the masses of working men at the bottom; none to women. Even the machines in the factories were said to be Social Democratic, so ready were the toiling laborers for social revolution.

Failure of the liberal Revolution of 1848 and success of the Franco-Prussian War in 1870–1871 from which Imperial Germany emerged led many members of German elites to believe in the effectiveness of Bismarck's "blood and iron" policies. Anglo-French liberal impulses gave way to nationalism and militarism as the popularity of the dueling fraternities attests. Germany's rapid industrialization during the second half of the nineteenth century was matched only by her increased militarization. The Krupp industrial empire moved into high gear to develop and produce new weapons of ever greater destructive capacity. Krupp's "Big Bertha" became the crown jewel of the empire. Enormous energy and ingenuity were invested in the northern shipyards to perfect the submarine and to build a navy for the Emperor, fueling an arms race.

Although continuing to discover, explore, and develop new frontiers of learning—in particular the historical critical method—most German intellectuals moved from a liberal to a neoconservative position when addressing social and political issues. Although academic freedom was progressively curtailed by the state, this step was not really necessary. All but a handful of academics actively worked to legitimate the Second Reich. These "German mandarins" developed a symbiotic relationship with the constitutional monarchy as the bearers of culture, the guardians of the national *Geist*, and the interpreters of the constitution. In their eyes the imperial regime was worthy of support to the extent that it protected and upheld the national *Geist* and its keepers.

Neither the conservatives nor the "liberals" really embraced democracy. For the conservatives, the sources of legitimate authority were Junker lineage and property ownership. For the liberals, the state was legitimate insofar as it rewarded the best and the brightest, that is, the culture bearers themselves. The difference was one of emphasis; both groups recognized the need for a coalition of wealth and learning in the face of proletarian unrest.

Only the Social Democrats continued to uphold French Revolutionary values of popular sovereignty, liberty, equality and fraternity (or solidarity). Although the German academics cherished the value of individualism, for them this concept increasingly assumed a mystical, supra-personal meaning and was seen to be embodied by the state as protector of the national *Geist*.

Notwithstanding Harnack's assertion that German Protestants were practicing "a religion without priests...a spiritual religion,"[1] the Evangelical Church of Germany was an important bulwark of the military-industrial order, and in turn, was supported by public revenues. Religious instruction of a Protestant variety was carried on throughout the public schools, and Catholic education apparently received public revenues at the regional level. As the Rector at Göttingen University, Albrecht Ritschl publicly spoke in favor of a controversial military spending bill. Later Adolf Harnack used his influence to assist the emperor in passing another military spending bill through Parliament. His loyalty to the emperor no less than his professional achievements eventually earned him the ennobling title of "von" in the year that World War I broke out.

The civil liberties of Catholics and Social Democrats, along with academic freedom, were curtailed. Anti-Catholic campaigns culminating in Bismarck's *Kulturkampf* in the 1870s outlawed religious orders and forced thousands of priests to leave the country. Upon the heels of the persecution of Catholics came the persecution and banishment of socialists until 1890. After the turn of the century with the Catholic Center party's exposure of brutal African colonial policies, anti-Catholicism resurfaced. Neither campaign of repression was successful but only served to turn the victims into martyrs in the eyes of the people and strengthen both Catholicism and Social Democracy. They also caused the National Liberal party to split, with the liberal dissenters to Bismarck's repressive measures leaving to form the Progressive party.

Anti-Semitism was also on the rise. In an age of German idealism, the Jew came to represent a preoccupation with crass materialism. Jews had great difficulty winning university posts; very few if any were to be found in the officer corps or the aristocracy. About the only paths to success open to them lay in the professions and entrepreneurship.

Although by the turn of the century a vigorous suffragette movement had arisen, the only party to respond positively to women's efforts to gain a modicum of political equality was the Social Democratic party, which added a suffragette leader to its national board. No German woman received a doctorate, much less a university chair, until the 1920s. The vast majority of German men, conservative and liberal, believed that woman's only legitimate role was to create a private shelter to which they could occasionally retreat from the *Sturm und Drang* of work and public life.

Therefore, the Social Democratic party stood for nothing less than social revolution—a challenge to the entire system of property and other relations of domination that underpinned the Second Reich. While neoconservatism pervaded the universities during Imperial Germany, Social Democracy kept alive the traditions of the French Revolution. It advocated popular democracy and a universal franchise that would include women, as well as abolition of the Prussian three-tier voting system based on income level. It demanded that the Reich's lower house of Parliament be vested with far greater powers than it currently enjoyed.

Social Democracy maintained that economic and other forms of inequality were the product of history, of some people exploiting others. With industrialization, economic scarcity for the first time in history could be eradicated and poverty abolished. The Social Democrats therefore supported class struggle on the part of the proletariat and upheld the right of trade unions to organize and strike. It also called for the eventual nationalization of industry, full employment, guaranteed housing, publicly funded medical services, labor protection legislation, social security benefits, and other reforms.

Under Social Democracy the arms race leading to World War I would have been drastically curtailed; what today we call the "peace dividend" would have been invested in public education and other public goods. Imperial colonial policies would have been reexamined.

Social Democracy also called for the separation of church and state, abolition of religious instruction in the public schools and the end to privileges then enjoyed by the Protestant churches. It did not, however, call for the abolition of religion itself; rather, it relegated religion to the private sector out of regard for civil liberties.

It is true that the Progressive Party also supported civil liberties. But the chasm that existed between the Social Democratic party and the other parties is demonstrated by the fact that none, not even the Progressive Party, was willing to enter into coalition with the SPD in 1912, the year the socialists won the largest plurality in the national parliament. Rather, they opted for parliament to remain stalemated, which had the effect of providing the emperor greater latitude as he and his warlords prepared for war.

The mass appeal of Social Democracy among Catholic and Protestant believers was enhanced by Kautsky's historical studies of Christianity. Kautsky published his two-volume social history of Christianity, *Forerunners of Modern Socialism*, in 1895, more than a decade before Troeltsch published his *Social Teaching* (1912). In his work Kautsky interpreted the communion of goods tradition of early Christianity as an anticipation of modern socialism. The practice of communism among the urban poor who formed the first Christian congregations was the heart of the gospel teaching for Kautsky. Christian communism failed because it did not and could not abolish unequal property in the means of production. Kautsky explained this failure in terms of constraints inherent in a preindustrial economy; he did not invoke the ahistorical theory of selfish human nature.

The internal contradiction between a communism of consumption and private property in the means of production increased as Christianity spread throughout the Roman world. This tension was eventually resolved in favor of the rich as they increasingly entered the church fold and came to dominate church affairs. A clerical hierarchy arose which, by virtue of a vow of "poverty," laid claim to church property originally designated for the poor. The practice of charity eventually replaced the communism of goods. Kautsky argues that the original communal tradition was so central that it was never entirely forgotten, but rather relegated to the margins, spiritualized, and yet periodically reintroduced through the emergence of religious orders and sects.

Kautsky also adduced evidence that the communist experiment of the early church weakened patriarchal family values and elevated women to leadership roles outside the family. With the later ascendancy of private over communally held property, the patriarchal family model reasserted itself. Patriarchy also gave shape to the development of clerical hierarchy.

With a growing minority of pastors and priests coming under the influence of Social Democracy, the Protestant churches attempted to make their own response to the Social Problem. In the early 1890s while the new emperor was in his "liberal" phase, the Evangelical Social Congress was formed. After the emperor's conservative shift in 1896, marked by his edict against "political pastors," the Congress took a conservative turn. The political activism of Göhre and Naumann gave way to a focus on private charity under the leadership of Harnack.

Christian socialists such as Leonhard Ragaz, who emphasized a gospel centered around the coming of the Kingdom of God *on earth* in a form compatible with Social Democracy, were particularly out of favor in Germany.

Troeltsch participated in this struggle between socialists and mainstream academics and clergy. Like his teacher Ritschl and older friend Harnack, he chose to actively support the Emperor's policies. In his address to the Evangelical Social Congress entitled, "Political Ethics and Christianity" (1904), Troeltsch approvingly cited the Emperor's edict against "political" pastors, thus joining forces with Harnack, who was then President of the Congress. He was not really advocating an apolitical alternative, however, for he urged his fellow Congress members to side with the Conservative/Liberal block.

Once World War I began, Troeltsch to his credit co-signed with Max Weber and a minority of other academics the Delbrück petition criticizing the Emperor's unlimited war aims. But Troeltsch's conformity to nationalist sentiment regarding the rights of hospitalized prisoners of war caused Weber to break off his close friendship with him.

Sitting in the Badenese Parliament as a member of the National Liberal party, Troeltsch was an active participant in a coalition of the Liberal and Conservative parties formed in 1905 to combat the Catholic Center and Social Democratic parties, which opposed brutal colonial policies in Africa and the runaway arms race. The more conservative of the two liberal parties, Troeltsch's National Liberal party also supported the call for a new *Kulturkampf* to suspend the civil liberties of Catholic religious orders. As a National Liberal, Troeltsch was politically to the right of Lujo Brentano's Progressive Party, as well as the Social Democrats; both these parties supported civil liberties for all.

While Kautsky wrote a social history of Christianity, making reference to both ideology and practice, Troeltsch used Dilthey's method of *Geistesgeschichte* to write a history of Christian social *teachings*. As one who embraced the neo-Kantian paradigm, questions of political economy were eclipsed for Troeltsch. He did not explore questions of how Christian social teaching eventually functioned to legitimate unequal property relations. Kautsky, on the other hand, analysed how the vows of poverty and celibacy arose and functioned in relation to the increasing ownership of church property by the clergy. Troeltsch makes no mention of such public policies as the Crusades, the witch-burnings of New England, the expulsion of Jews from Spain, or how such actions related, if at all, to Christian social teaching.

In *The Social Teaching*, Troeltsch argues that early Christianity never attempted to address the problems of poverty or oppression; that in fact the original gospel message had nothing to do with social reform of any kind. Christianity's primary focus looks beyond the problems of history or society altogether. It is concerned primarily with restoring the soul's relationship to God.

Though diverging widely from Kautsky in interpreting early Christianity, Troeltsch did agree with him on certain basic facts. He agreed that Christianity began as a movement among urban poor who had apocalyptic expectations of an imminent end to history after which the Kingdom of God would be ushered in. He agreed that these early believers practiced a communism of goods and lacked a work ethic or any orientation to questions of production.

But for Troeltsch, the social concerns of early Christianity were ancillary to its purely religious concerns. To the extent that the church dealt with social problems at all, it gave primacy to the individual soul. It did not weaken, but rather strengthened the patriarchal family and private property relations. The communism of the early church was a brief, ephemeral episode that passed quickly in favor of unequal property relations that Kautsky himself admitted had existed previously. Kautsky was correct to see that the early Christian communism of goods had to fail. He was incorrect to argue that under modern industrial conditions, socialism is a serious alternative that early Christianity anticipated.

Therefore, the social ethic of Christianity throughout its history finds ways to accommodate to the status quo. Contra Kautsky, Troeltsch followed Ritschl and Harnack in rejecting the Jewish prophetic and messianic antecedents to the early Christians, looking rather to their Hellenistic heritage. Because of his apocalyptic preoccupations, Jesus himself fails to provide ethical norms for the dominant church institutions; rather, Paul does so by recognizing the secular authorities to be divinely ordained and therefore to be obeyed. Thus, Paul accommodated Christianity to the existing order. There is no injunction in the gospel message against patriarchy, against war or the military, against social inequality, even against poverty or slavery. The idea that such established social institutions could ever be decisively modified is utopian; they are components of "reality" that transcend the possibilities of historical change.

Since Christianity strengthens patriarchal authority, it provides no legitimation for social equality; rather equality exists only "in Christ," that is, in the realm of the spirit only. The Christian ethic involves a double morality: one for those in authority and one for subordinates. Those (men) in authority ought to treat their subordinates humanely while subordinates ought humbly to accept their lot, and fulfill their duties obediently and industriously.

Troeltsch's interpretation of the Christian ethic recalls his earlier invocation of "authority, not majority" in his address to the Evangelical Social Congress of 1904. For Troeltsch, the theological meaning of redemption focuses upon the Pauline conceptions of predestination and election, which support the conservative view of social inequality as a fact of nature, ordained by God. He modified the conservative view by invoking the theological concept of personalism, which meant that authority based on personal cultivation and learning should replace authority based on blood and landed property. Here he expresses the "liberal" ideal of the German mandarins. The conservative ethic that affirmed hierarchical structures of authority, while thus modified, is still upheld. In Troeltsch's view, the Christian ethic does not legitimate democracy based on popular sovereignty.

Whereas Kautsky understood internal divisions within Christendom in terms of class conflict, Troeltsch understood them in terms of successful or unsuccessful accommodation to social "reality." Kautsky based his argument on history; Troeltsch, on nature. Troeltsch adopted Weber's typology of church and sect, adding mysticism as a new dimension. Here, he broke with Ritschl to follow the proto-fascist mystic, Lagarde.

According to Troeltsch, the difference between church and sect is the difference between those who accommodate and those who dissent from the status quo. Sectarians vainly attempt to usher in the Kingdom of God on earth, whether within their own circles or in the whole of society. He acknowledged that church and sect divide along class lines; the former governed from above by the ruling classes, the latter, from below by laboring peoples. Ragaz and other Christian socialists who confront the established order rather than withdraw from it are classified as *aggressive* sectarians.

While the church/sect dimension is defined sociologically, for Troeltsch, mysticism is defined in terms of a purely inward experience.

Mysticism is the essence of what he elsewhere calls religious individualism. It seems that Troeltsch himself was a mystic, and would have so
located himself on his own typology of religion. In theory, the mysti-
cal/non-mystical dimension is independent of the church/sect dimension and of politics generally.

Kautsky also accepted the validity of mysticism, understood in this
apolitical way, which he attributed to Schiller, for example. Thus, although Troeltsch frequently adopts the stance of defending the true
spiritual nature of religion from Marxist reductionism, in reality both
Troeltsch and Kautsky could agree on the authenticity of mysticism or
religious individualism. Futher, there was no inherent conflict between
Troeltsch's view that religious individualism was the *inner experiential* essence of Christianity, and Kautsky's view that the communism of
goods was its *sociological* essence. Troeltsch's real disagreement with
Kautsky was over the communism of goods *as such* and its modern
incarnation, Social Democracy.

In Kautsky's view, early Christianity with its communism of goods,
loosened family ties, and equalization of the sexes anticipated modern
socialism. Its inability to transform unequal relations of production resulted in this radical beginning being overtaken by traditional patriarchal structures of domination, which took on a new form with the rise
of clerical hierarchy. However, the power and centrality of the original
gospel of communism repeatedly broke through in prophetic voices of
dissent that called for a return to the original message.

For Troeltsch the reconciliation of the individual soul with God stands
at the center of the original gospel message and the communism of
goods is merely an ephemeral by-product. In fact, this communism is
significant only to the extent that it develops the virtues of the soul.
Thus, socialism is superseded by mystical individualism in Troeltsch's
interpretation. His emphasis on individualism by no means includes an
affirmation of popular democracy, however. Rather, German individualism refers to the sovereignty of the learned few. Christianity actually
added legitimacy to the patriarchal family structure as an appropriate
model for the state. Only *spiritual* equality is affirmed.

In summary, while mysticism and spiritual equality are compatible
with socialism and social equality, Troeltsch affirmed mysticism as an
alternative to socialism. In so doing, he distorted his own typology, in
practice conflating the theoretically apolitical mystical type with the
conservative church type.

The dominant history of the social teachings of Christianity, the history of the church type, is comprised of a series of "realistic" compromises with the status quo. The sects represent the dissent of an overly idealistic few and are not to be dignified through recognition of their "prophetic" status.

Finally, with respect to the Social Problem, the Christian ethic calls for acts of private charity. This is the most realistic recommendation, for the poor will always be with us. The Kingdom of God will never enter history; it is foolish to believe that the basic structures of society can ever significantly change for the better since they represent the natural order. The Kingdom is within us—a private oasis in a brutal public reality. It follows from Troeltsch's argument based on nature that the ruling class is not to be held responsible as the historical agent of oppression. All humans by virtue of their imperfect natures are equally to blame for the inequities of life.

"Brutal reality"[2] was exceptionally generous to Troeltsch. Born into a prominent doctor's family, educated in the most exclusive schools, Troeltsch was a charming, ebullient man who rose quickly through the academic ranks, and who generally supported his emperor's foreign and domestic policies. At the conclusion of *The Social Teaching*, published just two years before the outbreak of World War I, he imagined that another "abyss" was about to open. Troeltsch's use of imagery from nature evokes a sense of history as a product of natural forces beyond human control, rather than a product of social relations. Indeed, only a handful of socialist and pacifist dissenters would take a prophetic stand against the unprecedented slaughter that the emperor would initiate, that the European nations would carry out against one another, and that would bring about the destruction of the Second Reich.

Notes

1. Adolf Harnack, *What is Christianity?* (Gloucester, MA: Peter Smith, 1978), 268.
2. Troeltsch, *The Social Teaching*, 1012; GS1, 985.

14

Conclusion: Religious and Social Transformation

As humanity contemplates the unfolding of a new millennium, the future of our planet and of civilization has never been more uncertain. With a growing human population now exceeding 5.6 billion, a global corporate economy preoccupied with ecologically unsustainable growth, and the continued militarization of science and industry, humanity's clock may be running out. Given our current stressing of the earth's ecosystems, a projected doubling of population in the 21st century could plunge the planet into a new era of environmental degradation, poverty, and violence.[1]

What role can religion be expected to play in relation to these pressing global concerns? The answer to this question depends in part upon the lessons people of faith learn from the twentieth century, including its world wars; the Holocaust and other genocides; Hiroshima, Nagasaki, and the nuclear arms race; and the monstrosities of Stalinism and Third World fascism.[2]

In the midst of these nightmares, movements of religious awakening—including Gandhi's campaigns in South Africa and India, the Civil Rights movement in the United States, and liberation theology in Latin America—challenged underlying structures of social and economic power.[3] The ideological struggles associated with some of these movements bear a striking resemblance to the turn of the century debate between Kautsky and Troeltsch. Black and Latin American liberation theologies, for example, evoked a polemical rejoinder from sociologist Peter Berger that closely parallels Troeltsch's reply to Kautsky.

A brief comparison of Troeltsch and Berger, and how their ideas functioned to legitimize their respective power structures, will help put the subject matter of this book in a broader historical context.

Both thinkers proposed conceptual frameworks that purported to be politically neutral. In *The Social Teaching*, Troeltsch claimed to advo-

213

cate a middle way between Christian traditionalists like Martin von Nathusius and socialists like Karl Kautsky. Similarly, in *The Heretical Imperative* (1979), Berger proposed an "inductive" approach to religion as a middle way between the "deductive" affirmation of traditional religious authority and "reductive" interpretations of religious tradition that the author associates with liberal or socialist values.[4]

Upon closer examination, however, a political bias is apparent in Berger's definition of "religious experience," which is the basis of his inductive approach. Berger includes as "religious" the experience of virtually all phenomena believed to be of supernatural and otherworldly origin. The major exception, however, is divine liberation from earthly oppression, in spite of the centrality of this experience in the Bible, including the Book of Exodus, the Prophets and the writings of Luke.

This selective definition of religious experience then enables Berger to define as secular or nonreligious the oppression and liberation of African-Americans and Latin Americans who look to the Bible for a validation of their own experiences. Having excluded the relevant Biblical traditions from his initial definition of religion, Berger depicts liberation theologies based upon such experiences and traditions as "reductions" of Christianity to modern and secular ideologies.

As discussed in the present study, Troeltsch wrote *The Social Teaching* during the peak of social democracy in Germany, at a time when large segments of the general public and some important members of the clergy were rejecting traditional Christianity in favor of what today would be called "liberation theology." Responding to Kautsky's research on the communism of goods in the early church and throughout its history, Troeltsch interpreted Christianity as fundamentally a matter of the salvation of individual souls.

Although presenting his theological position as apolitical, it was of a piece with his politics. Troeltsch's verbal advocacy of equality (or even socialism) "in Christ" went hand in hand with his political opposition to social and economic equality for women, Jews, Catholics, working people, Africans in Germany's new colonial holdings, and indeed even for other Europeans in the way of German military ambitions.

Similarly, Berger wrote *The Heretical Imperative* in the aftermath of Martin Luther King, Jr.'s theology and during the peak of Latin American liberation theology. Inspired by such ideas, mass movements challenged racist structures in the United States and the complicity of the Catholic Church with right-wing regimes in Latin America and their links to the U.S. government and U.S.-based transnational corporations.[5]

As in the case of Troeltsch, an adequate interpretation of Berger's thought in the 1970s requires a reconstruction of its political context, which was the very real challenge that Black and Latin American liberation theologies then posed to the power structure of the United States. For Troeltsch, the challenge to the existing order came from the social democratic movement within Germany and internationally.

Both Troeltsch and Berger advocated a turning towards individual religious experience and salvation as an alternative to popular political variants of Christianity that sought to bring the Kingdom of God "on earth, as it is in heaven." Both sought to explain away revolutionary traditions within the Bible and to interpret the religious sphere as independent of politics. Both defended the patriarchal family and patterns of bourgeois privilege in the face of movements for women's equality and social equality generally, advocating spiritual equality as alternatives to material and earthly equality.[6]

In summary, both Troeltsch and Berger interpreted Christianity in such a way as to legitimize the dominant social orders in which they lived and disputed interpretations of Christianity that challenged those orders.

At the present time in history, to support the dominant social order is to participate in the destruction of civilization. The far-reaching economic, social, and political changes needed to secure a humane future will require far-reaching transformations of consciousness and values. Religious renewal can help bring about the needed consciousness and values, or, in the absence of such renewal, the religions of the world can remain part of the problem—continuing to legitimize wealth, patriarchy, and militarism.

More precisely, transformative and reactionary trends are contending within the very same religious traditions, and the relative strengths of these trends will determine the net impact of a given religion on the global crisis. Let us conclude this book with some examples, which give us glimpses into the future of religion.

There are undoubtedly numerous movements of authentic religious renewal in the world today. I will limit this discussion to examples with which I am personally familiar.

Michael Lerner and his associates at *Tikkun Magazine* are spearheading a far-reaching program of Jewish renewal. Lerner and Cornel West have engaged in pioneering Jewish-Black Christian dialogue. India's tradition of Vedanta, now understood as a science and technology of higher states of consciousness, is making measurable contributions to health and human development. Chiara Lubich and her associates in the international Focolare Movement are renewing the spirituality of love at the basis of Christianity and the apostolic communism of goods practiced by the early churches and by Catholic religious orders throughout the common era. American Muslims led by W. D. Mohammed are moving beyond Black nationalism and rediscovering the universal ideals of Islam. Tibetan Buddhism, suffering horrible repression by the Chinese government, remains a source of inspiration for millions in Tibet and throughout the world.[7]

The same world religions from which these life-affirming variants spring, however, simultaneously cast long shadows on the earth. Jewish and Muslim fundamentalists are seeking to sabotage the fragile negotiations between Israel and its Arab neighbors. The sacralization of motherhood in Catholicism and Hinduism undoubtedly contributes to excessive birth rates, while many believers of all religious traditions continue to heartlessly dishonor homosexuality—and mindlessly, in view of global overpopulation. White Protestant fundamentalists in Amarillo, Texas conflate Christianity with the cult of the Bomb, Catholic fundamentalists of "Opus Dei" maneuver in Rome to restore pre-Vatican II Catholicism, and Japanese cult leader Asahara presides over a highly destructive variant of Buddhism. A widespread refusal to reflect on the Holocaust deforms Christian education: admirers of Nazi theologian Emanuel Hirsch hold influential positions on theological faculties, for example, while the school of Johann Baptist Metz—who called for a reconstruction of Christian theology in response to Auschwitz—remains marginal.[8]

These brief samplings of authentic renewal on the one hand and reaction on the other illustrate the Janus-faced complexity of world religion today. A bewildering variety of such alternatives are likely to confront every religiously open-minded individual for decades to come. This was precisely the dilemma that Peter Berger so eloquently described in *The Heretical Imperative*. What was missing from that book, however, was any analysis relating such religious movements dialectically to structures of social, economic and political power.

Troeltsch, Berger, and others like them helped create conservative variants of religion that legitimized existing structures. Kautsky, Martin Luther King, Jr., and Latin American liberation theologians helped create social movements that shook the halls of power and inspired millions to work towards a humane future based on democracy, demilitarization, and racial, gender, and economic equality.

These same basic alternatives underlie the complexities of today's religious scene. Now—as then—more is at stake than the salvation of individuals. By the religious and political decisions we make, humanity is choosing the path to heaven or hell for the entire earth and its inhabitants.

Notes

1. Important books on the current global crisis include Lester R. Brown et al., *State of the World: A Worldwatch Institute Report on Progress Toward a Sustainable Society* (New York: W. W. Norton & Company, 1998 [updated annually]); David C. Korten, *When Corporations Rule the World* (West Hartford, CT and San Francisco, CA: Kumarian Press and Berrett-Koehler Publishers, 1995); and William D. Hartung, *And Weapons for All: How America's Multibillion Dollar Arms Trade Warps Our Foreign Policy and Subverts Democracy at Home* (New York: HarperCollins Publishers, 1994) For a spiritually informed, alternative response, see Robert Roth, *The Natural Law Party: A Reason to Vote* (New York: St. Martin's Press, 1998).

2. For a good example of the kind of reflection on history that can facilitate needed transformations of consciousness and values, see Robert Jay Lifton and Eric Markusen, *The Genocidal Mentality: Nazi Holocaust and Nuclear Threat* (New York: Basic Books, Inc., 1990); see also Ernest Mandel, *The Meaning of the Second World War* (London: Verso, 1986) and, Noam Chomsky and Edward S. Herman, *The Washington Connection and Third World Fascism* (Boston: South End Press, 1979).

3. See Dennis Dalton, *Mahatma Gandhi: Nonviolent Power In Action* (New York: Columbia University Press, 1993; Cornel West, *Prophesy Deliverance! An Afro-American Revolutionary Christianity* (Philadelphia, PA: The Westminster Press, 1982; Harvey Cox, *The Silencing of Leonardo Boff: The Vatican and the Future of World Christianity* (Oak Park, IL: Meyer-Stone Books, 1988).

4. Peter L. Berger, *The Heretical Imperative: Contemporary Possibilities of Religious Affirmation,* (Garden City, NY: Anchor Press/Doubleday, 1979. Berger's typology of the deductive, reductive, and inductive options for responding to the contemporary crisis of religion parallels Troeltsch's historical concepts of church, sect and mysticism. Like Berger's concept of the inductive option, Troeltsch's concept of mysticism is in theory neutral as between the other two but actually has a conservative twist, as is explained in chapter twelve. My critique of Berger and comparison of Troeltsch and Berger is based largely on a conversation with political scientist Brian D'Agostino.

5. This revolutionary movement within Catholicism has now been largely contained by the Vatican, which has systematically filled vacancies in Catholic bishoprics throughout the world with religious and political conservatives. While the preferences of Pope John Paul II are an important factor in this trend, broader social factors include the influence in Rome of "Opus Dei," a lay religious order with roots in Spanish fascism.

6. For Troeltsch's views on the family, social equality and democracy, see chapters ten and twelve of the present study. For an explicit polemic by Berger against equality and democracy as viable norms for developing societies, see "Underdevelopment Revisited" (Berger, 1984); for a defense of patriarchy and the bourgeois family, see *The War Over the Family: Capturing the Middle Ground* (Berger and Berger, 1983).

7. See, Michael Lerner, *Jewish Renewal: A Path to Healing and Transformation* (New York: Harper Collins, 1995); Michael Lerner & Cornel West, *Jews and Blacks: A Dialogue on Race, Religion, and Culture in America* (New York: Penguin Books, 1995); *Struggles in the Promised Land: Toward a History of Black-Jewish Relations in the United States*, eds. Jack Salzman and Cornel West (New York: Oxford University Press, 1997); Rabbi Arthur Waskow, "Religious Restoration or Religious Renewal," *Tikkun: A Bimonthly Jewish Critique of Politics, Culture & Society* (July/August 1997); Judith Plaskow, *Standing Again At Sinai: Judaism from a Feminist Perspective* (New York: Harper Collins, 1990; on Vedanta and higher states of consciousness, see the peer reviewed, published research compiled in *Scientific Research on Maharishi's Transcendental Meditation and TM-Sidhis Program: Collected Papers, Vols. 1–5* (Seelisburg, Switzerland: Maharishi European Research University, 1972–1991) (Vol. 6 forthcoming) and Robert K. C. Forman, ed. *The Problem of Pure Consciousness: Mysticism and Philosophy* (New York: Oxford University Press, 1990); on the Focolare Movement and W. D. Mohammed, see Chiara Lubich, *Jesus: The Heart of His Message* (Hyde Park, NY: New City Press, 1997; Jim Gallagher, *A Woman's Work: Chiara Lubich*; Chiara Lubich, "That Which We Have In Common," and Imam Warith Deen Mohammed, "God Is One" (excerpts from their May 18, 1997 talks at the Malcolm Shabazz Mosque in Harlem) *Living City* (July 1997), 36:7; Robert A. F. Thurman, *Essential Tibetan Buddhism*, 1st ed. (San Francisco, CA: Harper, 1995).

8. For a religious critique of homophobia, see Letha Scanzoni and Virginia Ramey Mollenkott, *Is The Homosexual My Neighbor? Another Christian View* (San Francisco: Harper & Row, 1978); on Christian fundamentalism and the Bomb, see A. G. Mojtabai, *Blessed Assurance: At Home With the Bomb in Amarillo, Texas*, (Albuquerque: University of New Mexico Press, 1986; on Christian fundamentalism more generally, see Charles B. Strozier, *Apocalypse: On the Psychology of Fundamentalism in America* (Boston: Beacon Press, 1995); on Asahara, see Robert Jay Lifton, "Reflections on Aum Shinrikyo," *The Year 2,000: Reflections on the End*, eds. Charles B. Strozier, Michael Flynn (New York: New York University Press, 1997), 112–20; for a critique of post-Holocaust Christianity, see Johann Baptist Metz, "Christians and Jews after Auschwitz," in Metz, *The Emergent Church: The Future of Christianity in a Postbourgeois World* (New York: Crossroad, 1981).

Bibliography

Adams, James Luther. "Ernst Troeltsch as Analyst of Religion." *Journal for the Scientific Study of Religion* 1 (1961): 98–109.

———. "Troeltsch, Ernst." *Encyclopedia Britannica*, XXII. London/Chicago: William Benton, 1963.

———. "Why the Troeltsch Revival?" *The Unitarian Universalist Christian* 29 (1974): 4–15.

Aldington, Richard. *Death of a Hero*. New York: Covici, Friede, 1929.

Antoni, Carlo. *From History to Sociology*. Translated by Hayden V. White. Detroit, MI: Wayne State University Press, 1959.

Bainton, Roland H. "Ernst Troeltsch—Thirty Years Later." *Theology Today* 8:1 (April 1951): 70–96.

Baranowsky, Shelley. *The Confessing Church, Conservative Elites and the Nazi State*. Lewiston, NY: Edwin Mellen, 1986.

Batty, Peter. *The House of Krupp*. New York: Dorset Press, 1966.

Baumgarten, Eduard. *Max Weber: Werk und Person*. Tübingen: J.C.B. Mohr, 1964.

Baur, Ferdinand Christian. *The Church History of the First Three Centuries*. 3rd ed. Translated by A. Menzies. London: Williams and Norgate, 1878–79.

———. *Paul, the Apostle of Jesus Christ, his Life and Work, his Epistles and his Doctrine. A Contribution to a Critical History of Primitive Christianity*. Translated by E. Zeller. London: Williams and Norgate, 1875–76.

Beach, Waldo and H. Richard Niebuhr, eds. *Christian Ethics: Sources of the Living Tradition*. 2nd ed. New York: John Wiley and Sons, 1973.

Bebel, August. *Aus meinem Leben*. Stuttgart: J. H. W. Dietz, 1914.

Benson, Constance L. "The Early Church in The Social Teaching: Troeltsch's Reply to Kautsky." Paper presented to the Trienniel Congress of the Ernst Troeltsch Gesellschaft, October 1988, Augsburg, Germany; also presented to the American Academy of Religion, National Annual Meeting, November 1990, New Orleans, LA.

———. "Mainstreaming the Radical Right: Ernst Troeltsch's Appropriation of Paul de Lagarde." Paper presented to the American Academy of Religion, Mid-Atlantic Region, March 4–5, 1993, Temple University, Philadelphia, PA.

———. "The Role of Race in Ernst Troeltsch's Analysis of World Religions." Paper presented to the American Academy of Religion, Mid-Atlantic Region, March 4–5, 1993, Temple University, Philadelphia, PA.

Bentley, James. "Three German Marxists Look at Christianity: 1900–1930." *Journal of Church and State* 22 (Autumn, 1980): 505–17.

Berger, Peter L. *The Heretical Imperative: Contemporary Possibilities of Religious Affirmation.* Garden City, NY: Anchor Press/Doubleday, 1979.

———. "Underdevelopment Revisited." (1984).

———. *The War Over the Family: Capturing the Middle Ground.* (1983).

Berghahn, Volker. *Der Tirpitz Plan.* Düsseldorf: Droste Verlag, 1971.

Blumhardt, Christoph. *Eine Auswahl aus seinen Predigten, Andachten und Schriften.* Edited by R. Lejeune. Zürich: Erlenbach, 1925.

———. *Metanoia* (September 1971).

Bock, Paul. Introduction to *Signs of the Kingdom: A Ragaz Reader*, by Leonhard Ragaz. Grand Rapids, MI: Eerdmans, 1984.

Bosse, Hans. *Marx, Weber, Troeltsch.* Munich: Kaiser Verlag, 1971.

Brentano, Lujo. *Hours and Wages in Relation to Production.* Translated by Mrs. William Arnold. New York: Scribners, 1894.

———. *Mein Leben im Kampf um die soziale Entwicklung Deutschlands.* Jena: E. Diederichs, 1931.

———. *The Relation of Labor to the Law of Today.* Translated by Porter Sherman. New York: G. P. Putman, 1891.

Breysig, Kurt. *Forschungen zur Geschichte- und Gesellschaftslehre.* Stuttgart: Cotta, 1929–32.

Bridenthal, Renate, et al., eds. "Introduction: Imperial Germany and World War I." *When Biology Became Destiny: Women in Weimar and Nazi Germany.* New York: Monthly Review, 1984.

Brose, Eric Dorn. *Christian Labor and the Politics of Frustration in Imperial Germany.* Washington, DC: The Catholic University of America Press, 1985.

Brown, Lester R., et al. *State of the World: A Worldwatch Institute Report on Progress Toward a Sustainable Society.* New York: W. W. Norton & Co., 1998.

Canney, Maurice A., ed. *Essay on the Social Gospel by A. Harnack and W. Herrmann.* Translated by G. M. Craik. London and New York, 1907.

Cassirer, Ernst. *The Philosophy of Symbolic Forms.* Translated by Ralph Manheim. New Haven, CT: Yale University Press, 1953–57.

Charlesworth, James H. *Jesus' Jewishness: Exploring the Place of Jesus within Early Judaism.* New York: Crossroad, 1991.

Chomsky, Noam and Edward S. Herman. *The Washington Connection and Third World Fascism.* Boston: South End Press, 1979.

Clayton, John, ed. *Ernst Troeltsch and the Future of Theology.* Cambridge: Cambridge University Press, 1976.

Coakley, Sarah. *Christ without Absolutes: a Study of the Christology of Ernst Troeltsch.* Oxford: Clarendon Press, 1988.

Cohen, Hermann. *Kants Begründung der Ethik.* Berlin: Dümmler, 1877.

Cort, John. *Christian Socialism*. New York: Orbis, 1988.

Cox, Harvey. *The Silencing of Leonardo Boff: The Vatican and the Future of World Christianity*. Oak Park, Ill.: Meyer-Stone Books, 1988.

Craig, Gordon A. *Germany: 1866–1945*. Oxford: Oxford University Press, 1978.

Curtius, E. R. *Deutscher Geist in Gefahr*. Stuttgart: Deutsche Verlags-anstalt, 1932.

Dalton, Dennis. *Mahatma Gandhi: Nonviolent Power in Action*. New York: Columbia University Press, 1993.

DeMause, Lloyd. *Foundations of Psychohistory*. New York: Creative Roots, Inc., 1982.

Dietrich, Wendell S. *Cohen and Troeltsch: Ethical Monotheistic Religion and Theory of Culture*. Atlanta, GA: Scholars Press, 1986.

Dilthey, Wilhelm. *Einleitung in die Geisteswissenschaften*. Leipzig: Duncker und Humbolt, 1883.

Dinnerstein, Dorothy. *The Mermaid and the Minotaur: Sexual Arrangements and Human Malaise*. New York: Harper and Row, 1977.

Dorrien, Gary. *Soul in Society: The Making and Renewal of Social Christianity*. Minneapolis, MN: Fortress Press, 1995.

Drescher, Hans-Georg. *Ernst Troeltsch: His Life And Work*. Minneapolis, MN: Fortress Press, 1993.

———. "Ernst Troeltsch und Paul de Lagarde." *Mitteilungen der Ernst-Troeltsch-Gesellschaft* III (Augsburg, 1984): 95–115.

Edwards, Paul, ed. *The Encyclopedia of Philosophy*. New York: Macmillan and Free Press, 1967, s.v. "Max Weber," by Peter Winch.

Eley, Geoff. *From Unification To Nazism: Reinterpreting the German Past*. Boston: Allen & Unwin, 1986.

——— and David Blackbourne. *The Peculiarities of German History, Bourgeois Society and Politics in Nineteenth-Century Germany*. Oxford: Oxford University Press, 1984.

Eliade, Mircea, ed. *Encyclopedia of Religion*. New York: Macmillan and Free Press, 1987, s.v. "Ernst Troeltsch," by Friedrich Wilhelm Graf.

Ericksen, Robert P. *Theologians Under Hitler: Gerhard Kittel/Paul Althaus/ Emanuel Hirsch*. New Haven, CT: Yale University Press, 1985.

Evans, Richard. *Rethinking German History: Nineteenth-Century Germany and the Origins of the Third Reich*. New York: HarperCollins Academic, 1987.

Fischer, Fritz. "Der deutsche Protestantismus und die Politik im 19. Jahrhundert." In *Probleme der Reichsgründungszeit 1848–79*. Edited by Helmut Böhme, 49–71. Cologne and Berlin: Kiepenheuer & Witsch, 1968.

———. *Griff nach der Weltmacht*. Düsseldorf: Droste Verlag, 1961.

———. *Krieg der Illusionen*. Düsseldorf: Droste Verlag, 1969.

Fischer, Kuno. *A Commentary on Kant's Critique of the Pure Reason*. Translated by John Pentland Mahaffy. New York: Garland Publishers, 1976.

————. *Geschichte der neueren Philosophie*. Heidelberg: C. Winter, 1909.

Forman, Robert K. C., ed. *The Problem of Pure Consciousness: Mysticism and Philosophy*. New York: Oxford University Press, 1990.

Frantz, Konstantin. *Der Föderalismus als das leitende Prinzip für die soziale, staatliche und internationale Organisation unter besonderer Bezugnahme auf Deutschland*. Mainz: Kirchheim, 1879.

————. *Die Religion des Nationalliberalismus*. Leipzig: Rossberg, 1872.

Freytag, Gustav. *Die verlorene Handschrift*. Leipzig: Hirzel, 1865.

Gallagher, Jim. *A Woman's Work: Chara Lubich*. Hyde Park, NY: New City Press, 1997.

Gayhart, Bryce A. *The Ethics of Ernst Troeltsch: A Commitment to Relevancy*. Lewiston, NY: The Edwin Mellen Press, 1990.

Gerdes, Hayo, ed. *Wahrheit und Glaube: Festschrift für Emanuel Hirsch zu seinem 75. Geburtstag*. Munich: "Die Spur", Itzehoe Herbert Dorbandt KG, 1963.

Gerth, H. H. and C. Wright Mills. "Introduction: The Man and His Work." *From Max Weber: Essays in Sociology*. Edited by H. H. Gerth and C. Wright Mills. New York: Oxford University Press, 1958.

Gieseler, Johann Karl Ludwig. *Lehrbuch der Kirchen-geschichte*. Bonn, 1831.

Gilcher-Holtey, Ingrid. *Das Mandat des Intellektuellen: Karl Kautsky und die Sozialdemokratie*. Berlin: Siedler Verlag, 1986.

Gläser, Ernst. *Jahrgang 1902*. Berlin: G. Kiepenheuer, 1931.

Glick, G. Wayne. *The Reality of Christianity: A Study of Adolf von Harnack as Historian and Theologian*. New York: Harper and Row, 1967.

Göhre, Paul. *Three Months in a Workshop: A Practical Study*. Translated by A. B. Carr. New York: Charles Scribner's Sons, 1895; reprint, New York: Arno Press, 1972.

Goetz, Walter W., ed. "Der Briefwechsel Gustav Schmollers mit Lujo Brentano." *Archiv für Kulturgeschichte*, vol. 30. Weimar: Hermann Böhlaus Nachfolgen, 1941.

Goldberg, Jeffrey. "Blindness or Insight? Is the Ernst Troeltsch Affair a Christian Coverup, or Merely a Matter of Grad Student Incompetence?" *Lingua Franca* (February 1994): 44–49.

Gough, J. W. *The Social Contract*. Revised ed. Oxford: Oxford University Press, 1957.

Grimm, Jakob and Wilhelm. *Grimms' Tales for Young and Old*. Translated by Ralph Manheim. Garden City, NY: Doubleday, 1977.

Groh, Dieter. *Negative Integration und revolutionärer Attentismus*. Frankfurt: Ullstein Verlag, 1974.

Grossman, Ron. "Doctorate Denied: Constance Benson's Standing as a Scholar is More than an Academic Question," *Chicago Tribune* (December 8, 1993): Section 5:1–2.

Harnack, Adolf von. "Das doppelte Evangelium in dem Neuen Testament." *Aus Wissenschaft und Leben*. Vol. 2. Giessen: A. Töppelmann, 1911.

————. "Ernst Troeltsch: A Funeral Address delivered on February 3, 1923." *Harnack and Troeltsch: Two Historical Theologians*. Edited and translated by Wilhelm Pauck. New York: Oxford University Press, 1968: 117–27.

————. "Die evangelisch-soziale Aufgabe im Lichte der Geschichte der Kirche (1894)." *Reden und Augsätze*. Vol. 2. Giessen: J. Ricker, 1904: 23–76.

————. *History of Dogma*. Translated by Neil Buchanan. New York: Russell and Russell, 1958.

————. *What is Christianity*. Translated by Thomas Bailey Saunders. New York: Harper and Brothers, 1957; reprint, 1978.

Hartmann, Eduard von. *Philosophy of the Unconscious*. Translated by William C. Coupland. London: Routledge and Kegan Paul, 1950.

Hartung, William D. *And Weapons for All: How America's Multibillion Dollar Arms Trade Warps Our Foreign Policy and Subverts Democracy at Home*. New York: HarperCollins Publishers, 1994.

Herbert, Ulrich. *Best*. Bonn: Dietz, 1996.

————. "Werner Best and the Intellectual Leadership of the Nazi SS." Paper presented at the City University of New York Graduate School, October 28, 1997.

Heuss, Theodor. *Friedrich Naumann, der Mann, das Werk, die Zeit*. Stuttgart: Deutsche Verlag, 1937.

Hintze, Otto. *The Historical Essays of Otto Hintze*. Edited by Felix Gilbert. New York: Oxford University Press, 1975.

Hitler, Adolf. "Basic Ideas Regarding the Meaning and Organization of the SA." In *Mein Kampf*, Vol. II. Translated by Ralph Manheim. Boston: Houghton Mifflin, 1925, 1971, 518–53.

Hodgson, Peter C. *The Formation of Historical Theology, a Study of Ferdinand Christian Baur*. New York: Harper and Row, 1966.

Hughes, H. Stuart. *Consciousness and Society: The Reorientation of European Social Thought 1890–1930*. New York: Alfred A. Knopf, 1961.

Husserl, Edmund. *Ideas Pertaining to a Pure Phenomenology and to a Phenomenological Philosophy*. Translated by F. Kersten. Boston: Kluwer, 1982.

Jacobs, Jack. "Karl Kautsky and the 'Jewish Question.'" Collected Papers Presented at the Internationale Wissenschaftliche Konferenz "Karl Kautskys Bedeutung in der Geschichte der Sozialistischen Arbeiterbewegung," 312–30, Bremen, 1988.

————. "Marxism and Anti-Semitism: Kautsky's Perspective." *International Review of Social History* 30:3 (1985): 400–30.

Kadzis, Peter. "Cornel West for the Defense," *The Boston Phoenix* (November 26, 1993): Section 1:1

Kähler, Martin. *The So-called Historical Jesus and the Historic Biblical Christ*. Translated and edited by Carl E. Braaten. With a Foreword by Paul J. Tillich. Philadelphia, PA: Fortress Press, 1988.

————. *Die starken Wurzeln unserer Kraft. Betrachtungen über das deutsche Kaiserreich in seiner ersten Krise*. Gotha: F. A. Perthes, 1872.

Kalthoff, Albert. *The Rise of Christianity*. Translated by Joseph McCabe. London: Watts & Co., 1907.

Karnick, Hannes and Wolfgang Richter. *Niemöller: Was Würde Jesus Dazu Sagen? Eine Reise durch ein Protestantisches Leben*. Frankfurt: Roderberg Verlag, 1986.

Kasch, Wilhelm F. *Die Sozialphilosophie von Ernst Troeltsch*. Tübingen: J. C. B. Mohr, 1963.

Kautsky, John H. *Karl Kautsky: Marxism, Revolution and Democracy*. New Brunswick, NJ: Transaction Publishers, 1994.

———. *The Materialist Conception of History*. Edited by John H. Kautsky. New Haven, CT: Yale University Press, 1988.

———. "The Political Thought of Karl Kautsky." Ph.D. diss., Harvard University, 1951.

Kautsky, Karl. "Der Antisemitismus." *Oesterreichischer Arbeiter-Kalender für das Jahr 1885*.

———. *The Foundations of Christianity*. New York: International Publishers, 1925; reprint ed., New York: Monthly Review Press, 1980.

———. "Social Democracy and the Catholic Church," *The Social Democrat*, Vol. VII. (London, 1903), 162–69, 234–43, 288–91, 359–62, 430–36.

———. "Die Sozialdemokratie und die katholische Kirche." 2nd ed. Berlin: Buchhandlung Vorwärts, 1906.

———. *Thomas More and his Utopia*. Authorized translation. New York: International Publishers, 1927.

———. *Die Vorläufer des Neuren Sozialismus*, 2 vols. Stuttgart: J. H. M. Dietz, 1895.

Ketteler, Wilhalm Emmanuel von. *Die Arbeiterfrage und das Christentum*. 3rd ed. Mainz: F. Kirchheim, 1864.

Korten, David C. *When Corporations Rule the World*. West Hartford, CT and San Francisco, CA: Kumarian Press and Berrett-Koehler Publishers, 1995.

Kupisch, Karl, ed. *Quellen zur Geschichte des deutschen Protestantismus (1871–1945)*. Göttingen: Musterschmidt Verlag, 1960.

Kutter, Hermann. *They Must; or, God and the Social Democracy; a Frank Word to Christian Men and Women*. Edited and translated by Rufus W. Weeks. Chicago: Co-operative Prints Co., 1908.

Lagarde, Anna de. *Paul de Lagarde. Erinnerungen aus seinem Leben für die Freunde zusammengestellt*. Göttingen: Kästner, 1894.

Lagarde, Paul de. *Aus dem Deutschen Gelehrtenleben*. Göttingen: E. Dieterichs, 1880.

———. *Ausgewälte Schriften*. Edited by Paul Fischer. München: J. F. Lehmanns Verlag, 1934.

———. *Bekenntnis zu Deutschland*. Edited by W. Rössle. Jena: E. Dieterichs, 1933.

———. *Deutsche Schriften*. 4th edition. Göttingen: Lüder Horstmann, 1903.

Lambi, Ivo N. *Free Trade and Protection in Germany, 1868–1879.* Wiesbaden: F. Steiner, 1963.

Lamprecht, Karl. *Deutsche Geschichte.* Berlin: Weidmann, 1912–13.

——. *Krieg und Kultur.* Leipzig: S. Hirzel, 1914.

——. *What is History?* Translated by E. A. Andrews. New York: Macmillan, 1905.

Lerner, Michael. *Jewish Renewal: A Path to Healing and Transformation.* New York: HarperCollins, 1995.

—— and Cornel West. *Jews & Blacks: A Dialogue on Race, Religion and Culture in America.* New York: Penguin Books, 1995.

Liebersohn, Harry. *Religion and Industrial Society: the Protestant Social Congress in Wilhelmine Germany.* Philadelphia, PA: American Philosophical Society, 1986.

Lifton, Robert Jay and Eric Markusen. *The Genocidal Mentality: Nazi Holocaust and Nuclear Threat.* New York: Basic Books, Inc., 1990.

——. "Reflections on Aum Shinrikyo." *The Year 2,000: Reflections on the End.* Edited by Charles B. Strozier and Michael Flynn. New York: New York University Press, 1997.

Lotz, David W. "Albrecht Ritschl and the Unfinished Reformation." *Harvard Theological Review* 73:3–4 (July-October, 1980): 342–44.

——. *Ritschl and Luther.* New York: Abingdon Press, 1974.

Lougee, Robert W. *Paul de Lagarde, 1827–1891: A Study of Radical Conservatism in Germany.* Cambridge, MA: Harvard University Press, 1962.

Lubich, Chiara. *Jesus: The Heart of His Message.* Hyde Park, NY: New City Press, 1997.

——. "That Which We Have in Common." *Living City* 36:7 (July 1997).

Lukes, Steven. *Individualism.* Oxford: Basil Blackwell, 1973.

Mackintosh, Hugh Ross. *Types of Modern Theology: Schleiermacher to Barth.* London: Nisbet and Co., 1937.

MacPherson, C.B. *The Political Theory of Possessive Individualism: Hobbes to Locke.* New York: Oxford University Press, 1962.

Mandel, Ernest. *The Meaning of the Second World War.* London: Verso, 1986.

Massing, Paul W. *Rehearsal for Destruction: A Study of Political Anti-Semitism in Imperial Germany.* New York: H. Fertig, 1949.

Mattmüller, Markus. *Leonhard Ragaz—Religiöser Sozialist, Pazifist und Theologe des Reiches Gottes.* Darmstadt: Lingbach, 1986.

Mayer, Arno J. *The Persistence of the Old Regime: Europe to the Great War.* New York: Pantheon Press, 1981.

McCann, Dennis P. "Ernst Troeltsch's Essay on 'Socialism.'" *Journal of Religious Ethics* 4 (Spring, 1976): 159–80.

Meeks, M. Douglas. Foreword to *Signs of the Kingdom: A Ragaz Reader,* by Leonhard Ragaz. Edited and translated by Paul Bock. Grand Rapids, MI: Eerdmanns, 1984.

Mehring, Franz. *Geschichte der deutschen Sozialdemokratie*. Berlin: Dietz, 1960.

Meinecke, Friedrich. *The Age of German Liberation: 1795–1815*. Edited by Peter Paret. Translated by Peter Paret and Helmuth Fischer. Berkeley: University of California Press, 1977.

———. *Cosmopolitanism and the National State*. Translated by Robert B. Kimber. Princeton, NJ: Princeton University Press, 1970.

———. *Erlebtes 1862–1901*. Stuttgart: K. F. Löhler Verlag, 1964.

———. "Ernst Troeltsch: 1. Nachruf," *Werke*, IV. Stuttgart: Koehler Verlag, 1965.

———. *The German Catastrophe*. Translated by Sidney B. Fay. Boston: Beacon Press, 1963.

———. *Die Idee der Staatsräson in der Neueren Geschichte*. Munich and Berlin: Oldenbourg, 1924.

Metz, Johann Baptist. "Christians and Jews after Auschwitz." *The Emergent Church: The Future of Christianity in a Postbourgeois World*. New York: Crossroad, 1981.

Meyer, Eduard. *Geschichte des Altertums* 5th ed. Basel: B. Schwabe, 1953–58.

Mill, John Stuart. *Principles of Political Economy*. Boston, 1848.

Miller, Alice. *For Your Own Good: Hidden Cruelty in Child-rearing and the Roots of Violence*. Translated by Hildegarde and Hunter Hannum. New York: Farrar, Straus and Giroux, 1983.

Miller, Donald E. "Troeltsch's Critique of Karl Marx." *Journal for the Scientific Study of Religion* 1 (October 1961): 117–21.

Mohammed, Imam Warith Deen. "God Is One." *Living City* 36:7 (July 1997).

Mojtabai, A. G. *Blessed Assurance: At Home With the Bomb in Amarillo, Texas*. Albuquerque: University of New Mexico Press, 1986.

Möller, D. "Kirche und Monarchie." *Quellen zur Geschichte des deutschen Protestantismus (1871–1945)*. Edited by Karl Kupisch, 143–44. Göttingen: Musterschmidt Verlag, 1960.

Mommsen, Theodor. *The History of Rome*. Translated by W. P. Dickson. London: E. P. Dutton, 1911.

Mommsen, Wolfgang. "Die latente Krise des Deutschen Reiches 1909–1914." *Handbuch der deutschen Geschichte*. Vol. 4. Edited by Otto Brandt, Oskar Meyer, and Leo Just. Frankfurt a. M.: Akademische Verlagsgesellschaft Atenaion, 1973.

Morgan, Robert and Michael Pye. *Ernst Troeltsch: Writings on Theology and Religion*. Atlanta, GA: John Knox Press, 1977.

Mosse, George L. *Toward the Final Solution: A History of European Racism*. Madison: University of Wisconsin Press, 1985.

Mott, Stephen Charles. *Biblical Ethics and Social Change*. New York: Oxford University Press, 1982.

Mueller, David L. *An Introduction to the Theology of Albrecht Ritschl*. Philadelphia, PA: The Westminster Press, 1969.

Nathusius, Martin von. *Die Mitarbeit der Kirche an der Lösung der soziale Frage*. Leipzig: J. C. Hinrichs, 1904.

Naumann, Friedrich. *Central Europe*. Translated by Christabel M. Meredith. New York: Alfred A. Knopf, 1917.

————. *Demokratie und Kaisertum*. 4th ed. Berlin: Schöneberg, 1905.

Niebuhr, H. Richard. "Ernst Troeltsch's Philosophy of History." Ph.D. diss., Yale University Microfilms, 1924, 1964.

————. Introduction to *The Social Teaching of the Christian Churches*. Translated by Olive Wyon. New York: The Macmillan Co., 1931; reprint, Chicago: University of Chicago Press, 1981.

Ollman, Bertell. *Alienation: Marx's Conception of Man in Capitalist Society*. 2nd ed. New York: Cambridge University Press, 1976.

Pauck, Wilhelm. *From Luther to Tillich: The Reformers and their Heirs*. Edited by Marion Pauck. San Francisco, CA, 1984.

————. *Harnack and Troeltsch: Two Historical Theologians*. New York: Oxford University Press, 1968.

Paul, Garrett E. "Why Troeltsch? Why today? Theology for the 21st Century." *Christian Century* (June 30–July 7, 1993): 676–81.

Paulsen, Friedrich. *The German Universities and University Study*. New York, 1906.

Plaskow, Judith. *Standing Again at Sinai: Judaism from a Feminist Perspective*. New York: HarperCollins, 1990.

Puhle, Hans Jürgen. *Agrarische Interessenpolitik und preussischer Konservatismus im Wilhelminischen Reich* (1893–1914). Hanover: Verlag für Literature und Zeitgeschehen, 1967.

————. "Parlament, Parteien und Interessenverbände 1890–1914." Chap. in *Das kaiserliche Deutschland*. Edited by Michael Stürmer. Düsseldorf: Droste Verlag, 1970: 340–77.

————. *Von der Agarkrise zum Präfaschismus*. Wiesbaden: F. Steiner, 1972.

Pye, Michael. "Troeltsch and the Science of Religion." Chap. in *Ernst Troeltsch: Writings on Theology and Religion*. Edited by Robert Morgan and Michael Pye. Atlanta, GA: John Knox Press, 1977.

Ragaz, Leonhard. *Dein Reich Komme*. 3rd ed. Zürich: Rotapfel, 1922.

————. *Das Evangelium und der soziale Kampf der Gegenwart*. Basel, 1906.

Ranke, Leopold von. *Universal History*. Translated by D. C. Tovey and G. W. Prothero. New York: Harper and Bros., 1885.

Reist, Benjamin A. *Toward a Theology of Involvement: The Thought of Ernst Troeltsch*. Philadelphia, PA: The Westminster Press, 1966.

Remarque, Erich Maria. *All Quiet on the Western Front*. Translated by A. W. Wheen. New York: Ballantine Books, 1987.

Rendtorff, Trutz. "In memoriam Wolfgang Trillhaas (1903–1995)." *Mitteilungen der Ernst-Troeltsch-Gesellschaft* IX (Augsburg, 1995/96): 1–2.

————. *Politische Ethik und Christentum*. Munich: Christian Kaiser Verlag, 1978.

Richmond, James. *Ritschl: A Reappraisal*. London: Collins, 1978.

Rickert, Heinrich. *Die Heidelberger Tradition in der Deutschen Philosophie*. Tübingen: J. C. B. Mohr, 1931.

———. *Kant als Philosoph der Modernen Kultur*. Tübingen: J. C. B. Mohr, 1924.

Rilke, Rainer Maria. *Poems*. Translated by Jessie Lemont. New York: Columbia University Press, 1943.

Ringer, Fritz K. *The Decline of the German Mandarins: The German Academic Community, 1890–1933*. Cambridge, MA: Harvard University Press, 1969.

———. "Higher Education in Germany in the Nineteenth Century." *Journal of Contemporary History* 2 (1967).

Ritschl, Albrecht. *The Christian Doctrine of Justification and Reconciliation*. Edited and translated by H. R. Mackintosh and A. B. Macaulay. New York: Scribner, 1900.

———. *Die Entstehung der altkatholischen Kirche*. 2nd ed. Bonn: Adolph Marcus, 1857.

———. *Geschichte des Pietismus*. Bonn: A. Marcus, 1880–1886.

Ritter, Gerhard A. and Jürgen Kocka, eds. *Deutsche Sozialgeschichte: Dokumente und Skizzen*. Vol. 2, *1870–1914*. Munich, 1974.

Rojahn, Jürgen, ed. *Marxismus und Demokratie: Karl Kautskys Bedeutung in der sozialistischen Arbeiterbewegung*. Frankfurt: Campus Verlag, 1992.

Roth, Robert. *The Natural Law Party: A Reason to Vote*. New York: St. Martin's Press, 1998.

Rubanowice, Robert J. *Crisis in Consciousness: The Thought of Ernst Troeltsch*. With a foreword by James Luther Adams. Tallassee: Florida State University, 1982.

Salvadori, Massimo. *Karl Kautsky and the Socialist Revolution 1880–1938*. Translated by Jon Rothschild. London: NLB, 1979.

Samuel, R. H. and R. Hinton Thomas. *Education and Society in Modern Germany*. London: Routledge and Kegan Paul, 1949.

Sanders, E. P. *Jesus and Judaism*. Philadelphia, PA: Fortress Press, 1985.

Sato, Shinichi. "Ernst Troeltsch und die soziale Frage im Wilhelminischen Zeitalter unter besonderer Berücksichtigung des Zusammenhangs zwischen Troeltsch und Gottfried Traub." *Mitteilungen der Ernst Troeltsch Gesellschaft* Vol. IV (Augsburg, 1989): 6–21.

Saul, Klaus. *Staat, Industrie, und Arbeiterbewegung im Kaiserreich*. Düsseldorf: Bertelsmann Universitäts-verlag, 1973.

Scanzoni, Letha and Virginia Ramey Mollencott. *Is the Homosexual My Neighbor? Another Christian View*. San Francisco: Harper & Row, 1978.

Scientific Research on Maharishi's Transcendental Meditation and TM-Sidhis Program: Collected Papers. Vols. 1–5. Seelisburg, Switzerland: Maharishi European Research University, 1972–1991.

Schiller, Friedrich von. "The Death of Wallenstein." In *The Works of Friedrich von Schiller*. Vol. 3–4. Translated by T. Martin et al. New York: Aldus Press, 1902.

Schmoller, Gustav. *Grundriss der Allgemeinen Volkswirtschaftslehre*. Leipzig: Duncker, 1900–1904.

———. *Die Soziale Frage: Klassenbildung, Arbeiterfrage, Klassenkampf*. Munich: Duncker, 1918.

Sills, David L., ed. *International Encyclopedia of the Social Sciences*. New York: Macmillan and Free Press, 1969, s.v. "Ernst Troeltsch," by Thomas F. O'Dea.

Simmel, Georg. *The Conflict in Modern Culture and Other Essays*. Translated by K. Peter Etzkorn. New York: Teachers College, 1968.

———. *On Individuality and Social Forms*. Edited and translated by D. N. Levine. Chicago: University of Chicago Press, 1971.

Skinner, Quentin. *The Foundations of Modern Political Thought*. Vol. 2, *The Reformation*. Cambridge: Cambridge University Press, 1978.

———. "Hermeneutics and the Role of History." *New Literary History* 7 (1975–6): 209–32.

———. "Meaning and Understanding in the History of Ideas." *History and Theory* 8 (1969): 3–53.

———. "Motives, Intentions and the Interpretation of Texts." *New Literary History* 3 (1972): 393–408.

———. Preface to *The Foundations of Modern Thought*. Vol. 1: *The Renaissance*. Cambridge: Cambridge University Press, 1978.

———. "'Social Meaning' and the Explanation of Social Action." *Philosophy, Politics and Society*. Series IV. Edited by Peter Laslett, W. G. Runciman and Quentin Skinner. Oxford: Blackwell, 1972: 136–57.

Sorg, Richard. *Marxismus und Protestantismus in Deutschland*. Cologne: Pahl-Rugenstein, 1974.

Steenson, Gary P. *Karl Kautsky 1854–1938: Marxism in the Classical Years*. Pittsburgh, PA: University of Pittsburgh Press, 1978.

Stegmann, Dirk. *Die Erben Bismarcks*. Cologne: Kiepenheuer und Witschl, 1970.

Stern, Fritz. *The Politics of Cultural Despair: A Study in the Rise of the Germanic Ideology*. Berkeley: University of California Press, 1961.

Stöcker, Adolf. *Christlich-sozial Reden und Aufsätze*. Bielefeld und Leipzig: Velhagen, 1885.

———. *Sozialdemokratie und Sozialmonarchie*. Leipzig, Velhagen, 1891.

———. "Unsere Forderungen an das moderne Judentum (19. September 1879)." *Quellen zur Geschichte des deutschen Protestantismus 1871–1945*. Edited by Karl Kupisch, 73–74. Göttingen: Musterschmidt Verlag, 1960.

Strozier, Charles B. *Apocalypse: On the Psychology of Fundamentalism in America*. Boston: Beacon Press, 1995.

Struve, Walter. *Elites Against Democracy: Leadership Ideals in Bourgeois Political Thought in Germany, 1890–1933.* Princeton, NJ: Princeton University Press, 1973.

Sybel, Heinrich von. *The Founding of the German Empire by William I.* Translated by Marshall L. Perrin. New York: T. Y. Crowell, 1890–98.

Taylor, Charles. *Hegel.* Cambridge: Cambridge University Press, 1975.

Tenfelde, Klaus. "Germany." *The Formation of Labour Movements, 1870–1914.* Vol. I. Edited by Marcel van der Linden and Jürgen Rojahn. Leiden: E. J. Brill, 1990.

Thurman, Robert A. F. *Essential Tibetan Buddhism.* 1st ed. San Francisco, CA: Harper, 1995.

Tödt, Heinz Eduard. "Ernst Troeltschs Bedeutung für die evangelische Sozialethik." *Zeitschrift für Evangelische Ethik* 10 (1966): 228f.

Tönnies, Ferdinand. *Community and Society.* Translated by Charles P. Loomis. New York: Harper and Row, 1963.

Treitschke, Heinrich von. *History of Germany in the Nineteenth Century.* Translated by Eden and Cedar Paul. New York: McBride, Nast, 1915–19.

Trillhaas, Wolfgang. "Repräsentant und Aussenseiter einer Generation: Nach dem Tode von Emanuel Hirsch," *Evangelische Kommentare, Monatsschrift zum Zeitgeschehen in Kirche und Gesellschaft* 5 (1972): 602f.

Troeltsch, Ernst. *Die Absolutheit des Christentums und die Religionsgeschichte.* Tübingen: J. C. B. Mohr, 1902.

———. "Die christliche Ethik und die heutige Gesellschaft." *Die Verhandlungen des fünfzehnten Evangelisch-sozialen Congresses.* Göttingen: Vandenhöck & Ruprecht, 1904: 11–40.

———. "Die christliche Weltanschauung und die Wissenschaftliche Gegenströmung." *Zeitschrift für Theologie und Kirche,* 4 (1984).

———. "Die geistige Revolution." *Kunstwart und Kulturwart* 34 (1921): 227–233.

———. *Gesammelte Schriften.* Vol. 1, *Die Soziallehren der christlichen Kirchen und Gruppen.* Tübingen: J. C. B. Mohr, 1912, 1923.

———. *Gesammelte Schriften.* Vol. 2, *Zur religiösen Lage, Religionsphilosophie und Ethik.* Tübingen: J. C. B. Mohr, 1913.

———. *Gesammelte Schriften.* Vol. 3, *Der Historismus und seine Probleme.* Tübingen: J. C. B. Mohr, 1922.

———. "The Ideas of Natural Law and Humanity in World Politics." In *Natural Law and the Theory of Society, 1500 to 1800.* Edited by Otto Gierke. Translated by Ernest Barker. Boston: Beacon Press, 1957.

———. "Meine Bücher." In *Gesammelte Schriften.* Vol. 4. Tübingen: J. C. B. Mohr, 1925.

———. "My Books." In *Religion in History.* Translated by James Luther Adams and Walter F. Bense. Minneapolis: Fortress Press, 1991.

———. "The Place of Christianity among the World Religions." In *Christian*

Thought: Its History and Application. Edited by Baron F. von Hügel, 1–35. London: University of London Press, 1923.

———. *Politische Ethik und Christentum*. Göttingen: Vandenhöck und Ruprecht, 1904.

———. *The Social Teaching of the Christian Churches*. Translated by Olive Wyon. New York: The Macmillan Co., 1931; reprint, Chicago: The University of Chicago Press, 1981.

Vollmar, Georg. *Über die nächsten Aufgaben der Deutschen Sozialdemokratie*. Munich: M. Ernst, 1891.

Wächter, Theodor von. *Die Stellung der Sozial-demokratie zur Religion*. Stuttgart, 1894.

Wagner, Adolf. *Grundlegung der Politischen Oekonomie*. Leipzig: C. Winter, 1892–94.

Waskow, Rabbi Arthur. "Religious Restoration or Religious Renewal." *Tikkun: A Bimonthly Jewish Critique of Politics, Culture & Society* (July/August 1997).

Weber, Marianne. *Max Weber: A Biography*. Translated by Harry Zohn. New York: John Wiley & Sons, 1975.

Weber, Max. *Economy and Society*. Edited and translated by Günther Roth, Claus Wittich, et al. Berkeley: University of California Press, 1978.

———. *Gesammelte Aufsätze zur Religions-soziologie*. Vol. 1. Tübingen: J. C. B. Mohr, 1920.

———. "Politics as a Vocation." *From Max Weber: Essays in Sociology*. Translated and edited by H. H. Gerth and C. Wright Mills. New York: Oxford University Press, 1918, 1964.

———. *The Protestant Ethic and the Spirit of Capitalism*. Translated by Talcott Parsons. New York: Charles Scribner's Sons, 1904, 1976.

Wedekind, Frank. *Prosa, Dramen, Verse*. München: Albert Langen, 1924.

Wehler, Hans Ulrich. *Bismarck und der Imperialismus*. Cologne: Kiepenheuer and Witsch, 1969.

———. *The German Empire 1871–1918*. Translated by Kim Traynor. Dover: Berg Publishers, 1985.

Weidlich, Tom. "A Thesis Fracas Comes Down to Procedure," *The National Law Journal* 17:36 (May 8, 1995): A12.

Welch, Claude. *Protestant Thought in the Nineteenth Century*. Vol. 2: 1870–1914. New Haven, CT: Yale University Press, 1985.

Wellhausen, Julius. *Prolegomena to the History of Ancient Israel*. Edited by W. Robertson Smith. New York: Meridian, 1957.

West, Cornel. *Prophesy Deliverance! An Afro-American Revolutionary Christianity*. Philadelphia, PA: The Westminster Press, 1982.

——— and Jack Salzman, eds. *Struggles in the Promised Land: Toward a History of Black-Jewish Relations in the United States*. New York: Oxford University Press, 1997.

Wichelhaus, Manfred. *Kirchengeschichtsschreibung und Soziologie im neunzehnten Jahrhundert und bei Ernst Troeltsch*. Heidelberg: Universitätsverlag, 1965.

Windelband, Wilhelm. *History of Philosophy*. 2nd ed. Translated by James H. Tufts. New York: The Macmillan Co., 1901.

————. *Präludien, Aufsätze und Reden zur Einleitung in die Philosophie*. Tübingen: J. C. B. Mohr, 1915.

Witt, Peter-Christian. *Die Finanzpolitik des deutschen Reiches von 1903 bis 1913*. Lübeck: Matthesen, 1970.

Wundt, Wilhelm. *Elements of Folk Psychology*. Translated by Edward L. Schaub. New York: Macmillan, 1928.

————. *Outlines of Psychology*. Translated by Charles Judd. New York: G. E. Stechert, 1902.

————. *Principles of Physiological Psychology*. Translated by Edward Titchener. New York: Macmillan, 1904.

Yamin, Jr., George J. *In the Absence of Fantasia: Troeltsch's Relation to Hegel*. Gainesville: University Press of Florida, 1993.

Index

academic freedom, 38, 42–44, 204
accommodation, ethics of, 56, 97, 99, 120, 134–135, 163–168, 174–176, 179, 183, 196, 209–210
Adams, James Luther, 6, 8, 10, 14
African colonies, 19, 21–23, 71, 172, 178–179, 196, 205, 214
aggressive sectarians, 83, 179–181, 183–186, 189–191, 210
agrarian communism, 141
Aldington, Richard, 113
alienation, 81, 126, 158, 181
Anabaptists, 87, 181–183
anarchism, idealistic, 158, 181, 183
Anglo-French Enlightenment, 39, 40–42, 96, 98–99, 116, 123, 156, 196, 204
Anglo-French liberalism, 39, 40–42, 96, 98–99, 106
anti-Catholic campaigns (*Kulturkampf*), 20–22, 51, 53–54, 71–72, 130, 144–145, 195–196, 205, 208
anti-Semitism, 6–7, 19–20, 23, 45, 51, 57–62, 69–70, 72–73, 80, 92–93, 103, 118–119, 129, 145, 148, 160–162, 205, 209, 213–214, 216
Antoni, Carlo, 104
apocalypse, 132–133, 161–163, 182, 209
Aquinas, Thomas, 57, 168, 170, 192
aristocratic principle, 115–118, 121–123, 125–126
aristocratic orders, 118–122, 125, 144, 160, 164, 168–169, 171, 174, 184–185, 191, 212
arms race, 28–29, 109–110, 112, 147, 204, 206, 208, 213
Augustine, St., 168, 192
"Authority not majority!", 116, 121, 124, 153, 160, 167, 175–176, 193, 210

Bainton, Roland, 8, 10, 90–92, 104

Baranowsky, Shelley, 13
Barth, Karl, 92
base-superstructure model, 120, 129, 184
Basilius, St., 136, 138
Batty, Peter, 113
Baumgarten, Eduard, 106
Baur, Ferdinand Christian, 91–92, 104
Beach, Waldo, 13
Bebel, August, 67, 73–74, 82, 144, 150
Benson, Constance L., 11, 13, 18–19, 106
Berger, Peter, 3, 11, 213–216
Berger's typology of religious experience, 213–214
Bernstein, Eduard, 71–72, 80, 82, 129
Birkner, Hans-Joachim, 7, 12–13
Bismarck, Prince Otto von, 27–31, 51, 53–56, 67–71, 73, 87, 130, 144, 204–205
Black Nationalism, 215
Blumhardt, Christoph, 81–83, 86
Bock, Paul, 86
Bomb, cult of, 216
Bosse, Hans, 199, 201
Brentano, Lujo, 30, 36, 44, 47, 49, 68, 73, 118, 159, 208
Breysig, Kurt, 36, 47
Bridenthal, Renate, 24
Brose, Eric Dorn, 32, 65, 85
Brown, Lester R., 217
Buddhism, Asahara, 216
Buddhism, Tibetan, 215
Bülow, Chancellor, 21, 29, 61, 130

Caesar (*Kaiser*), 75, 122, 140, 158, 162, 203
Caesar, cult of, 140, 158, 162, 203
Caesar, render unto… (Mt. 22:21), 75, 122
callings or vocations, 53, 56, 117–118, 169–170, 174

Troeltsch, "Die christliche Ethik und die heutige Gesellschaft," 126

Troeltsch, "Die christliche Weltanschauung und die Wissenschaftliche Gegenströmung," 106

Troeltsch, formative years, 87–89

Troeltsch, "Die geistige Revolution," 108

Troeltsch, *Gesammelte Schriften*. Vol. 2, *Zur religiösen Lage, Religionsphilosophie und Ethik*, 57–58, 64, 94–96, 106

Troeltsch, *Gesammelte Schriften*. Vol. 3, *Der Historismus und seine Probleme*, 40, 48, 89, 107–108

Troeltsch, "The Ideas of Natural Law and Humanity in World Politics," 39–40, 96, 106

Troeltsch, the legend, 87–108

Troeltsch, "My Books," 41, 48

Troeltsch, "The Place of Christianity among the World Religions," 92–93, 104–105

Troeltsch, "Political Ethics and Christianity," 115–128, 151, 153, 160, 162, 164, 193, 208

Troeltsch, *The Social Teaching of the Christian Churches*, 1–2, 7–11, 19, 21, 34, 36, 41–57, 71–72, 78, 89, 95–97, 109, 115, 119, 126, 130, 147, 151–201, 203, 209, 212–214

Troeltsch Society, 6–7, 9, 126–127

Troeltsch's racialist mission objective, 105

Troeltsch's sociology of race and climate, 98

Troeltsch's two-dimensional typology of religion, 186–189

two-kingdom theory, 82, 122, 171, 173, 175–176

Union Theological Seminary, New York City, 1

usury, 170, 172

utilitarianism, 88, 95, 155–156

Vatican, 51, 75, 130, 141–142, 146, 168, 170–171, 216–217

Vedanta, 215, 218

vocations or callings, 53, 56, 117–118, 169–170, 174

Volk, 7, 39, 44, 58, 60, 95–96, 103, 116

Vollmar, Georg, 71, 74

voting system, 29–30

vow of poverty, 141–143, 190, 207–208

Wächter, Theodor von, 78, 80–81, 86

Wagner, Adolf, 36, 47

Waldensians, 143, 180–181

war, ethics of, 61, 84, 97, 109–113, 117, 171–172, 183, 194, 196, 208–209, 212

Waskow, Rabbi Arthur, 218

Weber, Marianne, 107

Weber, Max, 3, 22–23, 36–37, 44, 52, 55, 88, 91, 96–98, 111, 113, 156–157, 163, 165, 177, 179–180, 186, 192, 208, 210

Weber and Troeltsch relationship, 96–98

Wedekind, Frank, 34, 46

Wehler, Hans Ulrich, 24

Weidlich, Tom, 11

Welch, Claude, 10, 14, 36, 47, 79, 83, 86

West, Cornel, 3, 11, 215, 217–218

Wichelhaus, Manfred, 98, 107

Windelband, Wilhelm, 35, 41–46, 64

Witt, Peter-Christian, 24

women, role of, 3, 19, 21, 23, 60, 73, 96, 104, 106–107, 118, 134–135, 169, 180, 204–207, 214–215

work ethic, 132, 172

working class, 17–19, 23, 67–86, 129–150, 156, 167–168, 180–192, 206

World War I, 97, 99, 109–113, 147, 194, 196, 205–206, 208, 212

Wundt, Wilhelm, 37, 89

Yamin, Jr., George J., 48–92

Zealots, 131, 160